THEIR
BRILLIANT
CAREERS

Fiction

The Weight of a Human Heart: Stories

Nonfiction

Alexander Fernsby: The Definitive Biography

Ordinary People Doing Everyday Things in Commonplace Settings: A History of Australian Short Fiction

Sacred Kangaroos: Fifty Overrated Australian Novels

Forthcoming

The Seasonal Journeys of Wilhelmina Campbell: The Amazing Story Behind the Least Known, Most Influential Writer in Modern Literature (with Anne Zoellner)

THEIR BRILLIANT CAREERS

THE FANTASTIC LIVES OF SIXTEEN EXTRAORDINARY AUSTRALIAN WRITERS

Ryan O'Neill

Lightning Books

Published by
Lightning Books Ltd
Imprint of EyeStorm Media
312 Uxbridge Road
Rickmansworth
Hertfordshire
WD3 8YL

www.lightning-books.com

First edition 2018
First published in Australia by Black Inc. 2016
Copyright © Ryan O'Neill 2016
Cover design by Peter Long
Text design by Tristan Main
Author photograph: Rachel Deverall
Photographs: page iv (Everett Collection_shutterstock),
   page 34 (LiliGraphie_shutterstock),
   page 70 (AnnaKostyuk_shutterstock),
   page 120 (Dark Moon Pictures_shutterstock),
   page 230 (MilanMarkovic78_shutterstock),
   pages 14, 48, 92, 106, 140, 152, 164, 180, 202, 218 (State Library of
Victoria)

British Library Cataloguing in Publication Data
A catalogue record for this book is available from the British Library

Printed by CPI Group (UK) Ltd, Croydon CR0 4YY

ISBN 978-1-78563-067-5

For my late wife, Rachel

Contents

FOREWORD

IN MARCH 1981 FRANK MOORHOUSE GAVE THE EULOGY AT
the funeral of his friend, the experimental writer Arthur ruhtrA.
Moorhouse ended his tribute by recalling something ruhtrA
had told him shortly before his death at the age of forty: "The
great need in Australian writing is still that it should go 'too
far' and resist blandness." In this book, with the same skill and
empathy he has so often displayed in his award-winning short
fiction and nonfiction, Ryan O'Neill gives us the lives of sixteen
writers, including ruhtrA himself, who followed this injunction.
Sometimes it was to the lasting gain of Australian literature;
often it was at great personal cost. These brief, expertly con-
densed biographies present a unique, fascinating overview of
the famous, infamous and forgotten from Australian literature's
last hundred and fifty years.

Addison Tiller, the bane of generations of Australian school-
children forced to study his short fiction, emerges here as a more

complex figure than "The Chekhov of Coolabah" once memorialised on the ten-dollar note. The struggles of Matilda Young, a poet still shamefully little read or celebrated in her own country, are recorded with a similar sympathy. The time has surely come for a full-length biography of Young, Australia's first Nobel laureate. It is unfortunate that Stephen Pennington, who also appears in this book, never had the opportunity to write a life of Young, as he had once planned. Sadly, Pennington's fame now rests on the one malicious act he committed in an otherwise blameless life, rather than on his extraordinary biographies. It is hoped that his inclusion here will refocus attention on his considerable record of literary achievement.

For all their flaws, Tiller, Pennington and Young emerge as essentially decent figures, but others are less admirable. There is little morality to be found in the biographies of such profoundly flawed human beings as Rand Washington, Edward Gayle, Francis X. McVeigh, Claudia Gunn and Robert Bush. Washington's and Gayle's sickening views on race still retain the power to appal, and it is disturbing to reflect that the works of both writers remain popular among large sections of Australian society. The equally unpleasant McVeigh and Gunn, on the other hand, are little read now, no doubt deservedly so, but their influence on Australian realism and detective fiction was significant, and their critical reappraisal is overdue. Robert Bush's beautifully written but ultimately self-serving autobiography, *Bastard Title* (2004), has obscured the claims of misogyny once made against the influential editor, so much so that a short-story prize was recently named in his honour. The life of Bush given here is a salutary reminder of the great editor's cruelty and duplicity.

As in his *Ordinary People Doing Everyday Things in Commonplace Settings: A History of Australian Short Fiction* (2001), O'Neill rescues a number of important writers from undeserved obscurity. Frederick Stratford is a name that should be better known, as either the country's most shameless plagiarist or its earliest postmodernist, or both. Another is Vivian Darkbloom, who inspired some of the best and worst books in Australian literature. The prolific Catherine Swan and the reclusive Helen Harkaway have for too long been relegated to the footnotes of scholarly articles, and it is especially gratifying to note that novels by both writers are scheduled to appear as Text Classics in 2017, with introductions, annotations and afterwords by O'Neill. Australia's "one-man avant-garde", Arthur ruhtrA, whose work is highly regarded in France but has always been treated with bewilderment and disdain in his native land, is also given his due.

The lives of Donald Chapman and Sydney Steele present unique challenges to a biographer. After recent books by Thomas Keneally, Peter Carey and Helen Garner, the critic Peter Craven argued that there could be nothing left to say about the Chapman affair, one of Australia's most enduring literary conundrums. While it must be admitted that O'Neill has come no nearer to uncovering the writer or writers behind Chapman, his life of the poet has unearthed significant new information about the rivalry between editors Paul Berryman and Albert Mackintosh, which provided the catalyst for the affair. In the case of Sydney Steele, an author whose talent was only matched by his misfortunes, it is immensely exciting to read a new account that dispels the whiff of brimstone which has for so long lingered around his memory. Like Simpson and his donkey, and Phar Lap, the bare facts of Steele's life were long ago transformed into myth. As early as 1890 it was whispered that he had sold his soul to the devil in return for becoming a writer of genius, yet by his death in 1945 all his work had been lost through carelessness, vindictiveness or bad luck. In this life of Steele, the first since Stephen Pennington's lost *Sydney Steele: Australia's Homer* (1961), O'Neill deftly outlines the development of the Steele legend while simultaneously debunking it.

Finally, it is impossible to be left unmoved by the life of Rachel Deverall, which is situated, thematically and structurally, at the heart of this book. Deverall's pioneering study on the short fiction of Lydia McGinnis, *Excavating the Basilica* (2001), is a classic of Australian literary criticism, yet there can be little doubt that even this great work would have been eclipsed by her *Squeaker's Mates: A History of Australian Women Writers 1800–2000*, had she lived to complete it. Deverall lived for books, and in the end a book destroyed her. O'Neill's biography of his late wife not only celebrates her early successes but also traces, with enormous sensitivity, the obsession which darkened the last years of her life, and which ruined her marriage, her career and, finally, her health. Had circumstances been different, hers might have been the most brilliant career of all.

Anne Zoellner

Rand Washington on Bondi Beach, October 1946

RAND WASHINGTON

(1919–2000)

With a cold blaster in one hand and a hot-blooded princess in the other, Buck Whiteman prepared to singlehandedly face the dark, slavering hordes of Cor!

From *Subhumans of Cor* (1937)

RAND WASHINGTON, BEST KNOWN FOR HIS HUGELY POPULAR *Cor* series of science-fiction novels and short stories, as well as his extreme views on race, was born Bruce Alfred Boggs on 11 August 1919 in Wollongong, New South Wales, exactly nine months after the end of the First World War. He was to claim later in life that the last shot fired in anger during the conflict had been his father impregnating his mother just before 11 a.m. on Armistice Day. Bruce's father, Mick, was a police constable, and his mother, Janet, worked as a maid in one of the wealthier areas of the city. The boy's childhood was defined by, on the one hand, the frequent, brutal beatings he received from his father, and on the other, his endless reading and rereading of the novels of H.G. Wells, which his mother first borrowed, then stole, for her son from the houses she worked in. Critics have been quick to seize on these facts to explain the sadomasochistic bent of much of Washington's writing, especially the *Cor* books.

Janet Boggs's petty thefts were eventually reported by a gardener, leading to her being sacked and her turning to alcohol. When her son was only eleven she died from cirrhosis. Bruce never forgot the gardener, or the fact that he was Aboriginal.

By the time of his mother's death, Bruce, having all but memorised the works of Wells, searched out the few pulp magazines that reached Australia from America, months and sometimes years after their original publication. The pulps were to have a transformative effect on the young man, both physically and psychologically. Seven months after sending a coupon cut from *Spicy Detective Stories* to New York, Bruce received the first instalment of "Hercules Strong's Twelve Lessons to Physical Perfection". Diligently following Strong's instructions for three years, Bruce had, by the time he was fifteen, succeeded in changing his physique to such an extent that (he once claimed) he was offered a job as strongman when a circus visited Wollongong in 1935.

Bruce's reading ranged across every genre the pulps offered, from cowboy stories, wilderness romances and medical dramas to science fiction, fantasy and horror. He was an early correspondent of the American writer H.P. Lovecraft, whose work he first came across in the October 1933 issue of *Weird Tales*. Bruce's first attempts at writing were horror short stories, and Lovecraft, always generous with his time, agreed to critique them. Though these early stories have not survived, Lovecraft's responses have, and demonstrate the older writer's acute literary judgment, tempered with forbearance at Bruce's ignorance of grammar and punctuation. As well as advising the boy to buy a dictionary and thesaurus, Lovecraft warned him that filling his stories with extremist views on race could, as Lovecraft knew

2

from personal experience, alienate editors. Bruce did not listen. Eventually, Lovecraft tired of the young Australian's repetitive jeremiads warning of "the mongrel races", and the correspondence lapsed after two years. Bruce always maintained he had simply outgrown Lovecraft and the weird after discovering his true love, science fiction.

Bruce's final communication with Lovecraft made no mention of the death of his father, Mick Boggs, which had occurred only two days before the letter was sent. Father and son had been on bad terms for months, ever since Mick had learned of Bruce's literary ambitions and had forbidden him from pursuing them. Instead he forced the young man to learn a trade, and Bruce was apprenticed to a car mechanic in November 1935. Mick Boggs was killed two weeks later while on night patrol in the warehouse district of Wollongong; his neck was broken and his head almost torn off. The murder was never solved. With the insurance payout from the Police Union, Bruce moved to Sydney, rented a one-room flat in Kings Cross and devoted his life to writing. He was nothing if not productive. In the first half of 1936 he wrote an estimated 300,000 words, submitting ten novellas and forty short stories to Australian pulps ranging from *Thrilling Housekeeping Yarns* to *Spooky Bush Tales*. These submissions, under the name Bruce Boggs, were swiftly rejected. The dismissal of his work made Bruce intensify his efforts, and he was eventually to produce an average of 500,000 words a year from the second half of 1936 to the outbreak of war three years later.

In July 1936, a month after adopting the pen name "Rand Washington", the young writer finally made his first sale, "The Rockets of Uranus V" to *Bonzer Science Stories* for five pounds.

This success encouraged Bruce Boggs to adopt the name Rand Washington permanently, and to concentrate his literary efforts on the burgeoning and increasingly lucrative Australian pulp science-fiction market. *Bonzer Science Stories* was one of two dozen pulps published by Siegfried Press, founded and managed by James Smith (born Johannes Schmidt), a German war veteran who had migrated to Australia in 1921. Smith was keen to expand into the novel market, and after accepting and publishing nine stories by Rand Washington in the latter half of 1936, he arranged to meet with the writer in January of the following year to discuss ideas for longer works. It was at this meeting that Washington was first introduced to the tenets of National Socialism; Smith presented him with a signed copy of an English translation of Adolf Hitler's *Mein Kampf* (1925), to which Siegfried Press held Australian publishing rights. The result of Hitler's, and to a lesser extent Smith's, influence on Washington's hitherto virulent but directionless racism can be seen in Washington's first novel, *Whiteman of Cor*, published in July 1937.

This book, the first in the seemingly endless *Cor* saga, was to set the template for all that followed. Buck Whiteman, a space scout employed by the nation of Ausmerica to seek new worlds for colonisation, is lost and shipwrecked on the hostile desert planet of Cor. Here, the "white race", led by the love interest in all the *Cor* novels, Princess BelleFemme Blanch, has been over-thrown and enslaved by the "Argobolin", described as "a savage, untrustworthy, genetically inferior tribe of evil blacks". After rescuing the princess and inciting a rebellion, Whiteman leads the new "White Masters of Cor" on a mission of extermina-tion against their erstwhile "Aboverlords". Despite the blatant racism directed towards Australia's Indigenous inhabitants, which permeates every page of the *Cor* books, and a writing style described by the influential critic Peter Darkbloom as "sub-literate", *Whiteman of Cor* was an immediate success, reprinted six times in 1937 alone.

Smith ordered Washington back to the typewriter, and over the next two years a further twenty-five *Cor* novels appeared, serialised in *Bonzer Science Stories* and its newly launched sister publications, *Bonzer Scientifiction Tales* and *Astounding True-Blue Science*, before being published as standalone novels. All were bestsellers and, along with the translation and publication of the *Cor* books into German by the publishing house C. Bertelsmann Verlag, beginning with *Der Weise Mann Von Cor* (1938), helped to make Smith a wealthy man. Unfortunately for Washington, he had signed over the rights to all future *Cor* novels to Smith in June 1937 for just two hundred pounds.

James Smith's good fortune was not to last. The outbreak of war in 1939, the paper shortages that followed and, most damningly, Smith's continuing and vocal support for Hitler resulted in the virtual bankruptcy of Siegfried Press by 1941. A year later Smith committed suicide by leaping through the closed window of his fifth-floor harbourfront apartment. Fortunately for Washington, Smith had written a new will on the night he died, naming Washington as his sole beneficiary and returning the *Cor* rights to their creator. In another stroke of good luck, Washington was exempted from military service because of his work in publishing, a reserved occupation.

Throughout the war years Washington rebuilt Siegfried Press (renamed Fountainhead Press in 1942) by capitalising on the Australian public's fear of Japan. *Whiteman of Yellos* (1943), the first book in a new series, saw Buck Whiteman and his insipid princess journey to the neighbouring planet of Yellos, where "yellow demons" had overthrown the race of "Purewhites". At the same time, Washington launched a new line of pulps, including *A Bonzer Homestead* and *Bonzer Down on the Farm Stories*, to take advantage of the public's nostalgia for simpler times. By the end of the Second World War, Washington was responsible for writing half a dozen science-fiction pulps, editing a further twenty bush, romance and medical-themed pulps, and overseeing the ghostwriting of the *Yellos* novels.

One of these ghosts was Sydney Steele, the famous Australian novelist, short-story writer and poet. Steele had fallen on hard times after returning from England in 1940. Destitute and miserable, he reluctantly agreed to write a *Yellos* novel for Fountainhead Press in November 1944, but Washington, who despised Steele for his involvement with the Communist Party, had no intention of publishing it. He wore Steele out with his demands for revisions, forcing him to rewrite the book twenty-three times in six months, at the end of which he exploited a loophole in their contract to reject the work without payment. Evicted from his room at a Sydney boarding house, Steele ripped up the manuscript and stuffed it under his clothes to help keep him warm through the winter. Of Steele's many lost works, the destruction of *Nippers of Yellos* is undoubtedly the least to be regretted.

Washington, exhausted by years of toil, decided in 1946 to hire an editor to look after his increasingly profitable romance line, which included *Sheilas in Love*, *Nurse Sheila Romances* and *Spicy Sheila True Confessions*. In June he arranged to meet with J.R. Hardacre, a frequent contributor to romance pulps, to offer him the position. Washington was stunned to find that Hardacre was the pen name of an attractive young woman, Joyce Reith. Though conscious that Washington's novels, stories and editorials were full of references to the weakness and helplessness of the female sex, Reith accepted the offered role. Washington proposed marriage to Reith numerous times throughout 1947 and 1948, but it was only when Reith's father was forced to declare bankruptcy after losing his uninsured bookshop in Newtown to a mysterious fire that she finally accepted. Washington and Reith married in June 1948, the same month that sales of Reith's romance pulps exceeded, for the first time, those of Washington's science-fiction magazines. After the wedding Washington gifted his father-in-law a substantial amount of money to clear his debts, an act of generosity memorialised in editorials in Fountainhead pulps.

The birth of the couple's son Galt in March 1949 inspired Washington to establish a new line of pulps, led by the flagship *Stupendous Bubba Stories*, to cater for the postwar baby boom. The romance and baby pulps, expertly edited and marketed by Joyce Washington, were to continue until the mid-1950s, and by that time were all that was keeping Fountainhead Press solvent. In 1956 it became clear to Rand Washington that the Australian pulp market was dying, and he reluctantly sold his company to Kookaburra Books for fifteen thousand pounds. Washington used the money to fund a new literary magazine called *Quarter*, modelled on American slicks such as the *Saturday Evening Post* and *Harper's*. Though initially apolitical, before long Washington's vituperative editorials alienated left-leaning writers, who organised a boycott of the magazine. By the end of its first year *Quarter* had published essays by

Washington denouncing poet Matilda Young's "bleeding-heart Bolshevism", as well as articles and opinion pieces by prominent conservative writers, including historian Edward Gayle, who took over editorship of the journal in 1960.

A few more *Cor* and *Yellos* novels appeared in the final years of the 1950s, but Washington was to complain in the letters pages of the few remaining SF pulps that it was becoming increasingly difficult to get his work into print. He blamed a "shadowy Aboriginal cabal in the publishing world" for the commercial failure of *Slave Girls of Cor* (1959). A book review by Guy Strong in *Overground* had called the novel "a farrago of sexy violence and violent sex, embodying all of our country's darkest impulses". Conservative commentators for the *Antipodean* and *Quarter* leapt to Washington's defence, with Edward Gayle arguing that the *Cor* novels were "a unique attempt to create a mythology for this great country, which has never had one", but an embittered Washington never completed another *Cor* story. Instead he turned his attention to nonfiction, penning a number of "tongue-in-cheek" travel books, including *I Got the Wog in Greece* (1962) and *Dago A-Go-Go* (1964), the popularity of which only increased after it was revealed Washington had never set foot in the countries he wrote so scathingly about.

Washington spent two years researching his next project, an exposé of organised religion. *Profits in Prophets: How to Make a Million from Founding Your Own Faith* was published in July 1968, to modest sales. He had long become inured to critical scorn, but the commercial failure of *Profits in Prophets* wounded Washington. At the beginning of August 1969, he told his wife that he needed some time alone and travelled to Uluru, where he spent days clambering up and down the sacred Aboriginal site.

On his last night there, camping under the stars, he claimed to have experienced a vision of a "Universal Galactic Controller" who existed outside our space-time continuum, and who had chosen Washington to spread his "Transvoidist Gospell" [sic]. The Gospell was found by Washington, neatly typed on foolscap paper, under a rock near his camp site. When Washington returned from Uluru, he wasted no time in spreading the Gospell, publishing pamphlets at his own expense and writing a long Transvoidist manifesto, which he insisted appear in *Quarter*; this brought about the resignation of the journal's editor.

Many derided Washington's conversion, paralleling exactly as it did the instructions he had given in *Profits in Prophets*. Yet Transvoidism proved popular among the jaded Sydney elite in the dying days of the 1960s. Washington purchased a large property in the Barrington Tops near Gloucester in rural New South Wales, and by April 1970 his movement had attracted over a hundred followers, including the son of a media baron, the wife of a state parliamentarian, and dozens of writers and artists. Transvoidism's doctrines were shrouded in mystery, but it was rumoured that by following its commandments, those faithful who attained the "fifth level" would be gifted eternal life. Only the most generous of adherents were initiated past the second level; Washington's wife, Joyce, had reached the first level before being killed in a car accident in May 1970. Her death, Washington told his followers, was a punishment visited on her for her lack of faith in the Universal Galactic Controller.

Washington's commitment to Transvoidism was tested by the return of his son, Galt, after fighting with the Australian Defence Force in Vietnam. Galt had stepped on a landmine in Hoi An and lost both legs and his left arm. Shortly before news of his son's injuries reached Australia, Washington had delivered a sermon claiming that the Universal Galactic Controller had bestowed miraculous powers on him, including the ability to cure cancer and to regrow damaged organs and tissue. With Galt's arrival at the compound in late 1972, Washington's disciples became increasingly insistent that he exhibit these powers. Washington put off the demonstration throughout 1973, claiming the Universal Galactic Controller did not like to be tested. His prevarication caused at least seventy followers to abandon Transvoidism.

Finally, on 6 February 1974, Washington announced he would perform a regeneration ceremony the next morning. That night all thirty of Washington's remaining disciples were struck down with severe stomach pains and diarrhoea. At first insisting that this was a sign of the Universal Galactic Controller's wrath, Washington eventually admitted to having doctored the evening meal with laxatives. He was arrested on 7 March 1974 and charged with reckless endangerment. Washington famously claimed he told the police, "They were giving me the shits, so I returned the favour." Transcripts of Washington's police interviews, however, do not include this statement; only his pleas to be released, and his attempts to blame the spirit of his dead wife for the doping, are recorded.

Washington was sentenced to three months in prison. After his release he returned to Gloucester, where Galt was still living. Legal action initiated by his former acolytes had almost bankrupted him and he was forced to sell his property in the Barrington Tops, yet he managed to hold on to *Quarter*. He toyed with writing another *Cor* novel, provisionally titled *Bad Trip on Cor*, but nothing came of it. Despite announcing the beginning or completion of half a dozen novels over the course of the rest of the decade, Washington published nothing, instead living off his son's disability and army pensions. It was not until 1982 that the short story "The Van[qu]ished", universally considered to be Washington's best work, appeared in the February issue of the shortlived but influential Australian science-fiction journal *Up Above, Down Under*. The story follows the experiences of a soldier in a future war fighting against a race of technologically advanced aliens. In the midst of battle, the soldier is bathed in an intense ray of red light; for a moment he thinks that he has been killed, but to his surprise he is uninjured. It is only weeks later, while on leave on Earth, that the terrible effects of the weapon become apparent. Parts of the soldier start to phase out of reality: first his left leg, then two days later his right, then one of his arms. As he waits for the rest of his body to vanish, the soldier's only comfort is memories of his mother. But she too has phased out of existence. She is dead. The story ends in the middle of a sentence; the soldier has disappeared.

"The Van[qu]ished" was a radical departure for Washington. It was the first time he had employed a first-person narrator, and his habitual leaden prose style had become translucent, deploying a complex structure, original metaphors and powerful symbolism. The story was unbearably moving, and critics even detected hints of homoeroticism in the description of the men in the narrator's unit. It has been suggested that the theme of the story, and its new-found subtlety and sensitivity, was Washington's reaction to the horrific injuries his son suffered in Vietnam. This theory, however, is undercut by Washington's private letters to Edward Gayle written around the time of the short story's composition, in which he describes his son as a "mewling, mollycoddled, limp-wristed mummy's boy, who should have lost his head along with his legs". "The Van[qu]ished" was selected for inclusion in *The Best Australian Science Fiction 1982* and subsequently won the Hugo Award for Best Short Story.

After winning the Hugo, Washington signed a contract with Tor to write three *Ace Star Specials*. The first of these, *A Kaleidoscope of Rockets* (1984), was a postmodern deconstruction of Golden Age SF, while the second, *The Sorceress of the Dawn* (1986), was an inventive fantasy novel that intelligently explored complex questions of race and sexuality. Both books received excellent, if bewildered, reviews from critics who had long dismissed the writer as a racist hack, and gave Washington his second Hugo and his first Nebula Award. The *Cor* series was meanwhile enjoying a new surge of popularity with disaffected youth in South America, and in 1988 the entire saga was translated and published by Black and White, a right-wing Argentinean publishing house, with introductions by the Guatemalan science-fiction writer Gustavo Borda. Washington's reputation soared, at least in South America, and he was invited to contribute stories and essays to a number of the continent's ultraconservative literary magazines, including *The Fourth Reich* and *History and Thought*. Before embarking on the third novel, Washington busied himself on a number of other projects. These included his long-promised autobiography, *The Last Shot*, co-written with Galt, and opinion pieces, usually protesting against multiculturalism and feminism, which appeared sporadically in the *Antipodean* newspaper.

The Last Shot was left unfinished. On 14 May 1989 Washington suffered a stroke which left him permanently paralysed, mute and completely dependent on his son. Providentially, Galt had been given full control over Washington's literary estate just the week before. *Quarter*, which had seen sales decline for years, was sold to News Limited; the proceeds were used to modify

Washington's house, including the purchase and installation of a chair lift. Galt also hired a full-time nurse, Alan Pieburn, to help him look after the old man.

The years after Washington's stroke saw Galt emerge from his father's shadow. In 1990 he brought out his first novel with New Dimensions, *How Time Cries*, which tells of a son's desperate attempts to use time travel to prevent the death of his mother. The novel was dedicated to the memory of Galt's own mother, Joyce Washington. In style, tone, the themes it examined and the skill with which it examined them the novel was eerily reminiscent of his father's two late works, *A Kaleidoscope of Rockets* and *The Sorceress of the Dawn*, and like those two novels it was nominated for, and won, the Hugo and Nebula Awards. In early 1996, Galt founded the "Rand Washington Trust", a charitable organisation that uses the considerable royalties from the *Cor* series to fund various progressive causes, from campaigning for gay marriage and Aboriginal land rights to providing legal representation for asylum seekers.

After his stroke, Washington, frail and confined to a wheelchair, became a fixture at demonstrations for social justice throughout Australia, always accompanied by his son and Alan Pieburn. In January 2000 all three flew to the Netherlands, where same-sex marriage had recently been legalised, and Rand Washington served as the best man at his son's wedding to Pieburn. Although he could not speak, Washington's emotions were displayed in the tears he shed throughout the ceremony.

Rand Washington died on 24 February 2000 while riding on a float at the Sydney Gay and Lesbian Mardi Gras. In accordance with his will, he was buried in Gloucester beside his wife, Joyce, with a copy of *Whiteman of Cor* in his coffin.

Matilda Young, August 1947

(1899–1975)

Iambic feet can dance in high heels too.

From "Poet in a Dress" (1939)

MATILDA LEANDER YOUNG, POET, FEMINIST AND AUSTRALIA'S
first Nobel laureate, was born in the Brisbane suburb of Oxley
on 10 October 1899, the only child of James Young, a Methodist
minister, and his wife, Clarissa. James Young was an Oxford
graduate who had published a volume of poetry in England in
1872, the same year he immigrated to Australia. Young was
a bookish, affectionate man who was held in high esteem by
his congregation, and he loved his "Tilda" dearly, reading her
poems by Robert Browning and William Wordsworth every
night before she went to sleep. In turn, Matilda idolised her
father, whose death from influenza in 1906, after ministering
to a woman dying from the disease, deeply affected her.
"I thought all men were like my father," she wrote in her autobiography *She'll Be Right* (1975), "but I learned too late that
no man was." After James Young's death Matilda read and
memorised his favourite poems. Writing also helped distract

her from her grief, and she composed odes in the style of John Keats as well as a humorous mock epic, "The Koaliad", none of which survive.

Less than a year after Young's death Clarissa married again, to Matilda's dismay. Her new stepfather was Aubrey Montague, the manager of a local bank. Matilda did not like Montague, and did not want to take his surname, though she finally relented due to her mother's tearful entreaties. Shortly after the wedding Matilda was sent off to the Rosewood Academy for Young Ladies, a boarding school, where she continued to write poetry, investigating different forms and metres. She excelled in English, winning her school's prize for composition each year without fail. Her stepfather discouraged her literary efforts, telling her that men were not attracted to clever girls and that she should put more time into embroidery and the piano. When Matilda returned home for the summer holidays in 1910, Montague forbade her from writing poetry. After she ignored him, he confiscated her writing materials and every scrap of paper in her bedroom. Matilda did not complain, but instead spent her days gathering berries for her mother's preserves and practising the piano, both activities that Montague approved of. It was only after she had returned to school that her step-father discovered a 600-line poem written on the wallpaper behind her wardrobe, in an ink Matilda had concocted from the berries. What particularly enraged him was that she had signed the poem "Tilda Young" rather than "Tilda Montague". When the girl returned home for the Easter holidays, her stepfather thrashed her for defacing his property; she received an extra caning for pointing out that it was her father who had paid for the wallpaper. Montague then made her spend a week pulling up blackberry bushes. Badly scratched and sunburned, Matilda began to experiment with distilling ink using tea-leaves and vinegar, and had soon made enough to write a series of sonnets with a quill on the wooden slats under her mattress. These too were found by Montague, two days before Matilda was to return to school, and the eleven-year-old was beaten again. The next morning her stepfather came across Matilda in the garden shed, where she was sharpening a large knife on a whetstone. The scene that followed was described in *She'll Be Right*:

> Montague threw open the door of the shed, and asked me what I was about. I told him that since he had taken away everything else from me, I was going to use blood to write my poems. Laughing heartily, he said, "Please, feel free to draw some blood from yourself for your silly rhymes. I doubt you have the courage."
>
> I looked up at him and replied, "It's not my blood I'm going to use."
>
> His face went very white, and he watched me for a long time, as I continued to sharpen the knife. Then he stepped back and gingerly shut the shed door. From then until the day he died, we did not exchange another word.

Matilda Young continued to write poetry throughout her adolescence, and in 1918 she was accepted into the University of Sydney to study English Literature and Music, supporting herself with a modest legacy left to her by her father. In her first week on campus Young spotted a small handwritten sign pinned to the noticeboard outside the English department, advertising a meeting of the university's Poetry Society that evening. When

Young arrived at the venue, a dusty classroom, she found only two others: Jack Sargent, a third-year philosophy student who was also president, treasurer and secretary of the society, and Paul Berryman, like Young a first-year English student. When no one else turned up the three went to a nearby restaurant, where Young and Sargent took turns reciting their own poetry from memory while the shy Berryman looked on. Young was quite taken by the dashing Sargent, impressed by the fact that he had a sonnet recently published in *Northerly*, Australia's oldest and most prestigious literary journal. Sargent told her he was from a property near Nyngan, deep in the bush, and held her spellbound with his tales of writing villanelles while mustering stock and repairing fences. Sargent, Berryman and Young continued to meet each week throughout the semester, and presently Sargent and Young fell in love. When Young completed her degree in 1921 they were married, with Berryman serving as best man. The eccentric Sargent made no objection to his wife's unconventional request that she keep her maiden name.

The couple moved to Newtown, where Young taught piano and Sargent found employment as an English teacher at a local grammar school. In the evenings they would write poetry, good-naturedly criticising each other's work and making fun of the verse they read in journals and newspapers. This was the happiest time in their marriage, but it was all too brief. Rather than the simple stockman she believed she had wed, Young's husband was something of a dandy, spending much of the household income on outfits for himself. Sargent's handsome looks, fashionable clothes and swaggering charisma ensured his prominence in the Sydney poetry scene. He even founded his own school, the Onomatopoets, which flourished for a time in the bohemian city in the 1920s. Sargent was a favourite of the literary patroness Vivian Darkbloom, who gave him small monetary gifts to subsidise his writing, and who bestowed on him the nickname "Fancy Jack", which everyone but Sargent's wife came to call him. And yet, despite his fame, Sargent found it difficult to get his work accepted. He submitted over one hundred poems to journals, magazines and newspapers from 1921 to 1923 but only one was published, and that had been heavily revised with his wife's help. In spite of the unwavering support of Matilda and his friend Berryman, Sargent gradually became soured by failure. In March 1924 he taught a class while intoxicated and was dismissed after vomiting in front of the headmaster. The loss of his job came on the same day that Young learned she was pregnant. Sargent was unwilling to find work, so Young took on more pupils, spending six days a week crisscrossing the city by tram. She hid her wages from her husband to prevent him squandering them on beer, cologne and expensive clothes.

Exhausted, Young continued to write poetry and began submitting her own work, all of which was met with polite rejection. Then, on the way to one of her lessons, Young caught the wrong tram by mistake and fell asleep, waking miles from her student's home. Weeping out of frustration she pulled a sheet of music from her bag and wrote "On the Tram", a free-verse poem that gave vent to her feelings of helplessness and despair. It was the first time she did not show her work to her husband. "On the Tram" would later become the most anthologised poem in Australian literature, yet *Northerly* initially declined to publish it. The poem was returned with a handwritten note from the editor, Albert Mackintosh, who declared that Young's "verselets showed some skill, but [were] sadly too feminine for our taste, and that of our subscribers".

Young, furious and humiliated, almost destroyed the poem, but instead waited five months before resubmitting it, this time under her husband's name. Within a week Mackintosh had sent her (or rather "Jack Sargent") a letter accepting the poem, praising it for "the masculine heft of the rhythm". "On the Tram" appeared in *Northerly* in September 1924. Young had only intended its publication to prove a point, but the money from the sale came just in time to prevent their eviction. Sargent was rarely at home now, preferring to spend his time drinking and exchanging gossip with Berryman and other cronies. When he did appear it was to demand money from his wife to pay the debts he had accrued with bars, restaurants and tailors.

Now eight months pregnant, Young left home at six o'clock most mornings and returned after dark. She would make herself toast for dinner and then spend two hours writing. She knew she would be unable to work for much longer, and there appeared no prospect of her husband ever getting a job. In October 1924 an anxious Young decided to submit more of her poems under Sargent's name, reasoning that they stood a better chance of being published if "written" by a man. Nine of these poems, including the poignant "Paper Targets", the technically dazzling "Look at the Whales" and the hilarious "We of the Synchronised Yawns", were accepted, bringing in enough money for Young and her husband to survive for a few months if they were careful. Unfortunately Sargent became aware of the publication of "On the Tram" in early November, when his friend Berryman congratulated him, declaring it the finest poem he had read in years. Drunk and enraged at what he saw as his wife's duplicity, Sargent returned to their flat to confront her. In the argument that followed, Sargent struck his heavily pregnant wife hard across the face, and threw her to the floor. Shocked at his own actions, he then made clumsy attempts to comfort her, bringing her a towel to press against her bleeding mouth and stroking her hair as she sobbed. He told her that he loved her, and that he forgave her, but that she must never do anything like that again. Young waited, resignedly listening to his ramblings until the early hours of the morning when he finally fell asleep. Then she left him.

She had no money for another place to stay, but friends from university put her up for a few days until her mother wired enough cash for a train ticket to Brisbane. Young returned to her mother's home in Oxley, where she gave birth to a daughter, Irene, on 17 November 1924. Aubrey Montague had died in 1922, and Young's mother told her she could stay as long as she wanted. In time Sargent learned where his wife had disappeared to, and in December he travelled to Queensland with the intention of bringing her back. Although he was careful to appear sober when he went to the Montague home, Young refused to speak with him. Sargent met the rebuff with dignity, but returned to the house that night and threw rocks at the windows, demanding he be allowed to see his wife and daughter. He was arrested and charged with being drunk and disorderly, and after spending a night in the cells was released. When he saw Young waiting outside the police station he assumed she had had a change of heart, but she returned her wedding and engagement rings to him along with the money for his train fare to Sydney. She was well aware no court would grant her a divorce, but she told him that she was no longer his wife.

Sargent returned to Sydney and, despite his protestations of love for his daughter, began no legal process to claim her. Instead, in February 1925, he avenged himself on Young by penning a page of obscene doggerel modelled after Dorothea Mackellar's "My Country" (1908), in which he described in explicit detail the sexual performance and preferences of his estranged wife. The loutish tone of the poem was signalled in Sargent's adaptation of Mackellar's title, as he removed the second, sixth and seventh letters of the last word. Sargent, with his friend Berryman's help and encouragement, sent the poem to the families of his wife's piano students, and to the editors of every newspaper and literary journal in Sydney, Melbourne and Brisbane. He dimly believed that destroying Young's reputation and sabotaging her literary ambitions would somehow result in her coming back to him, perhaps because she would have nowhere else to go. Instead he was to find himself an object of ridicule. In May 1925 the anonymously authored "Fancy of the Overflow" was circulated among the Sydney literati. The poem was brought to Sargent's notice by Vivian Darkbloom when he visited her to request a loan. Sargent listened in growing horror as Darkbloom read the poem aloud in front of the city's most influential editors and poets.

The speaker of "Fancy of the Overflow" is a young prostitute, lying down, bored and contemptuous, as the ludicrous Fancy grinds away on top of her for ten verses, of which the fifth reads:

I couldn't hardly feel him, why did Mother Nature deal him
Such a shrivelled little fellow hanging limp down there below?
I wanted him to ram me but instead he cried out "Damn me!
'Tis the first time this's happened to Fancy of the Overflow!"

"Fancy of the Overflow" made Sargent the laughing stock of Sydney. He was expelled from the Onomatopoets and dared not show his face in public for months. In that time he became addicted to opium as well as to alcohol, and one drunken night in November 1925 he confided in Berryman his plan to travel to Queensland to kill Matilda Young. Berryman, who blamed Young for his friend's troubles, made no attempt to dissuade him. It will never be known if Sargent was serious about his scheme. In January 1926 he was drinking in a Glebe bar with Berryman when Jim Taylor, the editor of the *Western Star*, complimented him on his excellent poem "On the Tram". Taylor was perfectly sincere; he was unaware that the poem had been written by Young, but Sargent lost his temper. In the ensuing melee Berryman's left arm was broken and Sargent was stabbed through the neck, dying within the hour.

Sargent's widow and baby daughter returned to Sydney for his funeral and stayed on afterwards, renting a small house in Sans Souci. Young found it impossible to resume teaching the piano, and the poems she submitted to newspapers and literary journals received no response. Albert Mackintosh, the editor of *Northerly*, had become aware of Young's deception in submitting "On the Tram" and was intent on using his considerable authority to ensure she would never be published again. Moreover, during her absence from the city, Paul Berryman had turned all of her former friends against her; Young was now generally held to be responsible for Sargent's decline and death, and no poet from the city's schools, collectives and movements would have anything to do with her. In response, Young formed "The Truants", a school of poets for those who refused to take part in the petty internecine quarrels of the Sydney literary world, but she was long to remain its only member. On her pension, Young's mother was unable to support her daughter any longer and so reluctantly Young had to resort to using pseudonyms again in order to have her work appear in print. Throughout 1926 and 1927 she wrote forty-five poems under a number of pen names, including Richard Hunter, Robert Manly and Henry Paterson, all of which were published.

Albert Mackintosh was quick to embrace this new generation of male Australian poets, dubbing them the "Sans Souci School" after the Sydney suburb where they all lived. Poems from the Sans Souci School garnered a great deal of attention and bountiful praise from reviewers and critics, leading Young to worry that she had gone too far. As long as Mackintosh and other editors continued to shun work she submitted under her own name, however, she felt she had no choice. Finally, in February 1928, Max Murray, editor of the *Billabong*, a new radical literary journal, contacted Young to commission some poems for the second issue, having been informed that "On the Tram", a work he greatly respected, had been written by Matilda Young and not Jack Sargent. Murray was no admirer of the established literary journals, whether conservative or experimental, and after meeting Young he asked her if he could publish her first collection. Young confessed to him then that she was behind the Sans Souci School. Murray was enchanted by the deception, but Young refused his repeated requests to make it public, until May 1928. It was then that *Northerly* published a review of three poems that had appeared under Young's own name in the recent *Billabong*. Young's most personal verses to date, "A Lover in Fortuna" and "But Mostly Air", with their uncompromising imagery and frank investigation of female sexual desire, were variously described as "filth" and "perverted trash", while "Flick of the Wrist", which the Nobel Committee would later praise as "one of the great poems of the twentieth century", was dismissed as "the hysterical ravings of a petty, shrewish mind". The review was written by Paul Berryman, who had recently been appointed deputy editor of *Northerly*.

The *Billabong* of July 1928 featured a long article by Max Murray, "La Belle Dame Sans Souci", which exposed both Young's deception and the gullibility and misogyny of Sydney's literary journals, with special attention paid to *Northerly*. Murray ridiculed the editors for being outwitted by a "mere woman" and questioned their credentials as men of letters. It was no surprise that when Young's collection, simply titled *Poems*, was published the following month, it was met with savage criticism from the same journals that had originally published and praised the work it contained.

The modernist poems in Young's first book were devoid of kangaroos, bushmen and billabongs, instead questioning the casual sexism ingrained in Australian society and the suffocations of suburban middle-class life. Her work was calculated to alienate conservative poets, but experimentalists also disparaged Young for her insistence on accessibility rather than opacity. The most damaging review, a venomous and brutal ten-thousand-word harangue by "PB and AM", appeared in *Northerly*, and its juvenile mockery upset Young more than any other. PB and AM concluded their critique:

> In her "book", would-be poetess Mrs Sargent
> (notwithstanding that she calls herself Young), does
> nothing but complain about her dead husband (who was,

it must be stated here, a great man unworthy of the slurs
cast at his memory), her child (poor tot!), her country,
and her life, so that one is tempted to think of her, if the
present critics can be forgiven for desecrating the work
of an infinitely superior artist, as a kind of *Whingeing
Matilda*.

She was not to learn of the fact until almost a decade later,
but Young's *Poems* had, at least, found admirers in England.
Sydney Steele bought a copy in London, and was so dazzled by
it that he destroyed his own half-finished poetry collection for
being moribund and old-fashioned and began writing another,
patterning it on Young's style. Steele gave Young's book to his
friend T.S. Eliot as a Christmas gift in 1929, and the American
mentioned it as one of his "Notable Poetry Books of the Year" in
a column in the *Sunday Times* of 28 December, along with collections by W.B. Yeats, Cecil Day-Lewis and D.H. Lawrence. On
Eliot's recommendation, the foreign rights to Young's collection were subsequently acquired by Faber & Faber, and the book
appeared in England in July 1931 and in America a year later.

In the meantime, Young continued to publish poetry
exclusively in the *Billabong*, including "Whingeing Matilda",
a celebration of the indomitability of Australian womanhood,
and "Irene", which analyses the helpless love Young felt for her
daughter. By January 1932 Max Murray and Young had become
lovers; Murray proposed to her on eleven separate occasions
throughout the year before Young agreed to marry. The couple wed in February 1933 but the poor state of Murray's lungs,
which had been damaged in a gas attack in France during the
Great War, necessitated the family leaving Sydney for the

clearer air of Katoomba. They purchased a bush property five miles from town, where Murray continued to edit the *Billabong* and Young wrote and spent hours tramping the property with Irene. All three were overjoyed to be away from the city. During the six years they spent in the bush, Young worked on the long sequence of anti-war poems that would become her masterpiece. "An Ecstasy of Fumbling" was inspired by her recent reading of Wilfred Owen's work and by her husband's anguished recollections of the war. This decade also saw Young touch upon two themes that would preoccupy her for the rest of her life: the degradation of the Australian bush and the mistreatment of Indigenous Australians.

Young's 1935 collection, *Yarramundi*, received only a single review in the Australian press, from the *Modrenist*, which dismissed its exploration of colonial exploitation and the ruin of the natural environment as "The Songs of a Cynical Sheila". The collapse of the *Billabong* in late 1939 meant that Young and her family could no longer afford to stay on their Katoomba property, and so, with some reluctance, they returned to the city. Regrettably, the enemies they had made meant that neither Young nor her husband could find employment in the literary world. Undeterred, they moved to Melbourne, where the outbreak of the Second World War found Young writing book reviews for the *Melbourne Eon*, while her husband worked as a copyeditor for the local office of the oldest publishers in the country, Berkeley & Hunt.

The 1940s were a wretched time for Young. Max Murray died suddenly of a cerebral haemorrhage in June 1942. Although he had suffered frequent debilitating bouts of depression, and often relied on his wife to nurse him when his lung problems flared up, he had adored his "Tilda", and theirs had been an unu-sually happy marriage. Young's love for her second husband can be seen in the poems she wrote in the weeks after his death but did not publish until twenty years later, including "The Meaning of a Dream", "The Unsaid" and, perhaps most movingly, the elegiac "Music for Broken Instruments". Young's loneliness after Murray's death was exacerbated by Irene's decision to move to Sydney to study teaching at the university. Before long, Irene was caught up in the excitement of student politics, and in January 1943 she joined the Australian Communist Party. Young thought of herself as a socialist, but she did not trust the communists, considering them traitors for their pact with the Nazis in 1939. Young had once been sounded out by Francis X. McVeigh, the head of the party's literature section, on whether she might join, but she had refused McVeigh's offers, both of membership and of taking her to bed. Young was dismayed when Irene dropped out of university in July 1943 to work as a secretary for the party's publishing arm, Steelman Press. Irene resented her mother's interference and stopped responding to her letters, in which Young implored her to return to her stud-ies. In late February 1944 Young travelled to Sydney, hoping to bring Irene back with her to Melbourne. The poet waited on the steps outside her daughter's flat for three hours before the police arrived with news of Irene's suicide. Earlier that morn-ing Irene had leapt from the Sydney Harbour Bridge. She left a brief note apologising to her mother for what she was about to do and expressing her love for her boyfriend, despite his appalling behaviour. An autopsy later revealed that Irene was pregnant. None of her friends had any idea who the mysterious boyfriend was.

Heartbroken, Young remained in Sydney after her daughter's funeral. Little is known of her life from 1944 to mid-1947, except that most mornings she could be seen walking up and down on the Harbour Bridge, stopping occasionally to peer into the waters below. At some point Young became convinced that her daughter's lover had been employed by Steelman Press. In early 1946 she was arrested twice: the first time for breaking and entering the offices of the Australian Communist Party's literature section, and the second for vandalism and theft, when it was discovered she had ripped out and stolen a page from the 14 December 1917 edition of the long-defunct *Clarion* held at the National Library of Australia's vast archives. Young's mother scraped together the money to pay her fines, and Young was released back into obscurity.

By 1947 interest in Young's poetry had been rekindled with the publication of half a dozen articles by Peter Darkbloom. Some critics believed Young was dead, but the appearance of a new poem, the bleak, cryptic "Prologue to the Death of a Pig: 1 November 1946", in *Lone Hand* in July 1947 announced her return to the world of letters. There followed the most successful period of Young's career. Her greatest enemies, Paul Berryman and Albert Mackintosh, had been humiliated by their part in the Donald Chapman affair and were no longer taken seriously. A new generation of editors was in charge of literary journals and, to Young's surprise, they were eager to publish her work. From 1948 to 1953 over a hundred new poems by Young appeared in Sydney's journals, magazines and newspapers, many of which were collected in *The Fallacies* (1954). This, Young's third and longest collection, received a handful of positive reviews in Australia but was hailed as a work of genius in England, America, France and Sweden, where it was translated by Tomas Tranströmer. Over the

years, Young's poetry had attracted numerous supporters overseas, including Albert Camus, Dylan Thomas, and Marianne
Moore, even as Young was still relatively unknown at home.

In October 1955 the Nobel Committee announced that
Matilda Young had won the Nobel Prize in Literature. The
news came as a shock to Young; at first she believed herself
the victim of an elaborate prank. Interviews with the newly
crowned Nobel laureate appeared in the London *Times*, the *New
York Times*, *Paris-Match* and even *Pravda*, which noted approv-
ingly Young's criticisms of Western imperialism. In Australia,
Young's achievement was barely remarked on, with only one
small newspaper, the *Western Sydney Advertiser*, mentioning it in
a small column on page nineteen under the inaccurate headline
"Sydney Housewife Wins Writing Competition". The substantial prize money for the Nobel allowed Young to devote more
time to the causes which were to define the remainder of her
life: feminism, the environment, and advocating for the rights
of Indigenous Australians.

Despite, or perhaps because of, her international prestige,
Young continued to be ignored by a number of elderly and conservative Australian writers and academics. Incredibly, not one
of her poems appeared in the three massive Australian poetry
anthologies of the 1960s, *Classic Australian Poems* (1961), *The Classic
Poems of Australia* (1965) and *Australia's Classic Poems* (1969), all
edited and dominated by men. Throughout this decade, Young
became more politically active, and her letters and articles decrying her country's sexism and racism became a regular feature in
progressive magazines and journals. The right-wing press, headed
by *Quarter*, resurrected Young's old nickname of "Whingeing
Matilda" in their attacks, even making slighting references to her

weight, which had increased steadily since her daughter's death.

In 1967, despite being past retirement age, Young was offered a post as a tutor in Australian literature at the University of Sydney, which she accepted with great humility. She initially intended to remain at the university for only one year, but Young stayed for six and was instrumental in lobbying for, and creating, a course which would examine only women writers, the first of its kind in the country. Her "Australian Women's Fiction Studies" was derided as "Bush Studies" by Edward Gayle in *Quarter* and faced hostility from male lecturers, but Young was vindicated when, within three years, "AWFS" had become the most popular course in the Arts faculty, and Young one of the most admired lecturers. Though teaching perhaps took too much of her energy, Young loved the work, and only left the university in 1973 when her failing eyesight and hearing made continuing impossible. That same year she sent Patrick White a letter of congratulations on his winning the Nobel Prize, noting wryly:

> According to the newspapers, you're the first Australian to win the Nobel. It's lucky you didn't write *The Tree of Woman* as the press would never have taken any notice of you!

White's response to this sally has been lost, although it is perhaps telling that he named a bitter, overweight woman in his next novel, *A Fringe of Leaves* (1976), "Mrs Young".

In spite of her ongoing health problems, including arthritis, rheumatism and a broken hip, Young continued to write poetry throughout the last years of her life, though most of her time was taken up campaigning against the Vietnam War. Her genius was finally, if belatedly, recognised in Australia, with the awarding of honorary doctorates from universities around the country. Berkeley & Hunt published her *Collected Poems* in 1974 and her autobiography, *She'll Be Right*, in 1975, both of which sold over 25,000 copies. A new generation of writers embraced Young, including the playwright Rainy Deverall, the feminist Germaine Greer and the writer Helen Garner. Shortly after the publication of Matilda Young's autobiography, her health deteriorated sharply, and she died in her sleep on 1 November 1975.

Arthur ruhtrA in Sydney, 1978

Arthur (signature)

(1940–1981)

Poor Arthur. The only constraint he couldn't overcome was his lack of talent.

> Georges Perec, in a letter to Italo Calvino,
> 29 November 1981

ARTHUR RUHTRA, EXPERIMENTAL WRITER AND FOUNDER OF the Australian avant-garde writing collective Kangaroulipo, was born Arthur Robinson on 30 August 1940, in the foreign literature section of his father's bookshop in Fremantle, Western Australia. His mother's labour had progressed so quickly that there was no time to take her to the hospital, so Arthur was delivered by his father, Oliver Robinson, with only the birth scene from Laurence Sterne's *The Life and Opinions of Tristram Shandy, Gentleman* (1759), which he happened to be reading, to act as his guide.

Arthur was to spend much of his childhood in his father's shop, a small space crammed floor to ceiling with dusty books on every conceivable topic. The main source of Robinson's income was the volumes he kept in an alcove behind a discreet curtain at the rear of the shop: novels that were banned or restricted in Australia such as *No Orchids for Miss Blandish* by James Hadley

Chase (1939), *The Kama Sutra of Vatsyayana* by Richard Burton (1883) and *My Secret Life* (1888) by "Walter". By the age of three, Arthur would often mind the counter while his father took a nervous male customer behind the curtain. At four, he had taught himself to read and had become proficient at the cross-words and word games on the puzzle page of the daily newspaper. Arthur was a very small child (he would never grow past five feet five inches) and faced bullying after he started school, despite attempting to teach himself martial arts from a book on jujitsu. He was shy, and a poor student; his teacher despaired of the boy ever learning his ABCs even as Arthur carried a twice-read *Ivanhoe* (1820) in his schoolbag.

Arthur's mother, Constance, doted on her young son and would pester him to play outside, but Arthur preferred to hide among the stacks, creating anagrams and acrostics. Constance's sudden death from septicaemia, when Arthur was eight, was a blow from which he never truly recovered. Oliver Robinson, in his grief, turned to alcohol, and from 1948 Arthur all but ran the bookshop, attending school sporadically, and only when his father was threatened with prosecution. During this time, Arthur became ever more absorbed by literature. Later he was to claim that his best friend in childhood was Huckleberry Finn, his first love Elizabeth Bennet, and that he had lost his virginity to Fanny Hill.

In 1954 Oliver Robinson was arrested for selling obscene publications, fined fifty pounds and sentenced to three months in gaol. In order to avoid being taken into care, Arthur created a fictional "Aunt Helen" to look after him, forging a birth certificate by following the instructions in a memoir by the early twentieth-century master forger W.D. Pascoe. His ploy was successful, and for years afterwards Helen Robinson appeared on Fremantle's electoral roll. Later in life, when he was accused by a critic of being unable to create a convincing female character, ruhtrA gave the example of his Aunt Helen. Arthur spent the term of his father's imprisonment alone in the shop. The police had confiscated the indecent books they had found, but were unaware that most of Robinson's stock was stored in a nearby warehouse. Arthur replaced the books the police had destroyed and hired a carpenter to put a door in front of the alcove. He painted the door blue and wrote across it in a childish scrawl, "Arthur's Room". He moved a chair and bed into the small space, papered the walls with comic-book covers, and stored the forbidden books under the mattress. Arthur could by now instantly recognise a customer who was after the special stock, and he would guide the man into his room and lift up the mattress so that he could make his choice. When the police raided the shop again, a week before Arthur's father was to be released from gaol, they merely glanced into the alcove. Although he was now fifteen, Arthur's short stature and reedy voice meant he could still pass for a nine-year-old. The police tousled his hair and left a polite note for his Aunt Helen, who, Arthur told them, had popped to the shops to buy him some lollies.

Oliver Robinson was released from prison in poor health and exhibiting the first signs of dementia. Once back at home, he rarely emerged from the small flat above the bookshop. Arthur continued to run the business; although the police returned to the premises twice in the next few months, they never found any forbidden publications. The shop turned a profit, just enough for Arthur and his father to live on, and by mid-1955 the boy, having read all of the books on the shelves, turned his attention to those kept in the back room. He was unimpressed by what he found there, swiftly becoming bored of such fare as *Common Sense About Sex* (1935) and *Tush in the Bush* (1942). One day, as he sorted the stock, he found a thick novel that had fallen between the bed and the wall. This was *Odysseus* (1923) by Frederick Stratford. For the next four days Arthur barely slept. He had never read anything like Stratford's novel and, though there was much of it he didn't understand, the book had a profound effect on him. Arthur believed his life truly began on the day he started reading the book; he came to refer to the time preceding this great event as B.O. (Before *Odysseus*). He read the book a dozen times over the next year, as well as the other novels Stratford had published in the 1920s. The accusations that Stratford had plagiarised the work of James Joyce, among others, made no impression on Arthur. He would never alter his conviction that Joyce, not Stratford, was the plagiarist. *Odysseus* had given Arthur his vocation: he would be a writer.

When Arthur was nineteen, his father died. Within a month Arthur had sold the bookshop along with all its stock. Inspired by the descriptions of Paris in Stratford's sixth novel, *The Sun Comes Up Too* (1926), he bought a passage to France, leaving Fremantle in November 1959 with only a suitcase containing a few clothes and his copy of *Odysseus*. He arrived in Paris in March 1960 and rented a small apartment off the Boulevard Saint-Germain. Hungering for experience, he frequented the cafés and brothels of the *Rive Gauche*, picking up the language so rapidly that he was fluent before a year had passed. During this time he commenced work on a memoir of his early life with the unfortunate title *My Childhood B.O.*, which was never finished. He also wrote poetry, usually in free verse, producing over eighty poems in his first year in Paris. He submitted them to the city's few English language literary journals, but they were rejected. Despite these setbacks, before long the diminutive Robinson had become a familiar figure on the fringes of the Parisian literary world, with his strongly accented French and his willingness to argue with anyone who disputed his strange notions about the authorship of *Ulysses*, including, on one occasion, an elderly Sylvia Beach, the original publisher of Joyce's novel.

Admiring Robinson's sincere absurdity, the vice-rector of the *Collège de 'Pataphysique* invited him to join in 1961, and there Robinson came into contact with the leading French artists, writers and intellectuals of the day, including Marcel Duchamp, André Breton and Raymond Queneau. It was Queneau who encouraged Robinson to put his arguments for the genius of Frederick Stratford into print. In November 1961, to mark his first publication, the polemical pamphlet *Shames Joyce: The Great Plagiarist*, Arthur changed his name, "marooning Robinson forever in obscurity", as he later recalled. He spent weeks considering a suitable nom de plume, until one day he caught a glance of his signature in a looking glass, and he became Arthur ruhtrA.

In 1962 ruhtrA met Georges Perec, who had written a mock-serious letter congratulating him on revealing Joyce to be nothing more than a copyist. Perec was then unpublished and working as an archivist in a research library attached to the Hôpital Saint-Antoine. The two men became friends, and ruhtrA encouraged Perec to complete his first novel, *Les Choses*, which went on to win the Prix Renaudot in 1965. ruhtrA, meanwhile, had abandoned poetry and was caught up in the first of his literary experiments. In June 1964 he published *Grosswords*, a collection of thirty cryptic crosswords in which every answer is a dirty word. The work enjoyed some success in France, and a measure of notoriety in Australia when a copy ruhtrA sent to Frank Moorhouse was seized by customs and destroyed, causing questions to be asked in the Australian federal parliament. Six months after the *Grosswords* scandal, ruhtrA completed his short-story collection *Waterworks*, written under one of the peculiar literary constraints he would become known for. Each story in the collection is exactly three thousand words long, and had been written after ruhtrA had drunk five litres of water. Though desperate to relieve his bladder, ruhtrA did not allow himself to go to the toilet until he had completed a story. *Waterworks* was published on 4 March 1965, by coincidence the same day as Perec's *Les Choses*.

Although it did not enjoy the success of Perec's novel, *Waterworks* did bring the Australian to the attention of Oulipo. **Ou**v*roir de* **li**t*térature* **p**o*tentielle* was an experimental collective of writers that had grown from the *Collège de 'Pataphysique*; among the aims of the group was to unite literature and mathematics, and to unleash creativity by the use of literary constraints. Raymond Queneau's *Exercises in Style* (1947), for example, retells the same trivial incident in ninety-nine different ways. ruhtrA was invited to meetings of the group as an observer throughout 1966, and in September of that year he made the fatal mistake of requesting to join, unaware that under the rules of Oulipo the only way to disqualify oneself from membership is to ask to become a member.

ruhtrA was dispirited by this rebuff, but generously warned his friend Perec so that he would not make the same blunder. Perec was invited to join Oulipo a month after ruhtrA was turned down, becoming a formal member in October 1966. ruhtrA was determined to convince the group to overturn their decision, and Perec promised he would do what he could to help. In January 1967 ruhtrA commenced writing his best known work, the novel *Long Time No See*, which he hoped would impress Oulipo sufficiently to invite him to join. *Long Time No See*, a picaresque satire of Parisian literary life, is also a lipogram; it does not use the letter C in any of its 734 pages. ruhtrA worked on the novel for two and a half years on a typewriter that had the C key removed. The money from the sale of his father's bookshop having run out long ago, ruhtrA could not afford to heat his tiny apartment, and so Perec allowed him to spend winter days in a quiet corner of his office, where he could write in relative comfort. Despite this gesture, the two men were not as close as they had once been. Their friendship, already strained by the success of Perec's *Les Choses* and acceptance into Oulipo, would be in ruins by the end of 1969.

On 19 June of that year, ruhtrA completed his revisions of *Long Time No See*, and was on the way to the local post office to send the manuscript to his publisher when he happened to glance in the window of a bookshop on the Rue Morgue. The display advertised Georges Perec's latest novel, *La Disparition*. ruhtrA was puzzled, as Perec had not told him he was working on a new book. When ruhtrA opened a copy, he saw what Perec had done. *La Disparition* was a lipogram; it never once used the letter E. Perec always claimed that he had been working on his novel before he met ruhtrA, and that the Australian had stolen the idea of *Long Time No See* from him just as his hero, Frederick Stratford, had stolen *Odysseus* from Joyce's *Ulysses*. ruhtrA, conversely, called Perec a thief and a plagiarist. "I should have known," he wrote in a letter published in *Le Monde* denouncing the French writer. "After all, Perec is an anagram of creep."

Betrayed, as he believed, by Perec and Oulipo, in January 1970 ruhtrA held the first meeting of his own experimental literary group, Kangaroulipo, at a small bar near Notre Dame Cathedral. ruhtrA modelled his collective on Oulipo, going so far as to copy their rules and structure, but with one difference: only Australian experimental writers could join. While this was a strong repudiation of the French avant-garde, it limited the number of eligible members. Just four writers were present at the inaugural meeting: ruhtrA; Lazaros Zigomanis, whose cut-ups of William Burroughs's *The Soft Machine* (1961) had attracted the ire of Burroughs himself; Kiralee Sutcliffe, who under the pen name "S" wrote "mathematical erotica", including the cult classic *Seven Ate Nine* (1969); and Erol Engin, poet and composer. At the meeting it was decided that the group would pursue experimental works with an Australian theme, explicitly rejecting the reactionary bush realism of such writers as Sydney Steele, Henry Lawson and Addison Tiller. Zigomanis worked on *Hanging at Picnic Rock*, an assemblage of a recently published novel by Joan Lindsay, while Sutcliffe repurposed the characters in Barbara Baynton's *Bush Studies* (1902). Engin elected to continue his work in progress, *Lazy Z*, a 500,000-word novel written under the constraint of not using the last letter of the alphabet. ruhtrA's contribution was to be a cento novel composed entirely of previously published works by Australian writers.

By the second meeting in September 1970, the group was a shambles. Zigomanis had resigned his secretaryship and fled Paris after a strung-out Burroughs ran him to ground in a café and threatened his life. Engin had abandoned *Lazy Z* after selling a book of traditional bush poetry, *Brumbies in the Gum Trees*, to Australian publisher Berkeley & Hunt. The only members to turn up for the meeting were Kiralee Sutcliffe and ruhtrA, who by then were living together. Throughout 1971 and 1972 Kangaroulipo met sporadically, never attracting more than half a dozen writers and resulting in few publications. *Long Time No See* received rejection after rejection from English and French publishers, and a depressed ruhtrA ceased working on his cento novel. Only the success of Sutcliffe's *Bush Studies*, which was later adapted into the film *Études de poils pubiens* (1972) starring Sylvia Kristel, enabled the couple to stay in the capital.

In January 1973 *Long Time No See* was finally accepted by New Dimensions, a small experimental Australian publisher, and this, along with the end of conscription, persuaded ruhtrA to return home. Sutcliffe paid for his flight on the understanding she would join him when she had finished her latest novel, but after arriving in Sydney ruhtrA wrote to Sutcliffe that he did not want to see her again, blaming her jealousy for the failure of their relationship. On its publication in June 1973, *Long Time No See* enjoyed faintly praising, if baffled, reviews, but sales were poor. ruhtrA had already spent his advance, and by August he was almost penniless. At the same time, the relaxation of censorship in Australia meant that Sutcliffe's previously banned novels appeared, including the bestseller *Ménages à Treize* (1972). For a few months the glamorous "S" became a figure of fascination in the Australian press, prompting ruhtrA to dash off a memoir of their time together in France, which was also published by New Dimensions. *The Possessive S* (1973), with its lengthy descriptions (mostly fabricated or exaggerated, according to Sutcliffe) of ruhtrA and Sutcliffe's sex life, proved to be the commercial success that had so long eluded ruhtrA.

Using the royalties from his memoir, and donations solicited from patrons in Sydney, ruhtrA launched a new avant-garde literary magazine, *Words, Words, Words*, in June 1974. In the first issue he published his Kangaroulipo manifesto, calling for more formal and thematic experimentation in Australian writing and the abandonment of the dry realism of the past. Although *Words, Words, Words* was advertised as a bimonthly publication, it appeared only twice a year in 1974 and 1975, and once in 1976. Each issue featured a long, provocative editorial by ruhtrA and a chapter from his work in progress, *Repression: A Novel Written Under Constraint*. The lengthy composition of this book was no doubt due to ruhtrA's typing it out with his nose while confined in a straitjacket for six hours a day. As well as his own work, ruhtrA published short stories by Murray Bail, Frank Moorhouse and Peter Carey, and poetry by Matilda Young, Anna Couani and others. His plan to serialise Frederick Stratford's *The Prodigious Gatsby* (1925) was foiled by copyright lawyers. The critical reaction to *Words, Words, Words* was hostile, especially after the third issue, in which ruhtrA parodied Raymond Queneau's *Exercises in Style* with a series of ninety-nine photographs featuring ruhtrA himself performing push-ups, jumping jacks and other calisthenics while dressed in a variety of outfits, from 1920s flapper to renaissance courtier. *Words, Words, Words* came to be seen as a vanity project, with literary critic Peter Crawley memorably rechristening it in the *Sydney Review* as *Turds, Turds, Turds*.

The journal's feeble sales and tepid critical reception were undoubtedly factors in ruhtrA's turning to narcotics in the mid-1970s. Within a few months, his drug use was no longer an inspiration but an addiction. In 1975 he published *Lines of Coke*, a collection of fifty sonnets, each written under the influence of cocaine. That same month, ruhtrA held the first meeting of Kangaroulipo on Australian soil, at a bar in Pyrmont. His speech, in which he dismissed Australian literature as "the acne on the greasy skin of an adolescent country", received a standing ovation from the assembled writers, who were mostly unpublished. ruhtrA expanded on this theme in the editorial of the final issue of *Words, Words, Words* in February 1976. For nine pages he excoriated the Australian poetry establishment and personally insulted several major figures from both the conservative and experimental sides of the poetry wars.

ruhtrA's attack achieved the near impossible: it united the poetry world, against him. Apart from the denunciations that appeared in newspapers and literary journals, ruhtrA also received more than fifty death threats, in both free and regular verse. Fearing for his life, ruhtrA demanded to be placed under police protection. When this was refused, he employed four members of the local Hell's Angels chapter to act as his personal bodyguards until the row had blown over. For months ruhtrA and his "Avant Guard" appeared at book launches and poetry readings in Sydney, their very presence a provocation to those present. The bikies also accompanied ruhtrA to court when he was sued for breach of copyright for his sexually explicit experimental novel *The Coming of the Harlequins*, which New Dimensions had published in January 1976. ruhtrA lost the court case and had to pay two thousand dollars plus costs to Helen Harkaway, the writer whose novel he was found to have copied. This meant he was unable to pay the bikies the money he owed them, and ruhtrA was later hospitalised with two broken legs after being attacked by four supposedly unknown assailants.

Although he made a full recovery, the experience left ruhtrA addicted to painkillers, which he supplemented with cannabis and cocaine, leading to ever more erratic behaviour. ruhtrA justified his drug use by claiming that he was working on a new project, an adaptation of his earlier *Lines of Coke* into novel form, in which every chapter was to be composed under the influence of a different drug or alcoholic drink. Only two chapters were written, "Absinthe", published in *Meanjin* in May 1978, and "Speed", which appeared in the short-lived counterculture magazine *Groovy!* in January 1979. By the end of the decade, ruhtrA had ceased attending meetings of Kangaroulipo, and in June 1980 he was deposed from his post as "eternal president" of the group. Kangaroulipo held two more meetings before disappearing for good. ruhtrA, ostensibly researching for the "Whisky" chapter of his book, was too drunk to notice.

Needing money to fund his drug habit, in November 1980 ruhtrA found work in a second-hand bookshop in Glebe, telling the owner his name was Arthur Robinson; he was still fearful he might encounter a poet he had insulted in his 1976 editorial. Things started to look up for ruhtrA; he cut back on his drinking and joined a methadone program to manage his drug use. He even began a new project, *Ed Soysus: An Anagrammatic Novel*, in which he intended to repurpose every letter in Frederick Stratford's *Odysseus* to create a new work. By 27 February 1981 ruhtrA had written two pages of his new book. When he went into the bookshop that morning, his first task was to clear out a room full of old stock that had been deemed unsellable. The first box he opened contained fifty copies of his own *Long Time No See*, which had remained unsold for eight years, even at five cents a copy. ruhtrA threw the books into the garbage.

That night ruhtrA went to a party being held by his neighbour, a psychiatrist, where large quantities of a fashionable new drug, MDMA, or ecstacy, were freely available. ruhtrA took three small pills, and in the early hours of the morning was found dead behind the bookshelves, where he had crawled during the night. Georges Perec, then living in Brisbane as writer in residence at the University of Queensland, attended ruhtrA's funeral, held on 4 March 1981. Also there was ruhtrA's close friend Frank Moorhouse, who delivered the eulogy, and ruhtrA's former lover, Kiralee Sutcliffe, now a lecturer in Gender Studies at the University of Newcastle. Perec had met Sutcliffe before, in Paris, and after the service asked her what had caused ruhtrA's death. Sutcliffe told him what she had heard from an acquaintance who had been present when ruhtrA's body was discovered, but her answer left Perec none the wiser. The Frenchman could not comprehend how someone could die from an overdose of e.

Addison Tiller in Sydney, January 1903

Addison Watts Tiller

(1874–1929)

"Wot a larf, eh Pa?" howled Pete. "Wot a larf!"
From "The Night We Walloped the Wallabies" (1903)

ADDISON TILLER, RENOWNED DURING HIS LIFETIME AS "THE Chekhov of Coolabah", was Australia's most successful short-story writer. Famous for his humorous depiction of bush life in the tremendously popular series of *Homestead* short stories, Tiller was born Henry Reginald Watkins on Christmas Day 1874 at Tiller Manor, near Bath, England. He came from a prominent local family that had made its fortune from the African slave trade in the eighteenth century, and at the time of Tiller's birth they owned twelve textile factories in Liverpool. Henry's mother, Mary, suffered from neurasthenia and was frequently bedridden for months at a time, so the boy spent much of his early life in the company of nannies, governesses and nursemaids. His first literary outpourings were directed to his mother's maid, Bessie, whom he begged to run away with him in perfectly scanned sonnets. (Henry's interest in female domestic staff was to become less innocent as he grew older.) With his father, Reginald, often absent in the north on business, Henry whiled away the time after lessons with the head gardener of the family estate, Thomas Boldwood, affectionately known to all as "Pa", and his young son and assistant, Peter. (Tiller would recall these names years later when writing his first short story, "Hacking out the Homestead".)

In 1878 Reginald Watkins formed a plan to seek his fortune in Australia. In preparation for their new life, Watkins took an interest for the first time in his son's education, ordering him to learn all he could about their new country. Accordingly, he purchased Harold Bachman's *Geography and Customs of the Antipodes* (1877) and set his son a number of pages to memorise each day. While young Henry enjoyed the sound of the exotic words he found in the book, such as Gabanintha, Toowoomba and Gerringong, he was never able to recall them when asked, which infuriated his father. It is no surprise, then, that by the time the Watkins family departed England in September 1879, Henry already despised his new home.

The Watkins family arrived in Sydney in February 1880 and swiftly established their household in a mansion in Potts Point. To Henry's horror, his father refused to hire a governess, and instead the boy was enrolled in the exclusive Calvin Grammar School, where his English accent and superior airs marked him out for mockery and bullying. Each day after school Henry was pursued from the school gates by a gang of boys, prompting him to learn by heart all the shortcuts and hiding places for three square miles. While retaining his native accent at home, Henry gradually adopted an Australian one at school, which served to mitigate the beatings from his classmates.

After school, Henry was expected to spend three hours a night with his father, learning the ropes of his importing

business. In the little free time left to him, the boy roamed
Sydney, friendless and alone. For years he was homesick for
the elegant terraces and spas of Bath. Sydney seemed to him
a shabby, uncouth place, its inhabitants vulgar and dirty. His
abstemiousness did not, however, deter him from consort-
ing with local prostitutes, and by the age of sixteen he was
constantly making excuses to escape his father's presence.
Actually, Henry was carrying on simultaneous affairs under
his father's roof: with his mother's maid and with the scullery
maid, both of whom he made pregnant in early 1891. When his
father was informed of the women's condition, he sent them
away with a month's salary. His son he disowned and disinher-
ited with immediate effect, and the young man found himself
out on the streets with nothing but the clothes on his back
and twenty pounds his mother had wrung into his hands as
they parted.

Henry Watkins had dabbled in poetry all his life, and
naturally his first thought was to make a living with his pen.
After letting the most expensive suite at the Russell Hotel, he
dashed off ten poems in the classical mode, including "Ode
to a Lorikeet" and the mock epic "An English Swain in the
Antipodes". While confident his work was of a standard to
appear in London's *Strand* or Edinburgh's *Blackwood's*, Watkins
was unwilling to wait the months such an acceptance would
require. Instead, he sent his effusions to the Australian journals whose titles had caught his eye on newsstands: the *Western
Star*, the *Cattleman* and the *Southern Cross*. To his astonishment,
his poems were rejected. Watkins had been reckless with his
savings, fully expecting to earn ready cash from his versifying,
and within a month the money his mother had given him was

spent. When he skulked back to the family home in an attempt to solicit more from her, Watkins's father coldly informed him that his mother had died the week before, no doubt from a broken heart. The two men would not speak again.

With the last of his savings, Watkins purchased as many back issues of the *Bulletin*, the *Stockman's Journal* and *Lone Hand* as he could find. Having been asked to leave the Russell Hotel due to non-payment of his bill, Watkins found a miserably damp basement room in Surry Hills, paying five days of rent in advance. He spent three of these days reading the journals from cover to cover, occasionally nibbling on a page or two in an attempt to stave off hunger pangs. The vernacular poetry of Henry Lawson and Banjo Paterson was beyond him, he realised, and instead he concentrated on the short fiction. He surmised that the stories most popular with editors and readers concerned the lives of ordinary, working Australians in the bush, told in a sentimental, humorous style. Watkins knew little of ordinary life, nothing about work, and had never been to the bush, but on the morning of 5 April 1891, after three hours of furious scribbling, he produced his first short story. "Hacking Out the Homestead" introduced the characters of Pa and Ma and their sons Pete and Norm as they left the city to build a shack on their new selection in the bush. Although elements of the story were clumsy, and some of its details manifestly inaccurate (Watkins believed a jumbuck to be a kind of parrot), it is remarkable how quickly he settled on the formula that would make his fortune. There was humour, if of a primitive kind, as Pa was kicked by a cow into the local creek, and then kicked again into a pile of manure, and at the climax of the story kicked once more into a bed of thistles. But there was also pathos, as the crude cabin the family had toiled for a week to build fell down around them at the first breath of wind. The characters could not be mistaken for anything other than Australian, if only for the number of times they said "strewth" and "fair dinkum". Moreover, the setting was positively crowded with gum trees, creeks, wallabies, possums and kangaroos. Watkins signed the story "Addison Tiller", borrowing the first name from his favourite English essayist and the second from his ancestral home in Bath.

Unable to afford postage, Watkins walked for miles in the pouring rain to the offices of the *Western Star*, on the way exchanging his worn but still fashionable suit for the faded, dirty clothes of a loafer. There, he handed his story to Jim Taylor, editor of the journal. From Taylor's editorials, Watkins knew he was no lover of the English, and so he was careful to speak to him in a broad Australian accent, brusquely demanding to be allowed to dry himself by the fire before departing. Taylor made no objection, retreating to his office with Watkins's story. As Watkins was about to leave, Taylor came running out and embraced him. "Addison, my boy," he cried, "you have the gum of the eucalyptus running through your veins!" When Taylor asked where Watkins hailed from, the young Englishman replied, "Coolabah"; it was the one place he could recall from Bachman's *Geography and Customs of the Antipodes*. Taylor offered to buy "Hacking Out the Homestead" on the spot and any other stories of a similar kind. Henry Watkins left the offices of the *Western Star* as Addison Tiller, with ten shillings in cash and a contract for a further eleven short stories.

"Hacking Out the Homestead" was a great success with readers of the *Western Star*, as were the Tiller family stories that appeared in each issue of the magazine for the next year, all describing the travails of Pa and Pete, Norm and Ma with the same blend of farce and poignancy. These dozen *Homestead* stories appeared at a propitious time for the newly born Addison Tiller. Henry Lawson and Banjo Paterson's *Bulletin* dispute had ignited a national debate about the bush. Tiller's work was singled out by Paterson in a stanza of his poem addressed to Lawson, "In Defence of the Bush":

> But you found the bush was dismal and a land of no delight
> Did you chance to hear a chorus in the shearers' huts at night?
> Did they not meet you with the welcome of a lordly
>   country seat?
> It's not in your precious city you'll find men like Pa or Pete.

Lawson's response, "The City Bushman", was more ambivalent about Tiller's creations:

> Yes, I heard the shearers singing "William Reilly" out of tune,
> Saw 'em fighting round a shanty on a Sunday afternoon,
> Pa and Pete I never saw, and that's a shame, it's true,
> But then that pair's as likely as a talking kangaroo.

Despite Lawson's criticism, the *Bulletin* debate helped establish Tiller as an important and authentic voice of the bush. Plans were made to collect his stories, and in November 1892 *On Our Homestead* was published by Allenby & Godwin, the country's most successful and respected publisher. The book sold out in a week and went through a further nine printings in the next year. Tiller's collection was a publishing sensation to rival

Fergus Hume's *The Mystery of a Hansom Cab* (1886) and Marcus Clarke's *For the Term of His Natural Life* (1874). Both Tiller and his publisher were keen to capitalise on their success, and more short-story collections followed: *Around Our Homestead* (1893), *Beyond Our Homestead* (1895), *Behind Our Homestead* (1897), *Towards Our Homestead* (1898) and *Athwart Our Homestead* (1900). Each of these *Homestead* books rigidly stuck to the established formula, and was received with great enthusiasm by the public and critics alike. An anonymous 1901 article in the *Bulletin*, believed to be by J.F. Archibald, acclaimed Tiller as Australia's national short-story writer; Archibald also later coined Tiller's famous nickname, "The Chekhov of Coolabah".

Tiller enjoyed staggering royalties from the very beginning of his writing career, but his prodigious spending on clothes and alcohol, as well as the large sums he used to pay off the housemaids he seduced and abandoned, meant he was always short of money. His finances were not helped by his uncanny ability to invest in stocks and shares that proved to be worthless. Two of the stories in *Opposite Our Homestead* (1903) were written as a crowd of furious creditors were pounding on the doors of his Brighton home, and *Concerning Our Homestead* (1904) was dedicated to "My long-suffering tailor". If pressed by a particularly irate landlord or cuckolded husband, Tiller would apply to his publisher for an advance on his next book, claiming the need to "go bush". These month-long "walkabouts" were largely spent in the brothels and opium dens of Kings Cross. Though Tiller was thirty by the publication of his eighth book about bush life, he had never been further west than Parramatta.

From his first appearance in print, Tiller took great pains to obscure "Henry Watkins" and preserve the fiction of "Addison

Tiller", aware of the disgrace and ruin that would follow if the public were to learn he was an English gentleman. He grew a thick beard, had his Byronic mane of dark hair shorn, dressed like a tramp and avoided all the old haunts where he might be recognised. Fearful of reverting in a moment of forgetfulness to his English accent, he relinquished it entirely. The death of his father in 1899 removed the final link with his old life, and he realised he would no longer have to worry about his true identity being uncovered. In the bars and pubs of Sydney, Tiller would encounter men who claimed they had known him in the goldfields, and throughout the 1890s he found himself fighting breach of promise suits from women he had never met, who lived in towns out west he had never visited. Though Tiller was a sociable man, he would often leave the parties thrown in his honour after an hour or so, to spend the rest of the night walking around Sydney alone. His knowledge of the city was encyclopaedic, but from time to time, to burnish his reputation, he would stop a stranger in the street, explaining he was a simple bushman who had lost his way, and ask them for help in finding the offices of the *Western Star*.

In 1909 Tiller was thirty-five. He had made and lost fortunes, all his books were in at least their tenth printing, and he enjoyed a literary reputation that eclipsed even Henry Lawson's. Yet he was despondent. He could not risk telling anyone his secret, and for years he had been considering a return to England, even going so far as to book passage on more than one occasion. Yet each time something forestalled his departure, whether the loss of another thousand pounds at the racetrack, or the appearance of another attractive maid to be bedded. He had written nothing since *Concerning Our Homestead* in 1904 when he was approached by the theatre producer Percy Runyon to dramatise *On Our Homestead*. Although Tiller was sick of Pa and Pete, he accepted the commission. He excitedly told Runyon of his conviction that the Tiller family could be used to explore other, more serious, facets of human existence.

The original script of the play, which took Tiller three years to write, contained the requisite clowning of the short stories, and the most famous stage direction in Australian drama: *[Exit, pursued by a cow]*. It was also on occasion discomfortingly gloomy. At the end of the first act, Pa, after being boxed around the ears by a kangaroo, sits in the middle of the stage and sobs, while Pete stands beside him muttering, "Nothin' to be done." More troubling was the play's final curtain, which left the two men lost in the bush, unable to find their way home. (Samuel Beckett's debt to Tiller's play is discussed in depth in Peter Darkbloom's 1954 article "Waiting for Pa and Pete".) The opening-night audience on 28 June 1914 was confounded by these serious interludes, and Runyon cut them for the play's second night, without informing Tiller. The inebriated author was ejected from the theatre after screaming abuse from his balcony while the audience laughed at Pa's antics.

In 1915, *On Our Homestead* was adapted into a 22-minute motion picture, again produced by Runyon, with whom Tiller was no longer on speaking terms. Retitled as *Pa and Pete on the Farm*, it was only the second motion picture to be produced in Australia. The film, like the play, was wholeheartedly embraced by a public distressed by the outbreak of war and longing for a return to simpler, more innocent times. Tiller himself claimed never to have seen the film, now lost, though his 1915 journal obliquely records a visit to the Alhambra theatre on 16 May of that year. The single word underneath this entry in Tiller's handwriting has been interpreted by literary historians as either "Bullocks!" – a reference to the climactic stampede scene in the film – or "Bollocks!"

During the war years Tiller published only one short-story collection, *Off Our Homestead* (1917), which saw Pa and Pete travel to Sydney, "the big smoke", to collect a bequest from a dead great-uncle. Through sheer guilelessness the pair is tricked out of all their money, which after many adventures they recover with interest, before returning home in triumph. Tiller had wanted to write about the city for years, and shuffled Pa and Pete off to the side in a number of the stories in order to more fully develop other characters in an urban environment. This decision perhaps explains why sales of *Off Our Homestead* were disappointing, though the reviews continued to resemble panegyrics. Henry Lawson, again unimpressed by Tiller's writing, confided in a letter to A.G. Stephens in November 1917 his belief that:

> The Pa and Pete stories have become a sacred cow in
> Australian literature, and a cash cow for Tiller. I am no
> friend of his, but a few of the stories in this book prove the
> man can write, though he has squandered his talents so far
> entirely in low comedy. I fear he will only stop producing
> his bloody awful *Homestead* books when the English
> language runs out of prepositions.

Lawson was perhaps the only reader in the country to detect the contempt and self-loathing that lay behind Tiller's prose. "Australia may love Pa and Pete," he once remarked to Sydney Steele, "but I'm damn sure Tiller hates them."

After the relative financial failure of *Off Our Homestead* Tiller resolved never to write another Pa and Pete story. It was the last collection of original Tiller family stories to be published for seven years, and the last of his work to be published by Allenby & Godwin. Now in his forties, Tiller had lost interest in the pastimes that used to occupy him, although he went through the motions of gambling and managing his investments, as badly as ever. He was lonely; despite offering outrageously high wages, he could persuade only old women to work in his household, due to his reputation as a rake. Always an impressive drinker of beer, at this time he moved on to spirits, and by the end of 1919 he was finishing a bottle of whisky a day. Only a looming bankruptcy obliged him to write more *Homestead* stories. In 1924 Tiller submitted what he swore would be the last of the Tiller family collections, *Outwith Our Homestead*, to his new publisher, Kookaburra Books. The stories marked a departure in style for Tiller. Slapstick was all but absent and an elegiac tone had replaced the usual archly humorous one. The caricatures of Pa, Pete, Norm and Ma even became, at odd moments, human. The final story in the collection was the infamous "He Leadeth Me Beside the Still Waters". Tiller's publishers begged him to amend this story, or even cut it from the collection altogether, but he refused, believing, correctly, that it was the best thing he had ever written. "He Leadeth Me Beside the Still Waters" sees the Tiller family leave the homestead in their rusty old Ford to spend a day by the creek. Pa disturbs a hive of bees, but by some miracle they don't sting him, and instead he is able to help himself to their honey. In the meantime, Pete confides to Norm his intention to leave their selection the next day to seek his fortune in the city. Pete decides to go for a last swim in the creek, and Pa, Ma and Norm watch as he shimmies up a nearby tree and dives headfirst into the water. He does not re-emerge. Pa and Norm wade into the creek and drag out Pete's lifeless body. The story ends with Pa cradling his dead son, whispering the twenty-third psalm into his ear.

The public hysteria following the death of Pete in "He Leadeth Me Beside the Still Waters" is comparable only to that which followed the demise of Arthur Conan Doyle's Sherlock Holmes at the Reichenbach Falls in "The Final Problem" (1893). Fourteen people in Sydney and twenty-eight in Melbourne were hospitalised with nervous prostration in the week after the book's release, and a mock funeral held for Pete Tiller in Brisbane reportedly drew a crowd of 2000 mourners. Within a short time grief turned to anger, and the letter columns of newspapers were flooded with correspondence condemning Tiller for his cruelty and heartlessness. Pa and Pete clubs were formed across the country, and countless petitions arrived at Kookaburra Books demanding that Pete be brought back to life.

For a time, Tiller was moved by the public's outpouring of emotion for the character he had created, but as the months passed and the furore refused to die down, it wearied him. The Pa and Pete clubs were encouraging boycotts of all his other *Homestead* books, and Tiller's one remaining pleasure, his twenty-mile daily constitutionals around Sydney, had to be curtailed because librarians, booksellers and prostitutes would shout obscenities at him as he passed. Within a month, his royalties were reduced to almost nothing, and within two months the little money he had saved had disappeared. Finally, in a terse letter to the *Bulletin* published on 6 December 1924, Tiller announced a new, and this time absolutely final, Tiller family book, *Return to Our Homestead*, in which, he promised, he would resurrect Pete.

Tiller wrote *Return to Our Homestead* in six drunken days at the end of December. The first story in the collection, "He Maketh Me to Lie Down in Green Pastures", is a direct continuation of "He Leadeth Me Beside the Still Waters". As Pa mumbles over Pete's body, his son jumps up from his arms and crows, "Wot a larf!" He had been shamming all along. The remainder of the story, and the other stories in the collection, were clumsy pastiches of previous Pa and Pete adventures. What little life Tiller had breathed into the characters in *Outwith Our Homestead* had dissipated. Pete's only function was to play cruel practical jokes on the rest of his family, constantly braying his catchphrase, while Pa was sadistically pricked, gored, scratched and bitten by the local flora and fauna as Ma looked on, shaking her head and laughing. *Return to Our Homestead* became the third-highest-selling book in the series.

Pa and Pete's Wireless Showcase Hour debuted in 1926 and was to run on Sydney's Radio 5XC for the next three decades. Eager to recoup the financial losses of the previous year, Tiller had agreed to work as a consultant on the show, spending an hour each week with the writers dispensing advice on how to portray his creations. The first eleven months of broadcasts were faithful adaptations of the Tiller family stories, but after these were used up the show degenerated into a parade of bad jokes and clumsy, crude double entendres, as demonstrated in the following exchange from the 15 November 1926 broadcast:

PA: Where's your mum, Pete?
PETE: She's squatting on Yorkey's Knob.
PA: I'm going to murder that Yorkey!

This was too much, even for Tiller, but his notes on the scripts were ignored, and he was no longer welcome in the studio. In a fit of rage, Tiller had destroyed the wireless in his home, and so on Saturday nights at eight o'clock, when *Pa and Pete's Wireless Showcase Hour* was broadcast, he would stagger drunkenly around the streets of Mascot or Bronte or Leichhardt until he found a house with an open window, and there he would listen as the family inside wept with laughter at the inanities spouted by Pa and Pete. When the sound of Tiller's mumbling grew loud enough to be noticed, he would be shooed away and move on to another house, and another window. In December 1926 Tiller attempted to enter the home of a family in Ashfield, in order, he said, to kill Pa and Pete, and he was arrested. A nervous breakdown followed, and Tiller was hospitalised for the first half of 1927. The doctors ordered a change of climate and told Tiller he should return to his home-town of Coolabah. The first annual Pa and Pete festival was scheduled to be held there later that year, and Tiller had been invited as guest of honour. Instead, the writer finally decided, at the age of fifty-two, to return to England.

Tiller sailed from Sydney in a first-class cabin in August 1927, remaining at the stern of the ship long after the city had disappeared over the horizon. It was the first time he had left Sydney in forty-seven years. He spent the long, solitary weeks of the voyage talking to himself in a mirror, trying to recapture the English accent he had not used for decades; he introduced himself to the other passengers as Henry Watkins. By the time the ship arrived in England four months later, Tiller had shaved off his beard, disposed of his old clothes, and had the ship's tailor make him an entirely new wardrobe.

Tiller arrived in London during the coldest winter in sixty years, and was met at the docks by Sydney Steele. Steele and Tiller shared a publisher in Kookaburra Books, who had asked Steele to keep an eye on Tiller. Though the men were contemporaries, and often mentioned in the same breath as Australia's two finest writers of prose, they had never before met. Steele had been warned about Tiller's eccentric behaviour, so he showed no surprise when instead of the bearded, ragged ex-sheepshearer he had expected, there stood before him a clean-shaven, immaculately dressed gentleman who spoke in a bizarre half-Cockney, half-Cornish accent and demanded to be addressed as Henry Watkins. Tiller rented a luxurious flat in Mayfair and was looked after by a personal valet and a cook, both of whom he eventually dismissed because they could not understand his accent. Steele was asked to help find a maid from Australia, and after much searching a young woman, originally from Cronulla, was found to serve Tiller.

On a snowy morning in January 1928, Tiller took the train from London to Bath to visit his ancestral home. Steele wanted Tiller's opinion on his novel, the high modernist *Uneasy Lies the Head*, and Tiller took the manuscript with him to read on the train. Upon arriving in Bath he spent hours wandering the streets of the city. Tiller Manor was gone; it had been destroyed in a Zeppelin raid during the Great War and the grounds had been sold to the council, which had erected housing for disabled veterans on the site. At the local cemetery Tiller found the grave of Peter Boldwood, the original Pete, who had been killed at Ypres in 1917. The vicar informed him that Thomas Boldwood, Peter's father, was still alive, and Tiller went to visit him at his great-granddaughter's house. The 99-year-old Boldwood remembered young Henry Watkins perfectly, but told his visitor that Watkins had died in Sydney in 1891, and there was a letter from Reginald Watkins to prove it. Tiller protested that he was indeed Henry Watkins, but the old man grew querulous. "Liar!" he shouted. "Listen to you. You're a foreigner." Tiller was asked to leave by the old man's great-granddaughter, and as he hurried away he could hear the agitated Boldwood continue to roar, "Bloody foreigner!" Tiller left a cheque for two hundred pounds with the vicar, asking that it be given to the Boldwood family. From Bath he sent a letter to his editor at Kookaburra Books, admitting that leaving Sydney had been the biggest mistake of his life and announcing his desire to return as soon as possible. He had been in England for just over five weeks.

Tiller made his way back to London the next day with a raging fever. He fainted on the train, and in the confusion his luggage, and the only copy of Steele's novel, went missing. He was taken home insensible with a bad chest cold that quickly developed into pneumonia. The best doctors in Harley Street were called in to examine him; all ordered complete bed rest for at least six months. Ill, forlorn and yearning for Sydney, on 3 March 1928 Tiller asked his maid to bring him paper and pen, and began to write. Sydney Steele, who remained on friendly terms with Tiller despite the devastating loss of *Uneasy Lies the Head*, assumed he was working on more Pa and Pete stories, but he was wrong. *The Lotus-Eater* was Tiller's last book, and his only novel. A radiant, poetic *Bildungsroman*, the novel tells the story of Simon Buller, a callow young Englishman exiled to Australia by his wealthy but emotionally stunted family. At first contemptuous of his new home and its inhabitants, Buller learns to love Sydney, and eventually his selfishness and greed are transfigured by the city into something approaching redemption. The novel's crystalline prose, complex, shifting point of view and indelibly evoked setting found many admirers in England when it appeared in 1934. T.S. Eliot wrote, "*The Lotus-Eater* is to Sydney as Mr Joyce's *Ulysses* is to Dublin," while E.M. Forster claimed that on long winter evenings he would read the novel to warm himself from its pages. *The Lotus-Eater* remained in print in Great Britain until after the Second World War, and was eventually reprinted as part of the Penguin English Library in 1993.

In the months he was confined to bed, recuperating and working on *The Lotus-Eater*, Tiller spent hundreds of pounds on maps, drawings and books about Sydney, though most of the astoundingly detailed descriptions in the novel were drawn directly from memory. On one occasion Steele visited Tiller and found him, so he thought, asleep with his manuscript spread out on the bed. But as Steele turned to leave, Tiller spoke, his eyes closed: "Wait a moment. I'm standing on the corner of George Street. I'm just crossing the road. Oh, it's the harbour! My God, what a sight!" Transfixed, Steele listened as Tiller roamed in imagination through the city he so loved. Steele traced Tiller's progress on a map, and when he gently corrected Tiller on some minor detail, the bedridden writer insisted that the map was wrong, as indeed turned out to be the case. One day Steele encountered Tiller's maid in the hall. Knowing Tiller's reputation, he expressed his wonder that she was still in his employ. The maid was puzzled: "Why would I leave?" she told Steele. "He's a nice old gent. He just asks me to read to him, that's all. For hours and hours I read the newspaper and things. He don't care. He says he just wants to hear my accent."

Writing for long hours each day, against his doctor's advice, Tiller completed the manuscript of *The Lotus-Eater* in early August 1928, dispatching it to his editor at Kookaburra Books with the scribbled note, "To hell with Pa and Pete – *this* is fair dinkum!" Though Tiller's publishers were initially reluctant to allow *The Lotus-Eater* to be published under the pen name of "Henry Watkins", they eventually agreed upon the condition that Tiller write another Pa and Pete book after he returned to Sydney. "I care not," Tiller recorded in his journal. "I would write nothing but the words Pa and Pete for the rest of my life if it means seeing *The Lotus-Eater* in print."

The Lotus-Eater was published in Sydney in February 1929. Tiller's wishes were honoured and his double identity remained a secret. Kookaburra Books poured money into an expensive advertising campaign, and even offered customers a discount on the next Pa and Pete book if they bought *The Lotus-Eater*. Sadly, the advertisements had little effect. *The Lotus-Eater* by Henry Watkins had sold just seventy-three copies by the end of April. Most of the print run was remaindered, and the novel was never reprinted in Australia. The book was reviewed only once, by Paul Berryman in the *Bulletin*, as

> the work of a patronising Pom who knows precisely
> nothing of Australia, and less about Sydney. Mr Watkins
> should have taken the time to read some of our famous
> local authors who can tell a good yarn without using too
> many fancy words. But lacking a firm hand on the *tiller*,
> Mr Watkins's novel drifts away from readability and is by
> and by lost from view in the straits of pretentiousness.

By a strange coincidence, directly under the review was an advertisement for *Pa and Pete's Wireless Showcase Hour* with an illustration of a grinning, cross-eyed Pete shouting, "Wot a larf!"

Mercifully, Tiller never knew of his novel's failure in Australia. In the early hours of 1 February 1929 Sydney Steele returned to his Westminster flat from a cocktail party at his protégé Graham Greene's house, when there was a telephone call from Tiller's doctor. The writer had suffered a massive stroke after learning his ill health would delay his return to Australia for a further six months. The doctor told Steele that Tiller had been calling for him all evening. "I can't see Sydney anymore," he had raved. "Where is Sydney?" Steele rushed to Tiller's apartment and was met at the door by the doctor, who informed him the patient was now resting. But when the two men tiptoed into Tiller's room they found he had somehow got out of bed and dragged himself across the floor to the bookcase. Tiller had died face-down in the opened pages of a large leatherbound book he had pulled from a lower shelf. After they had gently placed the body into bed, Steele glanced at the book on the floor. It was not he that Tiller had been calling for. The pages showed a reproduction of Grace Cossington Smith's painting of Sydney Harbour, *The Curve of the Bridge* (1928).

Tiller's will directed that he be cremated and his ashes scattered on the waters of Sydney Harbour, but such was the public grief in Australia that the federal government intervened, and the writer's wishes were ignored. His body was returned to Australia in late July 1929, and he was given a state funeral, attended by the premier of New South Wales and the Australian prime minister. Thousands of Sydneysiders lined the streets to pay their respects. His remains were then taken under military escort to Coolabah and laid to rest in an ornate vault in the town's small churchyard on 4 August 1929. The Addison Tiller Memorial Committee raised fifteen hundred pounds in just under a year, and two marble sculptures to commemorate Tiller's life and work were commissioned. The eight-metre-tall figures of Pa and Pete were completed in 1932 and set outside Tiller's last resting place, where they remain to this day.

Robert Bush and Lydia McGinnis on their wedding day, 5 August 1976

ROBERT BUSH

(1941–1990)

Bush's favourite copyediting symbol: "Delete"

ROBERT BUSH, EDITOR, WAS BORN IN WOODSTOCK, NEW SOUTH Wales, on 20 July 1941. His father, Herbert, was a butcher and a respected member of the local Masonic lodge, and owned a shop on the main street of the small town. Robert was the youngest of four brothers, all of whom were stocky and dark-haired like their father, while he was frail and willowy like his adoring mother, Mildred. He was a gifted child, able to read and write before he turned five. Robert's older brothers were not interested in books and took pleasure in tormenting him, encouraged by their father, who would laugh at their pranks. Robert's mother was too weak to protect him.

In later years, Robert Bush would edit out his brothers and father from his posthumously published autobiography *Bastard Title* (2004) by claiming that he was an only child and his mother a widow. Bush's father never knew what to make of his son. One of Robert's earliest memories was when he told his father that the sign on the shop window, "BUTCHER'S"', was grammatically incorrect. Herbert Bush laughed with his customers, who praised the serious little boy for his learning. When Herbert shut up shop that afternoon he took his son into the back yard and beat him with a belt, telling him that no one liked a smartarse.

Robert curried favour with his brothers by helping them with their schoolwork. He did this even before he started school; by the time he was seven, he was doing all their homework for them, reading their textbooks and writing their essays. The boy developed a talent for forgery; he was able to mimic his brothers' handwriting perfectly. In return for his help, they stopped beating him and allowed no one else at school to bully him. They could not defend him from the teachers, however, and Robert learned not to correct mistakes a teacher made on the blackboard. Realising that his cleverness only aggravated those around him, Robert stopped raising his hand to answer questions, and was careful to hand in mediocre work. Writing a bad essay took him hours, as he fussed over where to place each spelling mistake and run-on sentence.

He was fourteen when his next oldest brother left school, and having no need now of his writing skills, all his siblings picked on him once more. Robert observed that while his brothers talked endlessly about girls, none of them had girlfriends. Having just read *Cyrano de Bergerac* (1897), Robert suggested to his brothers that he write love letters for them, in return for a small payment and their leaving him alone. His brothers were sceptical, but eventually Robert's sensitive, lyrical letters won them the three most desirable girls in town. Robert gradually charged his brothers more and more for this service, and by the time he was sixteen he had saved enough money to run away from home.

In the early hours of 17 August 1957 Robert snuck out of his bedroom window with a large holdall. Before leaving town he corrected the sign on his father's shop with purple paint, and posted several letters. There was one for each of his brothers' fiancées, written in his brothers' handwriting, in which they confessed to various acts of sexual deviance Robert had cribbed from *Justine* (1791). Robert also sent a letter to the Masonic lodge; the contents were never disclosed, but his father was kicked out of the order a few weeks later and his standing in the town never recovered. These were only the first acts of vengeance Robert Bush would take in his personal and professional life; he was known never to forgive a slight.

It took Bush three days to hitchhike to Sydney, where he found a bedsit in Darlinghurst and worked at a number of odd jobs to support himself. Early in 1958 he secured a position in the mailroom of Berkeley & Hunt, publisher of Claudia Gunn and Alexander Fernsby. His predecessor had been an old man and very slow at his work; Bush soon learned that he could finish his daily tasks by noon. He would spend the rest of the day wandering around the office carrying an unaddressed envelope, eavesdropping on the editors, designers and publicists who worked there. Bush gloried in the peculiar terminology of publishing, confusing his mother in a letter in May 1959 by telling her he was working with widows and orphans amid alleys and gutters.

Within a few months Bush had assimilated a vast amount of publishing knowledge, but he had been so eager to leave Woodstock that he had missed his school exams, and his lack of formal qualifications precluded him from applying for an editorial position. Finally, fate intervened one evening in late 1961. As Bush was about to leave the office he walked past an editor's desk and saw there the final proofs of Claudia Gunn's latest novel, *A Cold Day in Helensburgh*, which had been signed off and were to go to the printers the following day. Idly, Bush leafed through the manuscript, until page twenty-three, where he came across the following: "'Yes, Inspector, the murderer was fortunate,' Arnaaluk ejaculated. "In fact, it was a veritable shit in the dark!'" Next morning Bush knocked on the door of the publisher, Claude Berkeley, and informed him of the error. The proofs were already on their way to the printer, and Berkeley cancelled the job just in time. Impressed by Bush's enthusiasm and his knowledge of even the most arcane aspects of the business, Berkeley offered the young man a junior copyediting position, which Bush gratefully accepted.

The senior copyeditors gave Bush their drudgework, including the proofreading of science textbooks and technical manuals. Bush worked conscientiously and never complained, developing a reputation for reliability and perfectionism. Within a year he had become an editor on the staff, working on novels such as *Parade of the Harlequins* (1964) by Helen Harkaway (with whom Bush had a brief affair), as well as Alexander Fernsby's *The Sydney Trilogy* (1963) and short-story collection *The Blind Sunrise* (1964). One sign of the trust placed in Bush was his being given special responsibility for editing the novels of Claudia Gunn, the source of a large proportion of the company's profits. Gunn had become more resistant to editing as she grew older, but Bush was able to charm her and, with the publication of *A Snowball's Chance* (1964) and the novels that followed, critics noted a marked improvement in the quality of her prose;

Gunn's detective Makittuq Arnaaluk no longer ejaculated every other page, and the holes in her plotting were, if not eliminated, at least made less conspicuous. Gunn dedicated *Murder at 32°F* (1967) to her editor; it was the only one of Gunn's numerous books not to feature a dedication to her husband, Quincy.

Robert Bush was less beloved by other writers, including the biographer Stephen Pennington. Bush was one of four editors who worked on Pennington's *Addison Tiller: Australia's Chekhov* (1963), and he outraged Pennington by demanding, a week before the book went to press, that he cut the 1200-page biography by one-third. Pennington responded by calling on Claude Berkeley to tell him he could not work with "the butcher" Robert Bush. Berkeley, who had Pennington in mind to write a biography of Alexander Fernsby, calmed the writer and assured him he would never have to accede to any cuts he found objectionable. Pennington insisted that this promise be given in writing and Berkeley complied, though he was to rue the day he gave such a guarantee, as volume after volume of Fernsby's biography emerged over the next four decades. Despite Pennington's dislike of Bush, he came to appreciate his exceptional abilities, even asking him to edit his massive biography of Fernsby. Bush's revenge on Pennington was simple: he made sure to leave one, and only one, spelling mistake in the volumes he edited, something Pennington always came across sooner or later, and which drove the biographer to distraction.

The nickname "the butcher" stuck even as Bush was appointed editor-in-chief in 1968, although no one ever said it to his face. Writers would often emerge in tears from a meeting with him, their novels heavily annotated in his trademark purple ink. Complaints were made to Claude Berkeley about

Bush's arrogance and intrusiveness, but on the one occasion Berkeley mentioned to Bush that he might perhaps be a little less high-handed, the editor threatened to resign and move to a different publishing house, taking Gunn and Fernsby with him. A chastened Berkeley gave him a pay rise; he was keenly aware of Bush's value to the firm. To further demonstrate his confidence, Berkeley asked Bush to take his place on the fund-raising committee for the Sydney Steele Centre, a memorial to the famous writer that was supposed to have been completed by 1966, the centenary of Steele's birth. Under Bush's guidance, and despite a seemingly endless number of setbacks, construction on the centre began in June 1968 six miles outside of Hazelbrook, New South Wales, the reputed site of Steele's demonic bargain.

Bush was instrumental in shepherding Berkeley & Hunt through the near collapse of the Australian publishing industry after the death of Catherine Swan in 1970. At his suggestion the firm purchased the rights to Addison Tiller's Pa and Pete stories from the ailing Kookaburra Books, then heavily cut and repackaged them. The collections were a great success when they were released in 1971. Moreover, it was Bush who persuaded science-fiction writer and religious leader Rand Washington to publish *The Transvoidist Gospell* (1970) with the company, a gamble that paid off when the tract sold in the thousands. Within five years of Bush becoming chief editor, Berkeley & Hunt's books were making a clean sweep of all Australia's major literary awards, and sales of foreign publication rights had increased dramatically. Writers who had vowed never again to speak to Bush sheepishly appeared outside his office to implore him to work on their next project.

In 1973, Berkeley asked Bush to edit a new annual anthology of short fiction to replace the recently defunct *Coast to Coast*. Bush initially refused, as he was overseeing the final stages of the construction of the Sydney Steele Centre, but when the centre, along with the last two samples of Steele's handwriting, was destroyed in a freak bushfire in July, he was happy to take on the task. Over two thousand submissions were received for *Australian Stories 1974*, and Bush spent six months winnowing them down to a shortlist, as well as continuing with his other duties as editor-in-chief. Bush's selections proved controversial; he rejected stories from Frank Moorhouse, Arthur ruhtrA and Peter Carey, while including a Makittuq Arnaaluk piece from Claudia Gunn and a sketch from Rand Washington. In addition, Murray Bail pulled his story "A, B, C, D, E, F, G, H, I, J, K, L, M, N, O, P, Q, R, S, T, U, V, W, X, Y, Z" from the anthology after Bush demanded the title be changed to "A to Z". *Australian Stories 1974* would be remembered for including the first publication by Sydney author Lydia McGinnis. Her short story "The Cockleshell", which tells of a family's disastrous visit to Manly beach, was the only piece in the anthology that Bush published unaltered. In a letter to McGinnis informing her that "The Cockleshell" had been accepted, Bush wrote, "It is as close to perfect as any short story I have read," and asked if he could see more of her work.

The publication of "The Cockleshell" in *Australian Stories 1974* and, even more significantly, Robert Bush's encouragement were extremely validating for McGinnis, who had been contemplating giving up writing for some time. She was thirty-three and had been writing seriously for seven years without being published. McGinnis was a dental nurse and had been married to Brian McGinnis, a taxi driver, for four years. They lived in a small apartment in Glebe, the setting of many of McGinnis's early stories. With a couple of failed attempts at a novel behind her, McGinnis decided to write short fiction after reading Alexander Fernsby's collection *The Blind Sunrise*, which had been edited by Robert Bush. "The Cockleshell" was her first story, and following its publication in *Australian Stories 1974*, McGinnis sent Bush the collection she was working on, *None of Them Knew the Colour of the Sky*. After reading the manuscript, Bush asked to meet McGinnis in person, and in November 1974 the writer came to Bush's office at Berkeley & Hunt. Bush told her that he enjoyed the stories and was keen to publish them but felt that they needed some work, and asked if she would be open to editing. McGinnis agreed, and for the rest of the afternoon they discussed her stories and how they might be improved.

From then on the writer and editor met at least twice a week, sometimes at Bush's office and sometimes at McGinnis's home in Glebe. Bush would bring an edited version of one of the stories and the pair would spend hours thrashing out the changes. The first was "The Cockleshell". McGinnis was well aware of Bush's reputation for literary butchery, and she leafed through the corrected manuscript nervously. With some relief she saw that the editor had only removed three commas and the last line of the story, a decision McGinnis could see at once improved the piece considerably. Nevertheless, it wasn't long before Bush's edits became more pronounced. He highlighted eight hundred words to cut from McGinnis's 4000-word story "Trinity", leading to an argument that raged on and off for a month, until a compromise of five hundred words was agreed.

Discussion of the removal of the word "coffee" from another story lasted for almost five hours. Although McGinnis fought for every syllable of her manuscript, she found herself gradually giving more and more ground to Bush.

However, Bush's changes to McGinnis's favourite piece in the collection, "Great Death Scenes in the Australian Novel", proved too much for her. He wanted to cut the story in half, including the first and last paragraphs, to change the protagonists' names from Cassandra and Robert to Kim and Bob, and to alter the title to "Platypus". In the end McGinnis lost her temper and hurled the story in Bush's face. The editor left without saying a word. McGinnis attempted to contact him on numerous occasions over the next two weeks, telephoning his office and waiting in the lobby of Berkeley & Hunt for hours at a time. She read and reread the revised version of the story, trying to convince herself that Bush's edits were changes for the better, until at last she decided that she could live with the new version. She sent Bush a letter apologising for her behaviour and asking that they might work together again. Bush relented, and the editing process resumed. Although no other piece in the collection would be changed as extensively as "Great Death Scenes in the Australian Novel", Bush's edits were comprehensive, often altering a story's setting and plot and the names of the characters, as well as cutting hundreds of words from the text.

The bitter argument over "Great Death Scenes in the Australian Novel" was the first of many that Bush and McGinnis would have over the next few months. On an edited draft of the short story "Nine O'Clock Shadow", McGinnis angrily crossed out her own name and scribbled "BY ROBERT BUSH". At different times McGinnis screamed, pleaded, and on one occasion threw an ashtray, cutting Bush above the eye. She told him she didn't recognise her own book anymore, and that she would be ashamed to have her name on the cover. Bush waited through her outbursts, listening to everything she said; when she had finished he would simply pick up his coat and start to leave. Each time, McGinnis begged him to stay and relented on his changes.

Throughout 1975 Bush spent much of his time working on McGinnis's collection. He handed over Claudia Gunn's final novel, *An Icicle for an Icicle*, to another editor without informing either Gunn or Berkeley, and Bush had to visit Gunn at "Mysteriosa" in order to mollify the famous author. Berkeley, meanwhile, was unhappy about the amount of time Bush was lavishing on a short-story collection from an unknown writer that would, if they were lucky, sell only six or seven hundred copies. Junior editors in the firm were beginning to complain of a lack of direction, and the publication of *Australian Stories 1975* was delayed into mid-1976 because Bush had not had time to read the submissions. In order to save McGinnis the ninety-minute trip to Bush's office, and Bush the trip to McGinnis's home, the editor suggested renting a hotel room halfway in between, where they could work all day without interruption from Bush's staff or McGinnis's husband. McGinnis agreed to the idea but did not tell Brian, who was already unhappy about how much time she spent writing.

Every Wednesday at 10 a.m., McGinnis and Bush met in the lobby of the Kennedy Hotel in Petersham. As a joke, they checked themselves in as Norman and Marion Dash ("N. Dash and M. Dash"). They would spend all day in the grubby hotel room, paper scattered everywhere, ordering room service for lunch. Work on the manuscript proceeded speedily, if not smoothly. Although McGinnis had all but surrendered to Bush's editing style, she would still become livid occasionally or even burst into tears, fearing that her book was being ruined. Bush continually reassured her that he only wanted to help. One day in July 1975, McGinnis saw that she was late for dinner with her husband, crammed a pile of papers into her bag, and rushed home. Later, when she was fishing for a tissue in the bag, she found a crushed-up letter from Bush among the manuscript pages. There was a thick red line through the contents of the letter, suggesting Bush had decided in the end not to give it to her, and she had picked it up by accident. In the letter Bush told McGinnis that he had fallen in love with her, and asked her if there was any chance she felt the same way about him. If she didn't, he emphasised, it would not affect their working relationship in the slightest. If she did, it would make him a very happy man. McGinnis's marriage to Brian had been falling apart for months. She barely saw her husband, and when she did they had little to talk about. He wasn't interested in her writing, and she wasn't interested in his football team; he wanted children and McGinnis didn't. By the end of the week, she had made her decision. The next time McGinnis met Bush in their room at the Kennedy Hotel, she returned his letter to him. Beside the thick red line through the text, she had written one word: stet.

The final edits on *None of Them Knew the Colour of the Sky*, now retitled *Basilica*, were completed at the beginning of November. Robert Bush and Lydia McGinnis were married the following year on 5 August 1976, after her divorce was granted and on the day *Basilica* went to press. (McGinnis chose to keep her ex-husband's name for her nom de plume.) Bush had saved much of his salary since working at Berkeley & Hunt, and the couple spent four months touring France and Italy for their honeymoon. In Turin they received a telegram from Claude Berkeley: "Congratulations, everyone worshipping at *Basilica*." McGinnis's collection of stories about stoic outsiders, told in an exquisite minimalist style, was proclaimed a modern Australian classic by reviewers, including the notoriously acerbic Peter Crawley. Publication rights had already been sold to St. Martin's Press in the United States and Faber & Faber in England, and French and German publishers were interested in bringing out translations. *Basilica* was reprinted three times by the year's end, becoming the biggest selling short-story collection since Addison Tiller's *Return to Our Homestead* more than fifty years previously. While Bush felt vindicated by the success of *Basilica*, McGinnis was left with a nagging feeling that the book was not truly hers. Bush had barely left a line of the collection alone, apart from "The Cockleshell", and it was this story that was unanimously singled out by critics as the best in the book. Still, McGinnis was understandably thrilled to see herself applauded in the *New York Times Book Review* and the *Times Literary Supplement*.

The couple returned to Australia in December 1976 and over the next four months *Basilica* made a clean sweep of the nation's literary awards. McGinnis began a new book, a novel, which she refused to show to her husband before it was finished. Bush was too overwhelmed with work to object; in February 1977 he was appointed publisher at Berkeley & Hunt after Claude Berkeley finally retired. The death of Claudia Gunn had put a large dent in the company's finances. Although Gunn's books were bestsellers, they never sold well when reprinted, and Berkeley's last decision as publisher, to reissue all fifty-nine of Gunn's books, had been a disaster. Sales were dreadful, and thousands of copies were pulped. The publication of Will Deverall's sensational *The Mystery of Claudia Gunn: An Unauthorised Investigation* in September 1977 only made matters worse. Fortunately, a film adaptation of Alexander Fernsby's *The Bloodshot Chameleon*, starring Robert Redford and Diane Keaton, was underway in Hollywood, and Bush bet everything on it, confident that it would lead to a renewed interest in Fernsby's oeuvre. Consequently, when *The Bloodshot Chameleon* was released in Australian cinemas in July, bookshops were well stocked with the novel, as well as reprints of all Fernsby's previous books and the first three volumes of his biography, released in a deluxe format.

Fortunately for Bush, *The Bloodshot Chameleon* was a box-office smash. Berkeley & Hunt sold 30,000 copies of the tie-in edition of the novel, which featured on the cover a photograph of Robert Redford emerging from a swimming pool. Sales of Fernsby's other novels rocketed, as did those of the three volumes of biography. By the end of 1977, Bush had once again saved Berkeley & Hunt from bankruptcy, but at a considerable price. Bush's autobiography, *Bastard Title*, and the letters McGinnis wrote to her friends at this time suggest the beginnings of the breakdown of their relationship. The couple saw little of each other all year. Bush left for the office at 5 a.m. and returned home at midnight. He worked most weekends, and though he had ostensibly given up his role of editor-in-chief, he still took a great deal of interest in all of Berkeley & Hunt's books, personally proofreading each one before publication. Bush hadn't smoked for years, but now he was getting through three packets a day and had started to drink heavily, beer at first but then spirits.

McGinnis did not realise the extent of her husband's problems for some time. Her novel was going well despite, or sometimes she feared because of, Bush's long absences from home. McGinnis had given up her job when she married Bush, and she was now able to write full-time, something she had dreamed of for most of her life. Although she missed Bush, her novel took up all of her attention. She rarely managed more than four hundred words a day, yet she felt satisfied that they were good words. *A Kingly Kind of Trade*, which takes its title from a line in Christopher Marlowe's revenge play *The Jew of Malta* (1590), tells the story of unassuming librarian Frankie O'Hara and the bizarre relationship that develops between her and a strange man she catches tearing pages from the books in her library. Written in a baroque style utterly distinct from the stories in *Basilica*, *A Kingly Kind of Trade* is closer to the gothic nightmares of Barbara Baynton's short fiction, and has echoes of the masochistic themes of the early novels of Alexander Fernsby.

Throughout most of 1977 and 1978 Bush and McGinnis saw each other only on weekends, which they would spend drinking wine and discussing writing and books, but never speaking of McGinnis's novel. Bush promised his wife that he would take time off to spend with her, and that he would give up smoking and cut down on alcohol. When he came to bed on weeknights, his breath reeked of mints and he awoke early every morning with a hacking cough. McGinnis worried, but he assured her that he was fine. On 23 January 1979, after sitting at her typewriter for ten hours straight, McGinnis finished *A Kingly Kind of Trade*. She had completely rewritten the manuscript nine times in the last six months and was now, at long last, satisfied. Still, she hesitated to show it to Bush, telling herself that she did not want to bother him with it. That night she went to bed and did not wake up until nearly one o'clock in the afternoon. In the living room she found Bush, drunk, with her manuscript. When McGinnis snatched it from him, she saw her own words were almost illegible under the annotations, deletions and alterations in his distinctive purple ink. McGinnis swore at him; Bush could not understand her anger and screamed at her in return. McGinnis took the manuscript, rented a hotel room, bought another typewriter and spent the next week retyping her novel before sending it to New Dimensions, who offered to publish without any changes. She did not return home for a month. When she did, she found a contrite Bush. He apologised and accepted with good grace her wish for the novel to be published by someone else.

A Kingly Kind of Trade appeared in September 1979. Sales were respectable and reviews, on the whole, complimentary. Yet there was a feeling that the novel, after *Basilica*, was something of a disappointment. While beautifully written, *A Kingly Kind of Trade* was, the reviewers suggested, perhaps too long and unfocused. Peter Crawley was blunter, saying, "With some judicious editing, McGinnis's gothic novel could have escaped its sad fate, which is to be more thick than goth." McGinnis fell into a severe depression. Her self-esteem, already damaged by Bush's interference in *Basilica*, was now all but destroyed. She came to think of herself as a fraud, someone whose writing could only succeed when reshaped by her husband. Although aware that she was being irrational, she blamed Bush for the failure of her novel. The reviews exposed the fissures in their marriage and by November, McGinnis was taking antidepressants while Bush was drinking ever more heavily.

On the night of 28 November 1979, Bush called McGinnis from the Berkeley & Hunt offices and asked her to pick him up. He told her it was because he couldn't wait to see her, but McGinnis suspected it was because he was too drunk to drive. He refused to get a taxi, so McGinnis, who had been in bed all day, put on a dressing-gown and went to fetch him. It was a rainy night, and Bush soon passed out in the passenger seat. On the highway, McGinnis, falling prey to the drowsiness caused by her antidepressants, also fell asleep. Their car drifted across two lanes before colliding with a truck and then another car. A badly concussed McGinnis regained consciousness in hospital two hours later with a broken left arm. Bush was not so fortunate, having crushed his right leg and suffered severe trauma to his head. He had been put in a medically induced coma, and as his next of kin McGinnis was asked to agree to an operation that would remove her husband's mangled leg below the knee. Bush emerged from his coma five days later, and McGinnis was by his bedside. When told that she had allowed them to cut off his leg, he was silent for a long time, before muttering, "And they call me the butcher."

After intensive physical therapy, including the fitting of a prosthesis, Bush was discharged from hospital in February 1980 and returned to work at the end of the month. McGinnis continued to blame herself for the accident, although her husband said he forgave her. Their marriage staggered on, with Bush adding painkillers to his list of addictions and McGinnis hospitalised a number of times for depression. She told her psychiatrist that she had come to realise she no longer loved Bush, but she felt she could not leave him. Finally, despairingly, she went back to the form that had given her her first success: the short story. She began a new collection in July 1980, returning to the themes that had informed *Basilica* before Bush had got to it. *The City of Fireworks* was made up of a dozen interlinked stories following six residents of the Sydney suburb of Ultimo. It saw McGinnis finally achieve the mature, original style that had been signalled but not entirely realised in *A Kingly Kind of Trade*. When the book was finished she presented it, nervously, to Bush. After four hours he looked up from the manuscript and gave his judgment. "It's a masterpiece," he told her. "Not a word should be changed." He asked if Berkeley & Hunt could have the honour of publishing the book, promising that her work would not be edited, and McGinnis agreed.

The months leading to the publication of *The City of Fireworks* were cheerful ones for McGinnis. She made great progress in her psychotherapy sessions, and as a result her medication was reduced. Bush started to attend Alcoholics Anonymous and was being weaned off his pain medication. For the first time in months, McGinnis could recognise herself and the man she had fallen in love with. They took long walks together to help Bush regain his strength, and talked into the night about the books they were reading. Bush involved McGinnis in every stage of the design of her new collection, and she was excited by how well it was coming together. *The City of Fireworks* was to be released on 15 September 1981. On the morning of 31 August, Bush left for the office, telling his wife that he would send a courier with the author copies of her collection later that day. Just after eleven, the courier arrived as promised, but the parcel seemed too thin to contain a dozen books. Standing on her doorstep, McGinnis fumbled open the package to find a single copy. At first she thought there had been a mistake. The cover was pink, not blue, and the book was called *Ultimo Thule* instead of *The City of Fireworks*. But her name was under the title. Frantically, she opened the book and read.

Four of her stories had been removed. The rest were heavily cut, reordered and rewritten. All the titles of the stories and names of the characters had been changed. On the front end-paper Bush had written, "I've had my way with it." McGinnis let the book fall to the floor. Part of her still hoped that her husband was playing a joke. Feeling nauseous, she ran the two kilometres to the nearest bookshop; displayed in the window were a dozen copies of *Ultimo Thule* by Lydia McGinnis. Her husband had not forgiven her for the accident after all. She walked home slowly, stepping over the open book that still lay on the doorstep of their flat. She went inside and wrote a note, then went into the kitchen, turned on the gas, and put her head into the oven. Her body was discovered at one o'clock by her husband, who telephoned the police and ambulance. The short note McGinnis had left in her idiosyncratic handwriting was written in purple ink: "I love you, but I'm sorry. I have to cut a long story short."

No one was aware that Bush's editing of McGinnis's last col-lection had been against the wishes of the author. Bush spoke of her suicide as a tragedy brought on by her depression. Over the next three years, in speeches he gave at the many ceremo-nies where he collected literary prizes on his late wife's behalf, Bush began, very gradually, to talk down McGinnis's role in her own writing. He explained that he was more McGinnis's collaborator than editor, and that his input had been crucial to the success of *Basilica* and *Ultimo Thule*. In newspaper profiles he was called "The Man Behind McGinnis", though some writers – including Stephen Pennington – spoke out against Bush's "self-mythologising". McGinnis's novel and her two collections of short fiction appeared on the syllabuses of universities around the country, and prominent feminist writers, including Germaine Greer, criticised Bush for his "appropriation" of McGinnis's life and writing, demanding that he release the original, unedited drafts of her books. Bush at first claimed that these drafts had been lost, and later that they had been destroyed at McGinnis's request. A number of letters from McGinnis to close friends came to light, showing the writer's ambivalence, and frequent hostility, towards Bush's editing. Finally, Bush stopped giving interviews altogether and, as publisher of Berkeley & Hunt and McGinnis's literary executor, he quietly allowed her work to fall out of print.

In July 1989 Bush agreed to his first interview in four years. The ostensible journalist, Rachel Deverall, was a student from the University of Sydney who had become obsessed with the life and art of Lydia McGinnis. Bush and Deverall met in Bush's office at Berkeley & Hunt. They had only spoken for a moment or two when Bush was called away to deal with a design issue. He apologised to Deverall, telling her he would not be long. After Bush left, Deverall took a chance and searched his desk. While she knew she was unlikely to find anything concerning McGinnis, she did not want to let the opportunity pass. Miraculously, in a thick folder in the first drawer she opened, Deverall found neatly bundled together McGinnis's original suicide note and the unedited manuscripts of *None of Them*

Knew the Colour of the Sky and *The City of Fireworks*. Deverall made good her escape with the documents before Bush returned. She spent the next three days staying at a friend's house, making forays to copy the manuscripts in print shops and libraries, all the time expecting to be arrested for theft. Bush never contacted the police, nor did he attempt to stop the circulation and eventual publication of McGinnis's manuscripts by Deverall and her small publisher Xanthippe Press. Deverall gave Lydia McGinnis's suicide note to the *Sydney Review*, which published a facsimile in its September issue. In the note, McGinnis wrote at length about what her husband had done to her, concluding that since Bush had edited her out of her own life, there was nothing left to live for. Upon finding McGinnis's body, Bush had hidden this note and written a new, much shorter one in McGinnis's handwriting.

The exposure of Bush's lies, the suppression and forgery of his wife's suicide note, and the revelation of the full extent of his cruelty towards her destroyed his reputation. He resigned from Berkeley & Hunt at once and withdrew from public life. His last months were spent alone. He had been diagnosed with lung cancer in June 1989 and died on 23 February 1990, a month after Lydia McGinnis's books were finally published as she had intended. There were few mourners to see him buried in Pine Grove cemetery, beneath a large marble headstone that read

Robert Bush

1941–1990

"But that was in another country,
and besides, the wench is dead."

The quotation was taken from *The Jew of Malta*, the same source as the title of McGinnis's only novel. In the years after his burial, and despite the best efforts of the groundskeepers in the cemetery, the headstone has been repeatedly vandalised to read:

> Robert Bush
>
> 1941–1990
>
> "   was   a   c unt ,
>
>   and   he   is dead."

Claudia Gunn at "Mysteriosa", December 1908

Dame Claudia Gunn

(1885–1975)

"We Esquimaux have one hundred different words for snow,"
ejaculated Makittuq Arnaaluk, "but only one for murder!"
From The Death of Vincent Prowse (1924)

CLAUDIA GUNN, THE POPULAR CRIME NOVELIST KNOWN AS
"The Antipodean Agatha", was born Claudia Calthrop on
12 August 1885 in Parramatta, New South Wales. Her father,
Alasdair, was a doctor and her mother, Clara, a former governess. Gunn was later to joke in her autobiography *A Red Herring*
(1960) that her knowledge of poisons came from her mother and
her writing style from her father, an observation that critics,
dubious of her grasp of both English and toxicology, were quick
to agree with. After qualifying as a doctor in 1853, Alasdair
Calthrop had been swept up by the gold rushes, spending a few
exciting if fruitless years fossicking in Echunga and Canoona
before returning to take up his practice in Sydney in 1861. His
rakish good looks and warm bedside manner found him many
patients among the wealthy families of Parramatta, and in 1873
he married Clara Brookes. The couple had all but accepted
their childless state by the time Claudia was conceived over a

decade later. Claudia's parents were affectionate and attentive, and her early years were halcyon. She was a bookish child, and she enjoyed spending hours leafing through her father's bound volumes of *Blackwood's Magazine*. It was in one of these dusty tomes that she happened across a story that had a profound effect on her, a reprint of Edgar Allan Poe's "The Murders in the Rue Morgue" (1841). The young girl then read Poe's other detective stories, "The Mystery of Marie Roget" (1842) and "The Purloined Letter" (1844) and, smitten with their protagonist, C. Auguste Dupin, resolved to become a detective. Weeks of nightmares in which a giant orangutan descended the chimney to cut her throat resulted in her mother forbidding her from reading more detective fiction. At school Claudia was considered to be a pleasant, clever child, although privately her teacher commented on her "sneaking manner" and her habit of eavesdropping whenever she had the chance.

When Claudia was ten, she was awoken by muffled cries coming from her parents' bedroom across the hall. The terrified child crept to their door and peeked through the keyhole. On the bed she saw her father lying on her mother, who appeared to be struggling for her life. As the distraught Claudia watched, the violence of her father's attack increased until he collapsed on her mother, who had gone limp. Claudia burst into the room and leapt on top of her father, scratching at his bare back as she screamed, "Murderer!" The hysterical child was carried to her bedroom by her mother, who was flushed and bedraggled but very much alive. Nine months later, Clara Calthrop died in childbirth along with her baby. In *A Red Herring* Claudia Gunn was to muse that her accusation against her father had been correct, only a little premature.

Alasdair Calthrop was overcome by a great melancholy in the years that followed his wife's death, and Claudia was left much to herself. The events she had witnessed in her parents' bedroom had cured her of her ambition to become a detective; she decided instead that she would write about detectives. With her mother dead and her father usually absent, she was free to read all the mysteries she wished. She began with *The Moonstone* (1868) by Wilkie Collins, then the Sherlock Holmes stories and novels as they appeared in the *Strand Magazine*, and also the Australian mystery stories of Waif Wander and James Skipp Borlase. Among the hundreds of pages of juvenilia she produced were dozens of short stories, including "The Sunstone", a Collins pastiche set during the gold rushes, and "The Swag Bag of Sherlock Holmes", which proposed that the English detective had travelled to Australia after his apparent death at the Reichenbach Falls in 1893.

In November 1902, at a ball in Double Bay, Claudia Calthrop was playing the parlour game "Murder" when she met Quincy Gunn. Claudia was the murderer and Gunn her first victim. Gunn was fourteen years Calthrop's senior, a former sailor who had worked his way around the world before returning to the city of his birth. A number of his nautical sketches had been published in the *Bulletin*, where he was now employed as a reporter. Gunn was already developing a reputation as a muckraker with his front-page revelations about corrupt customs officials and thieving dockworkers. Claudia was besotted by the handsome and exotic Gunn, who called often at the Calthrop house. In May 1903 Gunn asked Alasdair Calthrop for his daughter's hand in marriage. Calthrop, in great pain from the prostate cancer that would kill him within a year, refused the match. He told Claudia that he did not trust Gunn, believing him to be a fortune-hunter. Disconsolate, Claudia acceded to her father's wishes, and Gunn dropped out of sight. He returned to Sydney later that year, however, having researched an article featuring the reminiscences of gold miners around Echunga in the 1850s. After a private meeting, Claudia's father reconsidered Gunn's request. The couple were married on 13 January 1904.

The Gunns purchased a large house in Burwood and after months of renovations they held regular parties there, entertaining the cream of Sydney's society. Quincy was by now political correspondent for the *Bulletin* and politicians were frequent visitors to their home, which Claudia christened "Mysteriosa". The Gunns' weekend gatherings became legendary, and for years Claudia played the part of society hostess, setting aside her writing to help further her husband's career. Almost every weekend dozens of guests would congregate at "Mysteriosa" to dance, play tennis or croquet, eat fine food, borrow a book from Claudia's massive library of mystery novels (the largest in the Southern Hemisphere) and take part in the elaborate games she devised for their entertainment. Writers, editors, publishers, artists, composers, musicians and politicians all enjoyed the Gunns' hospitality, and the connections they made led to Quincy leaving the *Bulletin* to become editor of *Lone Hand* and then in 1912 chief editor of the *Southern Cross*, where he was to remain until his death nearly five decades later.

During the war, when she was not planning opulent parties, Claudia Gunn began writing what would become her first published novel, *The Death of Vincent Prowse*, but by 1916 work on the manuscript had stalled as Gunn cast around for a detective to solve her mystery. Originally the protagonist of

DAME CLAUDIA GUNN

The Death of Vincent Prowse was to have been blind, but Gunn was anticipated in this by the American mystery writer Ernest Bramah and his detective Max Carrados. For months Gunn toyed with the idea of writing about a deaf detective, then a mute detective, even briefly considering a blind-deaf-mute detective, before dismissing the idea as being too difficult to realise. She wondered if her novel would ever be finished. At last, in July 1923, Gunn and her husband went to see *Nanook of the North* (1922) at a cinema in Kings Cross. In *A Red Herring* Gunn recalled the birth of her detective:

> Watching Nanook hunting the walrus in the freezing
> Antarctic [sic], I suddenly envisioned an eskimo stalking
> a different prey in a different locale; no less a murderer
> in no less than the Australian bush. Thus was Makittuq
> Arnaaluk born, and the first of the cases he solved was
> *The Mystery of the Writer's Block.*

Gunn completed *The Death of Vincent Prowse* three months later and submitted the manuscript to Berkeley & Hunt. Publisher Erasmus Hunt had enjoyed some glorious weekends at "Mysteriosa", and wrote personally to Gunn to express his sincere regret that they would not be taking on her novel. Hunt explained that the market was flooded with English detective novels, and the public would simply not accept a mystery set in Australia, no matter how wonderfully written. Hunt's private handwritten report on *The Death of Vincent Prowse*, preserved in the company's archives, told a different story. He criticised the book for being "an awful mess" and confessed he was still unsure how some of the murders had been carried out. What was more, he thought the author was not certain either. Despite this rejection, Hunt was soon invited back to "Mysteriosa", where he enjoyed a private breakfast with the Gunns. When the novel was resubmitted six weeks later, it this time found an enthusiastic proponent in Hunt, who generously acknowledged his original mistake in turning the book down.

The Death of Vincent Prowse was published in January 1924. The sales were disappointing, even for a first novel, and the reviews indifferent, with one exception. Walter De Vere, literary critic for the *Western Star*, devoted five thousand words to ridiculing Gunn's novel in an article titled "The Death of Decent Prose", which echoed many of the issues Hunt had found in his original assessment of the novel:

> The plot is incoherent; at least three of the murders are left unexplained, and while the reader is assured time and again that the locked room Vincent Prowse died in has no secret entrances or exits, the murderer is later revealed to have escaped through a concealed panel behind a reproduction of the *Mona Lisa*. The investigating detective is an ass; for all his eating of tuna, the "brain food" that will help him solve the murder, his method of reasoning is neither deductive nor inductive but merely ineffective. The author assures us that Makittuq Arnaaluk is the world's first Eskimo detective, but I'm afraid he also holds a less noble distinction: he is undoubtedly the world's worst detective. The greatest mystery in the novel is how it was ever published.

Gunn had entertained De Vere many times at "Mysteriosa" and was saddened by the review. Still, she refused to say an unkind word about the critic, and was one of the first to defend him when De Vere lost his position at the *Western Star* amid rumours of grossly immoral conduct. At the same time the front wall of his house in Ryde was daubed in red paint with the words "DE VERE RHYMES WITH Q----". Matters came to a head in June when the police, acting on information received, arrested the critic and charged him with sodomy; eight male prostitutes came forward to testify against him. De Vere was granted bail but returned to an empty house. His wife, Judith, had left him, taking their four-year-old son, Billy, with her. On 22 September, the night before the commencement of his trial, De Vere was found dead in a cheap hotel in Milsons Point. Among his few personal effects was a heavily annotated copy of *The Death of Vincent Prowse*. Although De Vere was a Catholic, he was buried in a municipal cemetery four days later. The Sydney literati shunned the funeral. Apart from De Vere's estranged wife and son, the only mourners were Claudia and Quincy Gunn.

The publicity surrounding De Vere's suicide sparked renewed interest in Gunn's novel, and a second printing in November 1924. By then Gunn had completed two further Makittuq Arnaaluk mysteries, which were published in January and July 1925. *A Dish Best Served Cold* saw the detective confronted with the case of a retired colonel poisoned by a bowl of gazpacho, and *Ice in His Veins* featured the puzzle of how a man could freeze solid in the middle of the Great Victoria Desert. The critical reception of these two novels could not have been more different from that of Gunn's debut. The *Bulletin* proclaimed *A Dish Best Served Cold* to be the greatest Australian crime novel since Fergus Hume's *The Mystery of a*

Hansom Cab (1886) and bestowed on Gunn a nickname that she privately thought gauche, "The First Sheila of Crime". De Vere's successor at the *Western Star* went even further, calling the novel a masterpiece. Despite these and other almost impossibly enthusiastic reviews, readers took much longer to be convinced of the merits of Gunn's writing. Both novels sold fewer copies than *The Death of Vincent Prowse* had initially, and this time there was no sensational suicide to capture the public's interest and boost sales. Despite this, Berkeley & Hunt remained loyal to Gunn, with Erasmus Hunt particularly insistent that the company continue to publish her books, no matter how great the financial loss. His fidelity was to be rewarded, eventually. It was not until her twelfth book, *Snow Red* (1934), that sales of Gunn's novels started to climb, and her seventeenth, *Murder in Muloobinba* (1939), that she had her first bestseller, and was given the sobriquet, "The Antipodean Agatha". Readers did not appear to care that every one of the Arnaaluk stories follows precisely the same pattern. A murder occurs early in the novel, usually in the first chapter. The police, in the shape of Chief Inspector Phineas Blountley-Thicke, are perplexed, and reluctantly call in Makittuq Arnaaluk to consult on the case. Arnaaluk interviews the rapidly thinning group of suspects as the murderer strikes again, usually several times. All the while the detective consumes dozens of tins of tuna in order to stimulate his "thinking box" and mutters the occasional proverb, such as "Only a fool dances on thin ice." Finally, the last remaining suspects (or, in the case of *Death in a Cold Climate* (1959), the last remaining suspect) are called together and Arnaaluk reveals the murderer, to Blountley-Thicke's (if seldom the reader's) astonishment.

Though sales of Gunn's books continued to rise throughout the 1940s and 1950s, the novels proved far less successful
outside of Australia, with only two out of fifty-nine appear-
ing abroad. *A Dish Best Served Cold*, mystifyingly retitled *Death
of an Ice Blonde*, was republished by Faber & Faber in London
shortly after the outbreak of the Second World War. At that
time mystery novels were enjoying a boom, but sales of Gunn's
book were unexpectedly sluggish. Similarly, *The Case of the
Abominable Showman* (1941), retitled *Murder in the Circus* for the
American market, was met with little fanfare when published
by New York's Mystery House Paperbacks in 1944. The only
overseas review of any of Gunn's novels was dismissive. Mystery
critic Anthony Boucher devoted two sentences to *Murder in the
Circus* in his November 1944 column in the *Washington Post*:
"An arctic detective in the Antipodes can't catch a cold, never
mind a murderer. Less *Nanook of the North*, more *Badbook of the
South*."

In *A Red Herring*, Gunn devotes only a few pages to the years
between 1950 and 1959, observing that they were, on the whole,
so pleasantly uneventful that they could have been summarised
in three words: "We were happy." Every year on 13 January, her
wedding anniversary, another Arnaaluk novel would appear in
bookshops around the country beneath large purple signs featuring an attractive model with the slogan, "Start the New Year with
a BANG! Start the New Year with a GUNN!" The novel would
go through at least three printings and receive unanimously
admiring reviews. Quincy remained devoted and supported her
through the greatest sadness of her life: that she could not have
children. Despite this, the Gunns were content, and their legendary weekend parties at "Mysteriosa" continued to attract the

most talented, most famous and most powerful in the country. The decade was capped by Claudia Gunn being made Dame Commander of the Order of the British Empire in 1959.

The 1960s were less kind. Gunn continued to enjoy excellent health, but her beloved Quincy died in his sleep in August 1961. There followed an unseemly spat with Albert Mackintosh, the editor of *Northerly*, who rejected a poem Gunn had written in memory of her husband's passing. With Quincy's death, Gunn withdrew from public life, and there were no more parties at "Mysteriosa". Berkeley & Hunt brought out a new Arnaaluk mystery every year, although privately Gunn admitted to having had enough of the character, and of the letters she continued to receive from "do-gooders" objecting to his being called an Eskimo instead of an Inuit. In 1964 she confided to her agent, Oscar Musgrave, "Sometimes I wish M.A. would choke to death on a fishbone." A new generation of reviewers and writers agreed. The novels published after Quincy Gunn's death were received with antagonism and sometimes outright contempt, despite their being substantially better written, thanks to the editorial guidance of Robert Bush. Gunn's readers paid no attention to the reviews; sales of her novels reached their peak in 1968 with *Cold Comfort Harm*.

In 1972 Berkeley & Hunt approached the novelist with a proposal for an authorised biography. After some hesitation, Gunn assented, with the proviso that she could vet the biographer. Initially Stephen Pennington agreed to the project, confident that his lengthy life of Alexander Fernsby would soon be completed. By 1973 Gunn had lost patience with Pennington and instead turned to Will Deverall, a mystery critic and historian who had always looked kindly on Gunn's novels in his reviews.

In June of that year, Gunn invited Deverall to "Mysteriosa" to discuss the project. Satisfied as she was with the deferential Deverall, her decision to hire him was sealed by the presence of his four-year-old daughter, Rachel, who accompanied her father to the meeting. Gunn doted on the little girl and would often look after her during the time that Deverall spent researching in the basement archives of "Mysteriosa". Deverall completed the final draft of the biography in August 1975. On the last day of that month he went to "Mysteriosa" to personally deliver a copy of the manuscript to Gunn, who had, coincidentally, just finished her latest, and final, Arnaaluk novel, *An Icicle for an Icicle*. The biographer and his elderly subject had tea and cake together, then Deverall took his leave, telling Gunn he hoped she would enjoy the book.

The body of Claudia Gunn was found in her library the next morning by the butler. She had died at her desk while reading her biography; a heart attack had taken her on the last page. She was buried beside her husband in Cawdor cemetery. Obituaries recalled a kindly, eccentric woman who loved her husband deeply and was dedicated to the craft of mystery writing. *An Icicle for an Icicle*, which saw the death of Makittuq Arnaaluk, was published in December 1975, later winning the prestigious Gold Bludgeon from the Society of Australian Crime and Mystery Writers, an honour that had eluded Gunn while she lived. Though this would have seemed a propitious time to release Gunn's biography, Berkeley & Hunt remained tight-lipped on the matter, and it was rumoured that Will Deverall had taken the project elsewhere.

Deverall's biography, *The Mystery of Claudia Gunn: An Unauthorised Investigation*, was brought out in September 1977 by

New Dimensions following an unsuccessful court case in which Berkeley & Hunt attempted to prevent publication, citing breach of contract. The biography contained sensational revelations about the personal lives of Claudia and Quincy Gunn, including Quincy's serial philandering, Claudia's kleptomania and her affair with Vivian Darkbloom, and the Gunns' brutal treatment of their domestic staff. The most damaging disclosure was Deverall's discovery of a secret "blackmail chamber" that lay hidden behind a reproduction of the *Mona Lisa* in the basement archives of "Mysteriosa". When the Gunns had first renovated their house, they had added dozens of spy holes and secret passages from which they could observe the guests who came to their weekend parties. In twenty-six large filing cabinets, labelled from "Arson" to "Zoophile", the Gunns had amassed a staggering amount of evidence detailing the immoral and often criminal behaviour of hundreds of Australian writers and editors, critics, reviewers, booksellers, artists, politicians and publishers. The Gunns had used this information to terrorise anyone who stood in the way of Claudia's literary ambitions and Quincy's career in journalism. The entries stretched from 1905 to 1961, the year of Quincy Gunn's death, and presented proof of affairs, fetishes, addictions, embezzlements, manslaughters, assaults, cruelty to animals, espionage, fraud, pimping, prostitution, tax evasion, drunk-driving and vandalism. Many of the Gunns' victims had been forced to pay tens of thousands of dollars to buy silence, while others had been compelled to grant "favours", like Erasmus Hunt of Berkeley & Hunt, who had been coerced into publishing Claudia Gunn's first novel. Some, such as the writer Sydney Steele, had been destroyed. In late 1945 the elderly Steele threw himself and the only copy of his unpublished memoir from the Manly ferry and drowned after the Gunns threatened to reveal his dalliance with his goddaughter, Vivian Darkbloom, if he did not pay them two thousand pounds.

The Mystery of Claudia Gunn: An Unauthorised Investigation won the inaugural Pennington Prize for Nonfiction in 1978. The Society of Australian Crime and Mystery Writers voted to strip Gunn of the Gold Bludgeon a year later. Ambitious plans by the ABC to film the Makittuq Arnaaluk novels were shelved, and by 1980 all of Gunn's fifty-nine novels had fallen out of print. Within only a few years of her death, Gunn had disappeared from memory as completely as George Smythe, the doomed vicar in her *Albino in a Snowstorm* (1957). The sole critical appraisal of her work remains the devastating study *Who Cares Who Killed Vincent Prowse?* (1984), published by New Dimensions, which won the Society of Australian Crime and Mystery Writers Silver Hatchet Award in 1985. The book, written by Will Deverall, was the first to be published under his real name, which he had not used since he was four: William De Vere.

Francis X. McVeigh at the offices of the Australian Worker,
July 1937

FRANCIS X M.VEIGH

(1900–1948?)

*We must take the billy off the boil. We must put a bullet
through the head of "The Loaded Dog". The Snowy River
must be dammed, and the Overflow liquidated.*

From McVeigh's 1931 speech to the Conference of
Australian Communist Writers

FRANCIS XAVIER MCVEIGH, COMMUNIST PARTY MEMBER,
pamphleteer and writer of socialist realism, was born on
31 December 1900 at his parents' farm on the outskirts of
Toowoomba, Queensland. He was a month premature and was
not expected to survive more than a day or two, but Francis continued to live, though not to thrive. He was later to write that he
had come early so as not to be born an Australian, as the country
became a commonwealth the day after his birth. Francis was the
fourth child, and only son, of Ambrose and Catherine McVeigh,
who had emigrated from Scotland in 1895. Ambrose had been a
schoolteacher in Hawick; having lost his job because of his radical
politics, he had come to Australia in the hope it would prove a more
egalitarian society than Great Britain. Catherine was an illiterate
farmer's daughter from Aberdeen whom Ambrose married after
she fell pregnant. For all his socialist principles, Ambrose felt his
wife to be beneath him, and theirs was not a happy union.

Francis was a sickly child, and therefore exempt from the strenuous work of running a farm. He was bedridden for months at a time and spent his days reading and rereading the books his father owned: the novels of Émile Zola, the collected works of John Stuart Mill, and *The Communist Manifesto* (1848). In a speech to the Union of Australian Printers in 1935, McVeigh claimed that he had memorised Marx and Engels's pamphlet by the time he was six. But in a letter to Katharine Susannah Prichard in 1932 he confessed:

> Would you believe I never read the manifesto till I was fifteen? The first time I tried, I was five, and the opening line, "A spectre is haunting Europe – the spectre of communism", terrified me so much I had nightmares for the next six months. Every night I would wake up sobbing, "It's coming to get me! The commonism [sic] is coming!"

The McVeigh property was not a success. Though Ambrose worked hard, he had little knowledge of agriculture beyond that drawn from some old textbooks on animal husbandry he had bought in Toowoomba, and he refused to listen to his wife, who had grown up on a farm. Catherine worshipped her young son; he resembled her in his red hair and quiet ways. The friend-less woman could not help confiding in him how miserable she was, and how Ambrose McVeigh mistreated her, confidences Francis secretly reported to his father. By the outbreak of the Great War the family had lost their property and had moved to Spring Hill, a suburb of Brisbane. Ambrose was unable to find employment and they were reduced to living off the charity of the Catholic Church. Ambrose's radical beliefs did not extend to religion, and in November 1914, encouraged by the parish priest, he enlisted in the army, telling his son that he could not allow his family to starve. The money Ambrose McVeigh sent home after enlisting was sufficient, barely, for his wife and children to keep body and soul together. Francis's mother and three sisters found employment in factories, and Francis became a telegram boy. His health flourished with the exercise and fresh air, although in the first months of the job he was haunted by the faces of the women to whom he delivered pink telegrams, signalling the death of a loved one. After a year he was hardened enough that he lingered on the doorsteps of the devastated families, waiting patiently for his tip.

On 21 May 1917, the last of the telegrams Francis had to carry was addressed to his mother. Ambrose had been killed in France. Instead of delivering the telegram, Francis McVeigh rode his bicycle to the local Catholic church and smashed the stained-glass windows. He was arrested and imprisoned for two weeks; his first act upon release was to join the Industrial Workers of the World, a radical union calling for an end to the war. He took part in many anti-war demonstrations organised by the IWW, or the "Wobblies" as they were known. The earliest known photograph of McVeigh is of a protest that appeared on the front page of the Brisbane *Echo* of 14 August 1917. The young McVeigh can just be made out on the far left of the crowd, holding up a sign on which is printed, "War Profiteers Killed My Da". McVeigh held to this belief throughout his life, even on learning after the war from a soldier in his father's brigade that Ambrose McVeigh had died from syphilis contracted from a prostitute in Cairo, for which he had been too ashamed to seek treatment.

In late 1917 McVeigh volunteered to deliver the IWW's newspaper, the *Clarion*, which he would study from front to back each night before he went to sleep. He soon began to submit articles and, after a few false starts, his first published work appeared on 14 December 1917. The article was a celebration of the recent October Revolution in Russia, concluding with an open invitation to "Comrade Trotsky, hero of the proletariat" to visit Australia. Over the next three years McVeigh wrote hundreds of thousands of words for the *Clarion*, calling for higher wages, better conditions for workers and a general strike. When he submitted a column advocating armed insurrection against the New South Wales government, his editor refused to print it, fearing reprisals from the authorities. Disgusted, McVeigh resigned from the IWW in 1920 and later that year became one of the founding members of the Australian Communist Party. In his role as the party's director of literature, McVeigh grew ashamed of his mother and sisters, whom he thought of privately as "peasants". After sending them a one-off sum of ten pounds, he disowned them.

During the next two decades, McVeigh was instrumental in bringing dozens of Australian writers into the communist fold, including John Morrison, Judah Waten, Frank Hardy and Sydney Steele. Such was his influence that some writers would only publish their work after McVeigh, and by extension the party, had approved it. McVeigh's condemnation of Sydney Steele's unfinished novel *English Eucalyptus* as "bourgeois filth" in 1924 prompted Steele to destroy the only known manuscript of a book that his friend James Joyce had considered – even in its incomplete state – a masterpiece. As well as encouraging others to toe the party line, McVeigh himself wrote over two hundred and fifty pamphlets criticising various aspects of Australian literature, cultivating a reputation as a controversialist. Among his most incendiary works were "The Kulak's Wife: On the Class Traitor Henry Lawson", "The Forgetting of Wisdom: The Bourgeois Australian Education System" and the utopian "Pa and Pete on Our Collective Farm" (all published in 1926). McVeigh's position was secured in a purge of the party by the Communist International (Comintern) in 1927. The purge had been initiated a year earlier, when McVeigh sent the detailed files he had compiled on his comrades to Moscow. He further consolidated his importance to the party with the publication of a short-story collection, *The Red Flag* (1928), which envisages an Australia that has been collectivised and industrialised along the Soviet model. The stories feature plain-speaking, proletarian heroes who spend pages discussing Marxist dialectics, even when in the throes of passion:

> "Make love to me," the propertied woman begged Jones. "Give me your child!"
>
> The mechanic sneered at her. "Pah! You and your husband are capitalists. You produce nothing. You live on the sweat of others. Even your name is decadent: Vivian!"
>
> "Yes, I am bourgeois, I am decadent. Overthrow me!"
> He kissed her violently, and shoved her onto his cot.
> "You are ignorant!" he said.
> "Then teach me."
> "As Marx said, relations of personal dependence are the first social forms in which human productive capacity develops only to a slight extent and at isolated points. Personal independence founded on objective dependence

is the second great form, in which a system of general
social metabolism, of universal relations, of all-round
needs and universal capacities is formed for the first time.
Free individuality, based on the universal development of
individuals and on their subordination of their communal,
social productivity as their social wealth, is the third
stage."

"I'm yours!" she cried, drawing him down to her.

The success of the collection, which spawned a host of
similar works by left-wing Australian writers, was assured by a
sycophantic review in *Pravda*. Conservative critics in McVeigh's
own country predictably dismissed *The Red Flag* as an almost
unreadable instance of the Soviet "Boy Meets Tractor, Tractor
Breaks Down, Boy Repairs Tractor" school of fiction.

In 1929 the Russian translation of *The Red Flag* came to the
attention of Maxim Gorky, who had been personally tasked by
Stalin to promote the budding literary form of socialist realism. Gorky recognised in McVeigh's work a shining example of
this new form, and invited the writer to visit Moscow. McVeigh
left Australia for Russia in April 1930 and spent the rest of
the year there. During his visit he met notable Soviet writers
including Mikhail Sholokhov, Fyodor Gladkov and Andrei
Platonov, few of whom would survive the terror of the next few
years. McVeigh was also present at Gorky's house, along with
forty other writers from Russia, Germany, Great Britain and
France, in September 1930 when Stalin paid a visit. The general
secretary of the Communist Party told the assembled authors
they were "engineers of the soul" and instructed them to write
only stories that would encourage world revolution. Each of

the Russian writers in turn toasted Stalin, as did McVeigh, though he did not speak the language, and his translator had a great deal of trouble understanding his Australian accent. A photograph taken at the party, which shows McVeigh raising his glass to a mystified Stalin as Gorky looks on with a nervous smile, was published in the *1930 Soviet Literature Yearbook* and later reprinted on the front page of the *Australian Worker* on McVeigh's return from Moscow in 1931.

During his stay in Russia McVeigh was shown the wonders of communism, including a tour of the White Sea–Baltic canal, then under construction, which depended on the forced labour of nearly 100,000 "enemies of the people". The experience made a strong impression on the Australian. On returning to Moscow he wrote a detailed memorandum for his hosts suggesting numerous ways the efficiency of the prisoners might be increased. McVeigh included the formal letter of thanks from the Committee for Patriotic Works in his account of the trip, *Home Is the Worker* (1933), which categorically rejected the reports of horrific cruelty and death in the USSR. His long essay in praise of the project, "О реабилитации контрреволюционеров Благодаря упорной работе" ("On the Rehabilitation of Counter-revolutionaries Through Hard Yakka"), appeared in *Stalin's White Sea–Baltic Canal* (1934), alongside work by Gorky, Aleksey Tolstoy and others.

Upon arriving back in Sydney in June 1931, McVeigh called a general meeting of the Australian Communist Writers, a sub-branch of the party. His five-hour harangue on the urgent necessity of bringing socialist realism to Australia was reprinted in full in the *Australian Worker* but condemned in other national newspapers. McVeigh's opening words deriding Australia's literary tradition resulted in Iain Harkaway, the federal member of parliament for Lyne, New South Wales, calling for him to be charged with treason. Taking advantage of the controversy, the Comintern made unlimited funds available to McVeigh to advance the cause of communist literature in Australia. With this money, McVeigh established Steelman Press in July 1933, leasing a large office in Kings Cross and hiring dozens of staff, including several pretty young secretaries.

McVeigh had been galvanised by the successful implementation of five-year plans in the Soviet economy, and saw no reason why such a plan could not be used for literature. He set a target of ten million words to be published by the press in five years; the target was exceeded by over ninety per cent. Steelman Press brought out hundreds of socialist-realist novels, as well as providing sizeable grants to communist writers including Eleanor Dark and Katharine Susannah Prichard. Although they were always well reviewed by McVeigh in his regular column in the *Australian Worker*, the novels were boycotted by most other reviewers and literary critics, and all were published at a loss. Rumours circulated that a considerable slice of the Comintern funding was being used by McVeigh to buy the silence of his secretaries, whom he was in the habit of seducing and then sacking.

In the years before the outbreak of the Second World War, McVeigh's rhetoric was primarily directed towards attacking Adolf Hitler and defending the Moscow Trials of 1936 to 1938. In his columns he also condemned Rand Washington's short stories and novels as exemplifying the Nazification of Australian literature. McVeigh continued to denounce Washington and "his bestial overlord, Hitler" in speeches at Communist Party rallies throughout 1937 and 1938 and in a book of anti-Nazi essays, *The Black and the Red*, in which he argued that the most implacable enemy of fascism was not capitalism, but communism. *The Black and the Red* went to press on 22 August 1939, the day before the signing of the Molotov–Ribbentrop Pact, which guaranteed non-aggression between Germany and the USSR. When McVeigh heard the news he commandeered a car and raced round Sydney buying every copy of *The Black and the Red* he could lay his hands on. By late afternoon he had accounted for the last copy of the book, which he added to the others and burned along with the printing plates. His article for the *Australian Worker* the next day included a denunciation of the actions of Great Britain and France, which had drawn Australia into an imperialist war, and a review of Rand Washington's new novel, *Jackboots on Cor*, which McVeigh called "a magnum opus of science fiction." Steelman Press, with Siegfried Press, later jointly published a novel by Washington, *Whiteman of Mars* (1940), in which Buck Whiteman and the Shevikibol, the intrepid ant-like inhabitants of the red planet, agree to respect each other's cosmic borders after almost being tricked into war by the dastardly Argobolin.

In the early months of the Second World War, McVeigh returned to pamphleteering, writing a number of inflammatory works encouraging the members of trade unions such as the Miners' Federation and the Organisation of Waterfront Workers to go on strike. After the invasion of Russia by Germany on 22 June 1941 McVeigh's newspaper column advocated the arrest and execution of these same union members as "fascist stooges" who had deliberately sabotaged the war effort against the Nazis. In January 1944 the Comintern, dissatisfied with Steelman Press and perturbed by gossip about McVeigh's sexual improprieties, withdrew funding and the company was allowed to fold. A brief, blunt article in *Pravda* hinted darkly that sabotage was to blame. McVeigh was quick to respond, denouncing the wreckers by name. Sydney Steele and Irene Young, the daughter of the poet Matilda Young, were among the dozen party members employed by the press who were expelled for counter-revolutionary activities, which included a conspiracy to destroy McVeigh himself by spreading base, unfounded rumours about his private life.

Throughout the remainder of the war years, McVeigh sought to repair the damage the failure of Steelman Press had caused to his standing in the party by using his column in the *Australian Worker* to extol the gallant victories of the Russian armed forces and the almost supernatural genius of Stalin's military leadership. In 1945 McVeigh saw an opportunity to ingratiate himself further with the Comintern when Berkeley & Hunt announced their plans to publish George Orwell's anti-communist fable *Animal Farm* in November of that year. Using his influence with the Union of Printers, McVeigh threatened the publishers with a strike if they went ahead. Thanks to McVeigh's efforts, Berkeley & Hunt capitulated and *Animal Farm* did not appear in Australia until August 1946, when national feeling had begun to turn against the Communist Party. McVeigh reviewed the book in his column, calling it "a monstrous slander on the greatest of all nations, and the greatest of all men". McVeigh's only novel, *Return to Animal Farm*, appeared in print a week after Orwell's book, suggesting McVeigh had written it much earlier. Despite its title, *Return to Animal Farm* is not a sequel but a retelling of the events of Orwell's fable from the point of view of Squealer the pig, and follows the courageous Comrade Napoleon as he creates a socialist utopia after the Manor Farm uprising, which then spreads to all the other farms in the country. Although McVeigh reported that the print run of ten thousand copies sold out in two days, in all likelihood *Return to Animal Farm* sold only a fraction of that number. Its one lasting consequence was that the conservative press seized on the nickname "Squealer" for McVeigh.

On 12 January 1947 McVeigh's column in the *Australian Worker* informed his readers that he had been invited to return to the USSR. There he was to be personally honoured by Comrade Stalin with the International Workers' Award of Literary Glory, for his "Stakhanovite efforts at promoting the cause of social-ist realism". McVeigh flew first class to Indonesia, then Beijing and Vladivostok, where he took a luxury cabin on the Trans-Siberian express, arriving in Moscow on 11 July. A journalist saw him welcomed at Yaroslavsky rail terminal by three stocky men dressed in dark suits, then driven away in a black limou-sine. McVeigh was never seen again. That same month foreign subscribers to the *Soviet Encyclopaedia* were sent a slip of paper describing the mean cell volume (MCV) of red blood cells, which they were ordered to paste over the entry for McVeigh, Francis X.

The final fate of McVeigh remains an enigma, despite the opening of the NKVD archives after the collapse of the Soviet Union in 1989. No official record of what became of the Australian writer has surfaced, except for one suggestive entry in a partially shredded ledger recovered from the secret police archives, dated January 1947: "File received Sydney Embassy 1 November 1946, and forwarded to Comintern. F.X. McVeigh anonymously denounced as Trotskyite saboteur. Proof attached.

To be actioned." The "proof" of McVeigh's crimes, whatever it was, has been lost. It is unlikely that the circumstances of McVeigh's downfall will ever be known with any certainty, but a number of literary historians, including Rachel Deverall and Stephen Pennington, have maintained that the foreign zek (inmate) described in chapter four of the first volume of Aleksandr Solzhenitsyn's *The Gulag Archipelago* (1974) is the Australian writer. In this chapter Solzhenitsyn reproduces the account of a political prisoner who was held at a transit camp in Vorkuta in 1948:

> There is one zek in particular who stays with me. He was red haired, and very thin (as we all were, of course) and utterly lost. He was from Austria or Australia. I forget which. He spoke English and had no Russian, and his hands shook as he offered half his meagre bread ration to anyone who would write a letter for him to Comrade Stalin telling him that there had been a mistake. One of the thieves took him up on his proposal, and the foreigner wept with gratitude when he was handed back his precious scrap of paper with some Russian words scrawled on it. I peered down from my bunk and saw that the thief had written, "Stalin is a goatfucker" five times. When the foreign zek handed the note to the guards he was dragged away, screaming, as the thief roared with laughter. I don't know what happened to him after that.

McVeigh's successor as the Australian Communist Party's director of literature cleared out his office and destroyed all of his papers, including McVeigh's prized copy of the *1930 Soviet*

Literature Yearbook, which contained the photograph of him toasting Comrade Stalin. A replacement copy of the *Yearbook* was dispatched from Moscow including the same photograph of Stalin and Gorky, but with McVeigh airbrushed out. Yet the censors were careless: if the picture is examined closely, the faint image of McVeigh's raised right arm can still be seen on the edge of the frame, a ghostly glass of vodka in his hand.

Rachel Deverall in Paris, February 2005

(1969–2016)

If the history of Australian literature teaches us anything, it
is that behind every great female writer (Praed, Young, Mc-
Ginnis, Barnard et al.), there is a man holding her back.

From notes for the introduction to Deverall's unfinished *Squeaker's Mates: A History of Australian Women*
Writers 1800–2000

RACHEL DEVERALL, LITERARY CRITIC, HISTORIAN AND SCHOLAR,
was born in Melbourne on 17 May 1969. She came from a bookish family: her mother, Rainy, was a playwright and author of
popular farces including *On Words: A Play* (1984), a satire on
Kangaroulipo; her aunt Polly was an award-winning science-
fiction writer; her father, Will, was a mystery critic; and her
godmother was the poet Matilda Young. (The poem Young
wrote to mark the occasion of Rachel's christening, "The
Lamb", is considered among the finest of her late style.) As a
child, Rachel divided her time between the theatre where
rehearsals for her mother's latest play were taking place and her
father's study at home, where she loved drawing in the margins
of the dozens of detective novels that littered the floor. When
she was four, her father was commissioned to write a biography
of Claudia Gunn, and the family moved to Sydney. On many

visits Rachel accompanied her father to "Mysteriosa", where the elderly writer plied her with macaroons and jelly babies as her father worked in the archives.

Rachel enjoyed reading and writing, and her first stories were about a young gumshoe called Trudy Tective, who solved mysteries and uncovered secrets, but was always one step behind a shadowy arch-villain known only as the Bearded Man. One real-life secret revealed in 1975 was that Rachel's grandmother was not dead, as her mother had told her, but in a nursing home. From April 1975 to June 1976 Rainy and Rachel spent an afternoon every month with Vivian Darkbloom, Rainy's mother and Rachel's grandmother. Although Vivian did not know who they were, and could not remember them from visit to visit, the old woman was always happy to see Rachel, and would ask her to read aloud from one of the books that lined the shelves in her room. Rachel usually chose one of the *Little Viv* books to read from, a selection that made the old woman very happy. In late May 1976 Rachel wrote a new book as a present for her grandmother, *Little Viv Meets Trudy Tective*, but sadly Vivian Darkbloom passed away before their next visit.

At her death all Darkbloom's novels, collections of stories and volumes of poetry were left to Rainy, who passed them on to Rachel. It took the girl three years to read them. She laughed at Addison Tiller's *Off Our Homestead* (1917), was moved by her grandfather Peter Darkbloom's *Dancing in the Shadows* (1920), mystified by Frederick Stratford's *Odysseus* (1923) and bored by Francis X. McVeigh's *The Red Flag* (1928). Rachel also felt guilty because she could never manage to finish her grandmother's own novel, *Ivy Van Allbine: An Australian Vanity Fair* (1919), no matter how often she tried. Her mother had no answer as to why her grandmother owned only a handful of books by women. Rainy did not read many novels herself, and most of Rachel's father's mystery novels were also by men. Shortly after completing his biography of Claudia Gunn, he had shocked Rachel by making a bonfire of all Gunn's books in the garden.

Rachel's sense of fairness was outraged by the lack of books by women in her house, and she decided that since she had read only books by Australian men for three years, she would now only read books by Australian women for the same amount of time. She began with the boarding-school novels of Georgina Fairweather, and the series of abridged classics by Naomi Plume, but then pestered her mother to take her to distant second-hand bookshops, where her pocket money purchased dusty copies of novels by Marjorie Barnard, Katharine Susannah Prichard, Catherine Swan, Eleanor Dark and Madeleine White. The three years she was to spend reading work by Australian women lengthened to four, then five. Rachel filled dozens of exercise books with her reflections and observations and by the time she was fifteen, she had developed an excellent working knowledge of Australian women's writing from 1860 to the present day. Her favourite writer was a contemporary one: Rachel adored the short stories of Lydia McGinnis, and read McGinnis's first collection, *Basilica* (1976), over and over again. For her sixteenth birthday she asked her mother to go with her to the house where McGinnis had taken her own life after publication of her last book, *Ultimo Thule* (1981).

When she was seventeen, Rachel Deverall went to the University of Sydney to study Australian literature. The course bored her; she had long outgrown Lawson and Tiller, and her lecturer did not appreciate Rachel's polite interjections when he spoke about the poetry of Matilda Young. Deverall began to skip lectures and tutorials, although her marks remained as impressive as ever, and instead sat in on French classes so that she could at least learn something new. Her interest in the life and work of Lydia McGinnis intensified. The information available on the writer was sparse, and tightly controlled by McGinnis's second husband and editor, Robert Bush. Deverall read everything Bush wrote about McGinnis, much of it contradictory, and came to believe that Bush was hiding something about his wife's work. Her suspicions were further aroused when she read an old account of McGinnis's death in the *Daily Trumpet*, which mentioned that her suicide note had been written in purple ink. Deverall knew that McGinnis had an aversion to purple, perhaps because her husband had used that colour of ink when editing her manuscripts. This inconsistency prompted Deverall to investigate further.

Deverall had always looked older than her years, and carefully made-up and smartly dressed could pass for a young reporter. Under this guise she interviewed McGinnis's ex-husband, Brian, and the friends McGinnis had made in the Sydney literary scene, none of whom had a good word to say about Robert Bush. After a number of phone calls Deverall managed to secure an interview with Bush himself, claiming it was for a profile in the *Sydney Review*. During the interview Deverall stole evidence revealing the extent of Bush's meddling in his wife's work, and his forging of her suicide note. Deverall handed over McGinnis's unedited manuscripts to Xanthippe Press, and their publication led to Bush resigning from Berkeley & Hunt. Although officially the university frowned on her theft, Deverall was celebrated by the literary world for her role in Bush's disgrace. Robert Bush never pressed charges, and from time to time Deverall would wonder how he could have been so careless as to leave a stranger alone in his office with his desk drawers unlocked.

Deverall completed her degree in 1990 and won a full scholarship to study for a PhD shortly afterwards; her thesis was on the fiction of Lydia McGinnis. Over the next four years Deverall published thirteen articles comparing McGinnis's original stories with Bush's edited versions. Her conclusions were unexpected and divisive; Robert Bush's editing had, in almost every case, substantially improved McGinnis's work, and *None of Them Knew the Colour of the Sky* and *The City of Fireworks* were undoubtedly inferior to the reworked *Basilica* and *Ultimo Thule*. Deverall's judgment came under sustained attack from feminist academics, who accused her of falling under Bush's spell in the same way that McGinnis had, but Deverall stood by her analysis. After being awarded her doctorate she became a lecturer at the university; her first act was to resurrect and update Matilda Young's "Australian Women's Fiction Studies" course, which had been withdrawn after the poet's death in 1975. As well as Barbara Baynton, Elizabeth Jolley and Helen Garner, Deverall included the work of many critically neglected female writers, including Matilda Young herself, Lydia McGinnis and even Claudia Gunn. Deverall continued to publish critical articles on McGinnis throughout the 1990s, and her revised and expanded doctoral thesis, *Excavating the Basilica: The Short Fiction of Lydia McGinnis*, was published in 2001. In October of that year, Deverall's book won the Pennington Prize for Nonfiction, beating a strong field that comprised *Truth Goes Walkabout: The Great Aboriginal Lie* by Edward Gayle, *Kangaroulipo and Beyond: The Experimental Writers of the 1970s* by Lazaros Zigomanis and *Ordinary People Doing Everyday Things in Commonplace Settings: A History of Australian Short Fiction* by the author of this book.

Deverall straightaway commenced an ambitious new work, with the provisional title *Squeaker's Mates: A History of Australian Women Writers 1800–2000*. She spent months in the archives of the National Library of Australia, seeking out rare issues of nineteenth-century journals such as *Tegg's Monthly Magazine, Ha Ha! A Merry Magazine for Australians* and *Once a Month*. During the course of her research she found twenty-nine previously lost short stories by writers including Rosa Praed, Waif Wander and Louisa Atkinson. In the winter of 2003, shortly after her marriage to the author of this book, Deverall was contacted by a colleague at the University of Western Australia, who invited her to examine a cache of obscure nineteenth- and early twentieth-century Australian journals that had recently been discovered mouldering in the attic of a pub in Fremantle. Fortunately, the owner of the pub had some inkling of the artistic value of the trove and had donated them to the university rather than throwing them out.

Deverall flew to Perth in November 2003 and spent two weeks examining and cataloguing the contents of the journals, one of which, *The Looking-Glass Annual*, did not appear in any databases. This journal was particularly tattered. The cover was missing, as were the first three pages, and Deverall was unable to locate the place or date of publication. On a whim, she took *The Looking-Glass Annual* back to her hotel to read that night. It contained three short stories Deverall was already familiar with, and a complete novel, *The Summer Journey* by Wilhelmina Campbell, a writer Deverall, despite her knowledge of nineteenth-century Australian fiction, had never come across before. First, Deverall reread the short stories, so she was half-asleep when she began *The Summer Journey*, the picaresque tale of Quintus Collins, an Englishman convicted of forgery and transported to Australia in the early nineteenth century. Collins survives and eventually escapes the horrors of the convict system to become a drover, but when his wife, Clara, is killed by a snake he turns to bushranging to support his seven children. He then becomes a swagman, and is eventually reduced to stealing and killing sheep to avoid starvation. In one exciting sequence, after being cornered in a billabong by the police, Collins fakes his own drowning. At the end of the novel, after innumerable adventures, Collins remarries, makes a fortune digging for gold and returns to England, where his relentless egotism threatens to destroy his new family. Finally, Collins is found murdered in a hansom cab, and the novel breaks off before his killer is unmasked.

Despite her fatigue, Deverall stayed up all night to finish the story. It was well written and entertaining, stuffed with unbelievable incidents and action, and without doubt the most derivative book she had ever read. Campbell's novel contained elements of Catherine Helen Spence's *Clara Morison* (1854), Marcus Clarke's *For the Term of His Natural Life* (1874), Fergus Hume's *The Mystery of a Hansom Cab* (1886), Henry Lawson's "The Drover's Wife" (1892), Ethel Turner's *Seven Little Australians* (1894), Banjo Paterson's "Waltzing Matilda" (1895), Joseph Furphy's *Such Is Life* (1903), and dozens of other famous Australian poems, stories and novels from the mid-nineteenth to early twentieth centuries. Initially, Deverall theorised that "Wilhelmina Campbell" was a previously unknown alias of Frederick Stratford, and *The Summer*

Journey was his first, forgotten, published "work". However, the novel went beyond mere plagiarism; it did not simply copy word for word as Stratford had done, but repurposed a range of sources to create something new. Deverall estimated that the novel must have been written after 1903, and that the short stories that accompanied it, all written in the nineteenth century, were therefore reprints.

At first light Deverall returned to the university archives and continued her search through the towering piles of yellowed paper until she found the cover and contents page of *The Looking-Glass Annual*. The publication date presented her with an impossibility: the journal was dated January 1828, fully three years before the publication of the first Australian novel, Henry Savery's *Quintus Servinton: A Tale Founded Upon Incidents of Real Occurrence*. If this date was correct, then *The Summer Journey* was not only the first novel to be published in Australia, which was itself a remarkable discovery, but it had also anticipated by decades the work of Marcus Clarke, Henry Lawson and scores of others. After three days closely reading *The Summer Journey*, Deverall had identified a further one hundred and thirty-two similarities in plot, dialogue, character, symbolism and imagery to the most famous works of Australian literature up to Henry Handel Richardson's *The Fortunes of Richard Mahony* (1930). Still, Deverall could not quite bring herself to accept that almost every classic work of Australian literature in the nineteenth and early twentieth centuries had been derived from one forgotten novel by an unknown author published in an obscure journal in 1828.

Despite her eagerness to publish her find, Deverall was persuaded that the next step must be to establish beyond any doubt that *The Looking-Glass Annual* was genuine. Six months of painstaking enquiries resulted in her finding eight separate references to the *Annual* in literary journals published in 1829 and 1830. A review in *Lone Hand* in 1830 noted "Miss Campbell's amusing *Summer Journey*" while the December 1829 editorial in the *Women's Domestic Helper* admonished writers who "journeyed too far into summer, leaving the gentle reader perspiring by the wayside". Deverall also spent three thousand dollars from the savings account she shared with the author of this book having the ink and paper used in the *Annual* analysed by a forensic laboratory in Washington, D.C. A comprehensive chemical, physical and organic analysis, including radiocarbon dating, confirmed that *The Looking-Glass Annual* was published sometime between 1825 and 1835. Deverall's wildest theory had been proven correct: *The Summer Journey* was the hidden wellspring of Australian literature, and the greatest Australian writers had all secretly drawn from it.

Exhilarated by her find, Deverall spent the next four months scouring historical records for biographical information about Wilhelmina Campbell, her labours uncovering only a few scant facts. Campbell was born in Parramatta in 1810. Her father was a forger from Battersea in London, whose death sentence was commuted to transportation to Australia for life, and her mother was a laundress who had been transported for receiving stolen goods. Nothing was known of Campbell's childhood or education. *The Summer Journey* was apparently her only publication; at least Deverall could find no others. The only additional record of Campbell's life was her marriage to a Frenchman, Victor Wernier, in Parramatta on 9 January 1835. With her marriage Wilhelmina Wernier disappeared from historical records, but

Deverall did not give up. In late 2004, conscious that she needed to exhaust every avenue before publishing her research, she determined to travel to France to investigate the Wernier family in the hopes of establishing a connection with Wilhelmina. The language posed no problem; she was fluent in French, having studied it informally at university when she was supposed to be attending English lectures. The trip also served as a long-delayed honeymoon for Deverall and the author of this book.

Deverall spent weeks searching the *Archives nationales* in Paris, Fontainebleau and Aix-en-Provence, but found no mention of the Wernier family. Disheartened, Deverall and the author were preparing to return to Australia when she glanced at her copy of the Werniers' marriage certificate. The "W" was florid, and smudged; it might perhaps be a "V". Deverall paid a final visit to the archives. Within a few hours she had uncovered vital new information: Victor Vernier had returned with "*une femme australienne*" to the family estate in Vimy (Pas-de-Calais) in February 1836, where Wilhelmina gave birth to a son, Hugo, born 3 September that same year. Unfortunately the records were incomplete, the town hall having been destroyed during the Great War. Deverall could find no more details about the Verniers, but it was enough to encourage her to stay in France and continue her research, while the author returned home to Sydney.

In January 2005 Deverall mentioned Hugo Vernier during a conversation with an acquaintance who lectured in French literature at the *Université Paris-Sorbonne*. The name struck the lecturer, who recalled that a writer called Hugo Vernier had been the hobbyhorse of one of his professors when he was himself a student in the late 1960s in Beauvais. The professor, Vincent Degraël, told his story to his students again and again: in the last week of August 1939 he had been on holiday at a friend's villa in Le Havre, where he had by chance come across a book called *Le Voyage d'hiver (The Winter Journey).* It was a slender volume, the first part describing the narrative of a young man's surreal journey to an island on a lake, and the second, longer section made up of a mixture of poetry, maxims and paradoxes, a form familiar to Degraël from the works of Léon Bloy, Tristan Corbière, Rimbaud, Mallarmé, Verlaine and other canonical nineteenth-century French writers. Degraël had assumed the author of *Le Voyage d'hiver* to be a plagiarist, until he noticed the publication date of the book, 1864. Years later, in the many lectures he gave about his revolutionary findings, Degraël insisted to his students that these nineteenth-century writers

> were nothing but the copyists of a genial and neglected
> poet who, in a once-in-a-lifetime work, had known how
> to bring together the very substance from which three or
> four generations of authors would find their nourishment!

After taking notes on the book, Degraël had returned to Paris to pursue his research, but before he could do so he was drafted into the army. He was unable to return to the villa in Le Havre until after the war, only to find it had been destroyed and *Le Voyage d'hiver* lost. Although he continued searching for the rest of his life, he was never to find another copy of the book; the only additional fact he did uncover was that five hundred copies of *Le Voyage d'hiver* had been published in Valenciennes by the Hervé Bros., Printers-Booksellers. The unfortunate Degraël eventually died in a psychiatric hospital in 1974.

On learning about Degraël, Deverall wasted no time in locating his only living relative, a nephew who resided in the prosperous Paris suburb of Neuilly-sur-Seine. Fortunately Pierre Degraël had been fond of his uncle, and had kept his effects in storage after he died. It was his great pleasure to allow Deverall access to the papers. Among the hundreds of manuscripts Degraël had amassed during the decades he was gripped by his mania, Deverall found a heavy binder bound in black cloth, labelled simply and in a careful hand, *Le Voyage d'hiver*. The first eight pages detailed Degraël's researches, while the rest of the four hundred pages were blank. Her heart pounding, Deverall read Degraël's few notes. On the bottom of the sixth page she found two queries the Frenchman had written: "*Pourquoi tant de kangourous? Qu'est-ce que c'est un billabong?*" Degraël had been perplexed by the references to Australia in the *Le Voyage d'hiver*; he had not known that Hugo Vernier's mother was Australian.

In June 2005 Deverall paid a visit to the Genealogical Library in Paris, where she ascertained that a Hugo Vernier had been buried in the cemetery of a small church in the village of Lourmais in Brittany. The church had been destroyed in the Great War, then rebuilt; its register of births and deaths lay forgotten in a bricked-up basement which was only revealed after renovations at the turn of the century. The information in the register would have astonished Degraël, but it only confirmed Deverall's theory. Hugo Vernier had died when he was two. He could not have written *Le Voyage d'hiver*. The only explanation was that his mother, Wilhelmina, had written the book and published it under her dead son's name. Deverall had now been in France, alone, for eighteen months; she had exceeded the terms of her sabbatical, and the University of Sydney demanded that she return to work.

Deverall resigned from her post at the university and remained in France, combing through the historical records of the towns around Vimy for any other mention of Wilhelmina Vernier. After a discouraging nine months amid musty archives in sleepy regional centres, she uncovered a bundle of uncatalogued papers in a forgotten room in the local government offices of Arras. Though she learned nothing of Wilhelmina's life in the tumultuous years between 1836 and 1863, which saw the fall of the July Monarchy and the Second Republic, she confirmed that in 1871 the Verniers were in Paris during the last days of the Second Empire and the rise of the Paris Commune. Victor Vernier was killed on the barricades when the French army retook the city during "The Bloody Week" of 21 to 28 May 1871. Sometime afterwards, the widow Vernier sold all of her husband's estates, but instead of returning to Australia she decided, for reasons unknown, to travel to England.

Deverall flew to London in May 2006, going straight from the airport to the British Museum. There she searched for two titles, *The Spring Journey* and *The Autumn Journey*. Her conjecture was rewarded with the publication details of *The Autumn Journey* by Wilhelmina Campbell (she had obviously reverted to her maiden name after her husband's death), published by McAdam & McAllister in London in 1873 in an edition of four hundred copies. Barely able to suppress her excitement, Deverall filled in the form to request a copy from the stacks. Sadly, the librarian informed her that the book was lost. Deverall contacted Oxford's Bodleian Library, Cambridge University Library and the Trinity College Library in Dublin, but while they all held publication information about the book, none possessed a copy. She haunted auctions of rare books and became a familiar and increasingly forlorn figure among the bookshops of Charing Cross Road, always asking after *The Autumn Journey*. In January 2007, Deverall's mother and father died within a month of each other; the money and property she inherited allowed her to prolong her stay in England. Deverall's purgatory finally ended when a disreputable dealer informed her he had located an extremely rare copy of *The Autumn Journey* that could be hers for ten thousand pounds. Deverall went to her bank and completed the necessary paperwork to empty the accounts she held in Australia. Within the week, she had presented the dealer with a bank cheque for the required amount, and she held *The Autumn Journey* in her hands.

The title page of the slim, slightly water-damaged volume was stamped, faintly, "Ex Libris Halifax, Hickleton Hall, May 1899". Deverall recalled a newspaper article she had read, about two weeks previously, reporting a violent robbery in Hickleton Hall in Doncaster, the ancestral home of the third Earl of Halifax. A janitor had been seriously assaulted, and a number of rare books stolen. Deverall decided that she did not care. She returned to her hotel room and, after locking the door, read *The Autumn Journey* from beginning to end. It was written in the same elegant, oblique, fragmented style Degraël had described as belonging to *Le Voyage d'hiver*, and followed a similar structure. The first section describes a nightmarish city in the thrall of a great terror from which the narrator barely escapes with his life. The second section consists of eighty-nine vignettes and sketches, from a few lines to a paragraph long. Though Deverall was no expert in English literature, she quickly identified themes, plots, characters and dialogue that would later form the basis for Anthony Trollope's *The Way We Live Now* (1875), Anna

Sewell's *Black Beauty* (1877), Henry James's *The Portrait of a Lady* (1881), Robert Louis Stevenson's *Treasure Island* (1883), H. Rider Haggard's *She* (1886), Arthur Conan Doyle's *A Study in Scarlet* (1887), Rudyard Kipling's *The Man Who Would Be King* (1888), Thomas Hardy's *Tess of the D'Urbervilles* (1891), H.G. Wells's *The Time Machine* (1895), Bram Stoker's *Dracula* (1897), and Joseph Conrad's *Heart of Darkness* (1899) and *Nostromo* (1904). There was not an atom of doubt left in Deverall's mind; Wilhelmina Campbell was the most important and influential writer since William Shakespeare. Further analysis, she was certain, would reveal yet more authors, British, Australian and French, who had plundered Campbell's body of work.

The endpapers to *The Autumn Journey* contained a barely legible message written in pencil: "Spoke to Jardin, bookseller. No other books by W.C. extant. Jardin met W.C. once in 1879. Discouraged by failure of TAJ, she spoke of going to America. Damn shame." Deverall followed this clue, requesting access to the Cunard Line's records, which was granted in October 2007. In the company archives, she examined the passenger lists of every ship that had left a British port for America from 1879 onwards. Deverall found Wilhelmina Campbell recorded as a second-class passenger on the RMS *Umbria*, sailing from Liverpool to New York on 8 November 1882. On her way out of the archives, through the Cunard offices, Deverall was already calculating how she could scrape together enough money for a plane ticket to New York. In the foyer, her attention was caught by a model of the RMS *Umbria*; above it was a gold plaque, which stated that the ship had been lost in a storm crossing the North Atlantic on 18 November 1882. Thus ended Wilhelmina Campbell's final journey.

Deverall spent a further year in England and France, vainly searching for additional information about Wilhelmina Campbell, and at long last returned to Sydney at the end of January 2009. Ignoring the author's attempts to meet her, she bought a rundown one-bedroom house in Petersham, a twenty-minute train ride from the library at the University of Sydney. In her new home she marshalled her work on Wilhelmina Campbell: *The Looking Glass Annual* she had stolen from the University of Western Australia, her precious copy of *The Autumn Journey*, six boxes from Vincent Degraël's archive that his nephew had allowed her to take from Paris, and her own records, which now amounted to two thousand closely handwritten pages. Deverall spent months organising her voluminous research in preparation for writing her book on Wilhelmina Campbell. Then, disaster struck.

On the evening of 7 November 2009, Deverall returned from the university library to find her house in flames. The fire service was already there, and they prevented the hysterical Deverall from entering the burning building. Though she had transcribed most of her notes and made an electronic backup, Degraël's work on *Le Voyage d'hiver* was lost, as were the only copies of *The Autumn Journey* and *The Looking-Glass Annual* containing *The Summer Journey*. Deverall was inconsolable. A few days later she was admitted to the Southside Clinic, a private psychiatric hospital, where she remained, undergoing treatment, for almost two years.

An investigation into the fire concluded that it had been started deliberately; kerosene had been splashed around the living room and a match used to set it alight. The police interviewed Deverall after she had been at the hospital for six months, endeavouring to find out whether she had any enemies.

Regrettably, this set off an episode of persecutory delusion and paranoia in which Deverall refused to speak to any of her friends and family for over a year, convinced that someone she knew had deliberately sabotaged her research. For some months in 2010 Rachel regressed to her childhood; she became convinced that she was Trudy Tective, the sleuth she had made up when she was five years old, and that the Bearded Man, her nemesis, had concocted a diabolical master plan to steal her secret files.

The insurance company completed its own investigation in August 2010, reluctantly paying out Deverall's policy that December. After months of therapy and many relapses, Deverall left the clinic in October 2011, still under medication for depression and anxiety. She rented a dingy apartment in Hornsby and spent her days trying to reconstruct from memory the contents of *The Summer Journey* and *The Autumn Journey*, or in the stacks at the university library, reading her way through every journal, novel and newspaper published in Australia from 1820 onwards, seeking references to Wilhelmina Campbell she might have overlooked. She subsisted on the little money she made from freelancing for a number of Australian publishers, mainly line-editing and creating indexes for scholarly texts. Though serious research was beyond her now, she was employed as a research assistant and proofreader on *Sacred Kangaroos: Fifty Overrated Australian Novels* (2013) by the author of this book.

In late 2013 she began to complain of blurred vision and migraines. Despite the fact that reading had become an agony to her, she continued to spend at least thirty hours a week on her "research", sitting alone in the stacks at the university library, sifting through reels of microfilm and ancient bound volumes of journals, looking for the words "Wilhelmina Campbell".

Eventually her migraines became so excruciating that she could barely get out of bed in the morning; only then did she agree to see a doctor. Tests revealed that she had a brain tumour; unlike in the case of her biological grandfather, Alexander Fernsby, in 1964, this time there was to be no error. Rachel underwent surgery in February 2014, but not all of the tumour could be removed; although she endured debilitating bouts of radiation treatment, the cancer continued to grow. Her condition was pronounced terminal in January 2015, and her health slowly deteriorated over the next twelve months. During her last days she occupied herself with compiling the index for this book, a task which she completed on the morning of 14 February 2016, two hours before she passed away.

Catherine Swan, circa 1950

Catherine Swan

(1921–1970)

Lord Mountford's eyes met those of Lady Olivia across the crowded oh fuck I spilled my gin and tonic ballroom.

From *Lady Olivia's Secret* (1967)
by Anastasia Beaumarchais

CATHERINE SWAN, PROLIFIC WRITER OF SHORT STORIES, novels and nonfiction, was born in Lakemba in south-west Sydney on 8 May 1921. Her father, Septimus, was a poorly paid clerk who drifted from job to job, invariably being given the sack when his heavy drinking told on his work, and her mother, Claire, was little more than a cipher, endlessly nursing, cleaning and cooking for her large family. Catherine was the seventh of fourteen children; much later she would lament the fact that her father could not get paid for the one thing in life he was good at. When Septimus was in work, young Catherine was tasked by her mother with creeping into his bedroom as he slept to snatch some of his wages from his trouser pockets, before he could spend it all on drink. If she was caught, she would get a beating. Catherine always tried to help her mother; she would change nappies, make dinners and settle her younger brothers and sisters every night by telling them stories. She borrowed characters and plots from the lessons she had at school, when she was not needed to help around the cramped family home. Catherine's tales combined knights, detectives, Martians, kings, explorers, princesses and talking animals; anything that would amuse her siblings. She could go on for hours, stop in the middle of a sentence when everyone was asleep, and start at precisely the same point the next night.

When she was fourteen Catherine started going out with a young man who worked in a store that sold and repaired typewriters. She allowed him to paw her and in return he let her into the store after hours so that she could teach herself how to type. Through the window of the store, across the street, was a poster of a beautiful, elegant woman advertising the latest Claudia Gunn novel. Catherine would stare at the advertisement, wishing that it was the model who was kissing her, and not some spotty-faced man. This was the moment she realised that she was attracted to women. When Catherine could type at eighty-five words per minute, she decided she no longer needed the young man and broke off their relationship. At age fifteen, but looking years older, she found work as a typist in an office in the centre of Sydney. Her delicate good looks attracted the attention of the men in the office, with whom she mechanically flirted but otherwise ignored. Catherine gave almost all of her wages to her mother to help feed and clothe her siblings; the little she permitted herself to keep was spent on pulp magazines, which allowed her to escape into a fantasy world for an hour or two.

On the bus to and from work, in her lunch hour and before going to sleep, Catherine read everything from *Modern Bloke* to *Astounding Housewife Adventures* and *Wonder Stories of the*

Outback. In July 1938, when reading that month's *Bonzer Science Stories*, Catherine came across the short story "Eugenicists of Cor" by Rand Washington. It was printed alongside an interview with the science-fiction writer in which he boasted of his recent literary and financial successes. Washington's story was so badly written that Catherine was inspired to write a work of "scientifiction" herself. For three nights she hid in the toilets of her office until everyone else had left, and then emerged to type out her story, "The Time Remainer", which she submitted to *Bonzer Science Stories* as the work of "Charles Swan". Though ineptly constructed and awkwardly written, the central conceit of the story was ingenious: advances in technology have created a world in which time machines are as cheap to buy as a packet of cigarettes. The narrator is too timid to travel in time; he lives in a world that is constantly metamorphosing because of the changes to the time stream, but only he is aware of the differences. One day he is married and living in an Australia ruled by Mongols; the next he is single and riding a dinosaur to work. "The Time Remainer" was accepted by *Bonzer Science Stories*, who paid Catherine six pounds, the equivalent of two weeks' wages. The money could not have come at a better time, for a janitor had reported Catherine's nocturnal writing and in November 1938 she was sacked for misuse of company property. That same month, Rand Washington published *Time Masters of Cor*, which blatantly plagiarised the central ideas of "The Time Remainer".

Septimus Swan died from liver failure in February 1939. With the small endowment his family received at his death, Catherine bought a second-hand typewriter. From the first she wrote for nine hours a day, six days a week, a schedule she followed religiously. Her first sales came immediately, and stories by Catherine Swan appeared in *Saucy Mystery, Bush Sweetheart* and *Fantastic Farming Adventures* in May, August and September 1939. Swan soon realised that she could have even more work published if she adopted a pseudonym. In fact, she took on at least thirty, including Harry Stagg, Jake Holliday, Guy Strong, Juliet Love, Edith Lamoure and Madeleine White. Under her male pseudonyms, she submitted to magazines such as *Bonzer Bachelor Tales, Private Dick: The Magazine of Detection* and *Six-Shooter Stories*, and as a woman to *Jackaroo Romance, Stirring Secretary Stories* and *Scary Spinster Yarns*. In her first two years of writing professionally she sold two in every ten stories, but this proportion grew markedly as she came to know what editors were looking for. The dozen short stories and three novellas in the April 1940 issue of *Tear-jerking Tales of Motherhood* were written entirely by Swan, under various pseudonyms. She was under no illusions that she was producing great literature; she called herself a hack and was proud of it. But her stories were better written and plotted than those of most pulp writers of the time, including the most successful, Rand Washington. Before long Swan acquired a literary agent, Oscar Musgrave, who coordinated her many submissions.

By the end of 1940 Swan was making enough money to move her siblings and mother into a four-bedroom home in Chatswood, and to rent a flat for herself in St Leonards, where she could write in peace. During this time she had relationships with a few women she met at a discreet bar in Kings Cross, but none of these liaisons lasted longer than a month or two. Throughout the 1940s, her output for the pulp market steadily increased, and by the end of the decade Swan had worn out four typewriters. Most of her income went to support her brothers and sisters at school and university, and to ensure her mother had a comfortable retirement. In 1943 her contributions to the romance magazines published by Fountainhead Press caught the attention of another pulp writer, J.R. Hardacre, and the two struck up a correspondence. Hardacre pressed for a meeting and when, in October 1943, Swan finally agreed, she was thankful to find that Hardacre was actually a woman called Joyce Reith.

The two became friends and, some time towards the end of 1943, lovers. They were cautious, aware of other lesbian writers in Sydney whose lives had been blighted by blackmail. In order to further camouflage their relationship, in early 1944 Swan married her literary agent. Oscar Musgrave was an Englishman and homosexual and was happy to take part in the pretence. The newlyweds set up house together, and Reith would often spend nights and weekends "visiting" the couple. Over the next two years, Swan and Reith collaborated on hundreds of stories, saving enough money to purchase a property near Leura, in the Blue Mountains west of Sydney, where they could be alone together. Nonetheless, Swan's generosity towards her family and other writers who had fallen on hard times meant that she was always short of cash.

In 1946 Rand Washington, as publisher of Fountainhead Press, met Reith and offered her the editorship of the company's romance line. The market for science-fiction and mystery stories was drying up, and the position afforded a large salary. Despite Swan's protests, Reith accepted the job and was soon fending off marriage proposals from Washington. Swan asked her to quit, but every time Reith handed in her resignation, Washington offered her a pay rise. In 1948, Reith's father faced ruin after a fire destroyed his business, and Washington offered to clear his debts if Reith would marry him. Swan begged Reith not to, promising to give her the money if she would only wait a few months until Swan had sold some more stories. But Reith was afraid her father's health would not stand the strain, and she and Washington wed in June 1948. Reith fell pregnant at once. With the birth of her son, Galt, in March 1949, Joyce Washington told Swan that she would not leave her husband.

Swan was heartbroken and threw herself into her writing, averaging an incredible one million words a year for the next decade. With the decline of the pulp market in the early 1950s, Swan abandoned the short story and turned to the long form, writing a huge number of science-fiction, fantasy, Western, boarding-school and mystery novels under her many pseudonyms. She also worked on Sundays, a day she had previously reserved for relaxation; now, she devoted Sundays to writing nonfiction. For her first project she conjured the new pen name of Naomi Plume and created a series of abridged versions of classic books for children, including *A Child's Finnegans Wake* (1948) and *A Child's Remembrance of Things Past* (1949).

Plume's publisher, Kookaburra Books, requested more popular works from the writer. Although she had never finished secondary school, Swan was able to absorb and synthesise complex ideas and interpret them for general readers. She produced wide-ranging introductions to science, history, philosophy, technology and language, all while completing a new novel every two weeks. Her *Introduction to Australian Literature* (1953) popularised the tale that Sydney Steele had made a deal with Satan, selling his soul in exchange for immense literary gifts, only to be tricked and lose everything he ever wrote. Swan took more care over her nonfiction than her novels, which she continued to write because they paid better and were easier to "knock out", as she said. On one occasion she wrote to the *Sydney Review* as Catherine Swan to protest the journal's glowing reviews of Westerns by Tex McAllister and boarding-school novels by Georgina Fairweather, two of her own pseudonyms.

In 1955, Swan published the work she was most proud of: *Cor Blimey* was a blistering and bilious parody of the *Cor* novels that so enraged their creator, Rand Washington, that he ran a full-page editorial in all his pulp magazines fulminating against Swan. Joyce Washington wrote to Swan, asking her not to attack her husband again, and Swan grudgingly agreed, although the titles of many of her 1950s novels referred obliquely to her frustration: *Why Won't She Leave Him?* (1952), *Murder in Washington* (1954) and *Pain in the Mars* (1957).

Even Swan herself was sometimes confused as to which of her numerous pen names wrote which books; she relied on Oscar Musgrave to keep track. Swan's publishers were unaware that an increasing number of books in their fiction and nonfiction lines were by one writer. In 1960, for example, thirty of the fifty titles published by Kookaburra Books were by Swan or one of her alter egos. A year later, at only forty, she was diagnosed with arthritis in her finger joints. She hired three secretaries, and had them sit in three separate rooms of her house; throughout the day she would walk back and forth between rooms, dictating three different books. In this way Swan was able to increase her already phenomenal daily word count. Inevitably, Swan sometimes renamed or forgot characters as she went along, or left plot threads dangling. Usually her husband picked up these mistakes; if he didn't spot them, the editors and proofreaders at her publishers would. However, on one notorious occasion Swan dropped her drink while dictating to a secretary, who faithfully transcribed the writer's profanity. The obscene phrase, nestled amid a scene describing a ball in Regency-era Bath, went unnoticed by editors at Kookaburra Books and no doubt shocked the many admirers of Anastasia Beaumarchais, under which name Swan wrote *Lady Olivia's Secret* (1967).

By the end of 1968 Swan had published millions of words of fiction and nonfiction, encompassing nine of the ten classes of the Dewey Decimal System, excluding only religion. She was also one of the most prolific letter writers in Australian literary history; she responded to every piece of fan mail she received, and often sent five or six letters a day to friends or to one of her siblings. It is estimated that between 1948 and 1969 she wrote over eight thousand letters to Joyce Washington, but while a handful of Joyce's replies remain, all Swan's letters were later destroyed by Rand Washington. Joyce Washington's surviving letters repeatedly allude to Swan's entreaties to leave her husband, explaining that she could not while her son was a minor; Rand had once told her that if they ever divorced, he would find a way to gain custody of Galt and would turn the boy against his mother. From time to time Joyce even went so far as to defend her husband, telling Swan that he was not as bad as Swan thought; he was a decent father to Galt, and almost always kind to her.

Swan waited impatiently for Galt Washington to grow up. She would see Joyce two or three nights a year, but they had to be careful. Rand Washington was a jealous man. When Galt was conscripted and sent to Vietnam in 1969, Joyce still refused to leave her husband, at least until Galt had returned home safely. She told Swan that she felt sorry for Washington; his last book had flopped and he had become a figure of fun in the Australian science-fiction community. Late in 1969 the Washington marriage took a bizarre turn when Rand established his own religion. Swan scorned Washington's claims to enlightenment, even as his Transvoidist Gospell was embraced by a number of prominent Australian writers, artists and celebrities. She was greatly troubled when Joyce told her that Washington had bought a property in the Barrington Tops and was gathering disciples. There was no telephone at the property, and Joyce's letters ceased on her moving there.

Swan decided that it was high time to expose Washington for the charlatan he was. In January 1970 she began researching a short biography of the writer. Over the next few months she travelled to Washington's hometown of Wollongong to speak to his few surviving childhood friends; in Sydney she interviewed Helga Smith, the elderly widow of James Smith, Washington's first publisher. She also located a number of Transvoidist apostates, and gathered as much information as she could about the bizarre and often contradictory doctrines of Washington's religion. Swan told her husband that she had made disturbing discoveries about Washington and was worried about Joyce's wellbeing. In early May she wrote a letter to Joyce, the contents of which remain unknown; Joyce did not reply. Swan then informed the police of her suspicions that something had happened to her friend. A constable from Gloucester police station was sent to the Washington property; he reported that Joyce Washington was in good health.

On 10 May 1970, Swan told her husband she could wait no longer. Early that morning she set off from Sydney. It was raining heavily, and when she was twenty miles from Gloucester she was delayed by a flooded road. There was a long detour; it was evening before she arrived in the town, and dark by the time she drove up the narrow, unsealed road to Washington's property. The rain worsened as Swan arrived at the Transvoidist compound, where Washington was leading a group of followers in meditation. She demanded to speak to his wife, and Washington made no objection. Joyce emerged from one of the small bungalows when she heard Swan calling her name. The two women embraced, then went into the house together. When they came out fifteen minutes later, Joyce Washington was carrying a suitcase. Washington did nothing to stop the pair as they walked to Swan's car, but before Joyce got in, he called out to her over the sound of the rain, telling her that the Universal Galactic Controller would rebuke her unless she repented of her transgression. Joyce looked at Swan, who smiled at her. The two women got into the car and drove away.

Their bodies were recovered two days later by a police search party, who had been alerted to Catherine Swan's disappearance by her husband. The brakes in Swan's car had failed, and the vehicle had slipped off the road two miles from Washington's property and plunged a hundred metres down a ravine, killing both women. A police investigation ruled out foul play and the tragedy was declared an accident, although doubt was cast on this finding in 1982 when it was revealed that both the investigating officer and the coroner had been practising second-level Transvoidists.

The tragic death of Catherine Swan, and with her the dozens of writers she had created, had the unexpected effect of bringing the Australian publishing industry to its knees. At the time of her death, the top twenty bestselling fiction and non-fiction books were all by Swan or one of her noms de plume.

Four of the major publishing houses, including Berkeley & Hunt and Angus & Robertson, had unknowingly based nearly their entire catalogues on the work of one writer. With Swan's demise, these companies lost not just one but nearly all of their most successful authors. By the end of 1970, all of the books Swan had submitted before her death had been brought out, and her publishers scrabbled to find new talent to fill the void. Sales of Australian fiction and nonfiction plummeted in 1971. Kookaburra Books went bankrupt, Berkeley & Hunt and New Dimensions barely survived, and Angus & Robertson did not recover its share of the market until 1980.

Oscar Musgrave died in 1974, leaving few records concerning his wife's incredible output. Thanks to the research of Rachel Deverall, over six hundred books and fourteen hundred short stories, written under fifty-five different pen names, have been identified as the work of Catherine Swan, though there remains no full-length critical study of her writings. Swan's research notes on Rand Washington were never found.

Frederick Stratford, circa 1907

Frederick Stratford

(1880–1933)

Life; Brisbane; this moment of June.

From *Mrs Galloway* (1925)

FREDERICK STRATFORD, THE BOLDEST AND MOST SUCCESSFUL plagiarist of the twentieth century, was born in Cardiff, New South Wales, on 22 June 1880. (As the academic and novelist Peter Darkbloom was later to note, "Even the name of Stratford's birthplace was lifted from somewhere else.") Frederick's father, Laurence, was a customs and excise officer who worked at the port of Newcastle. His mother, Helen, kept house for the family, which comprised four sons and three daughters. Frederick was a taciturn boy, often overlooked among his more outgoing siblings. When Frederick was five his father was transferred to Sydney and the family moved with him to the city. Frederick began his education at Calvin Grammar School, also attended at the time by Henry Watkins, the future short-story writer Addison Tiller, although there is no evidence the two knew each other. Frederick was an unremarkable student. After three years, his teachers still did not know his name, and although he was not bullied, he had not made any friends. He simply went unnoticed.

One evening in June 1894 Frederick was sent by his mother to bring his father home from the local pub. Frederick found Laurence Stratford asleep on a stool at the bar. As he tried to wake him, a fight broke out nearby. A jeering crowd gathered around two brawling men as Frederick watched, mesmerised and appalled. Finally there emerged a victor, a tall, blond-haired man who stood on a nearby table, took out a much-folded piece of paper, and started to read from it through bloodied lips. Although he could not be heard over the noise of the bar the man continued to talk, and gradually the room fell silent. Frederick and the fifty or so drunkards listened, spellbound, as the man declaimed a poem. Sometimes they laughed, and at other times they had to wipe tears from their eyes. Frederick's father came to during the final verse; he applauded with the rest as the man finished and climbed down from the table. Frederick's father explained that the victorious fighter was a bush poet called Sydney Steele whose verses had recently thrust him into the limelight. There were even rumours that Steele had bargained away his soul in return for becoming the greatest writer in the country. Frederick stared at the grinning poet, the centre of attention, surrounded by wellwishers. There can be no doubt that as soon as he glimpsed that world, he wanted to belong to it. He quickly realised that there were two ways to achieve his aim: through violence, which was out of the question, since he was peaceable and timorous by nature, horrified by the mere sight of blood; or through literature, which is a surreptitious form of violence, a passport to respectability, and can, in certain young and sensitive nations, disguise the social climber's origins. He opted for literature and decided to spare himself the difficult years of apprenticeship.

Frederick helped his father home, then slipped out of the house again (as usual, no one noticed) and returned to the bar. He waited outside long into the night until Sydney Steele emerged, unsteady on his feet, his torn shirt still damp with sweat and blood. Frederick followed Steele to his home, lingering in some nearby bushes until the candles in the house were extinguished, before creeping towards the only open window. Inside, the poet was snoring on a cot, his trousers hanging from a hook by the windowsill. Carefully, Frederick reached in and snatched the wad of papers from the back pocket of the trousers, then turned and ran. The next morning was a Saturday, and Frederick spent the morning leafing through the purloined manuscript. It was called *Bush, Beer and Ballads*, and the twenty-five poems it contained were written in a neat, almost feminine hand. Frederick copied out the poems, then destroyed the original. That Monday he showed two of the poems, "The Stringybark" and "Charlie Cobb's Shadow", to his English master, who had barely spoken to him in the past. The teacher was excited by the poems, and encouraged Frederick to enter them into the school poetry competition. Frederick did so, and within the month had been awarded first prize. His family were impressed, and his teachers finally seemed to know his name.

Flushed with success, Frederick submitted "The Stringybark" to the *Western Star*, whose editor, Jim Taylor, replied with a letter praising the work and asking Frederick to come to his office that Friday to discuss terms for publication. When Frederick arrived, a furious Sydney Steele was awaiting him. Taylor had recognised

"The Stringybark" as Steele's work the moment he read it, and he informed the poet that he had found his thief. Frederick broke from Steele's grasp and sprinted home in terror, where he quickly disposed of *Bush, Beer and Ballads* down the dunny. When Steele and Taylor banged on the door of his house an instant later, Frederick flatly denied their charges. After a heated argument with Frederick's father, the police were called. Taylor and Steele had no proof that Frederick had stolen the poems. Before they were moved on, Steele begged the boy for the manuscript, telling him it was the only copy he possessed, and he could not remember most of the poems in it. Again, Frederick denied any wrongdoing, and finally the two men departed. Throughout the course of his long life, Steele was to attempt to reconstruct *Bush, Beer and Ballads* many times, always without success.

Cowed by the experience, Frederick made no further attempt to enter into the literary world for four years, and he gradually faded into the background of his school and of his family. There were nights when he cried with rage. Then he began searching for a solution, and he didn't let up until he found one. He told his father of his wish to follow him into the customs service and, after passing the entrance examination at the age of eighteen, Frederick Stratford became a junior officer, working under his father at Circular Quay. One of Stratford's first tasks was to confiscate a three-volume set of the collected short stories of the French writer Guy de Maupassant, which had been ordered from London by A.G. Stephens, editor of the *Bulletin*. Stephens was incensed when customs informed him that the books had been destroyed, all of Maupassant's work having been banned by the censorship office; he was moved to write an article decrying the incident, which appeared in the *Bulletin*'s "Red Page" in July 1898.

A few weeks later, Stephens received a short story called "The Locket" from a contributor identifying himself only as "F.S." The story tells of a poor woman, Mary Smith, who borrows her rich friend's gold locket to wear at a party, and loses it. Too frightened to tell her friend, Mary instead borrows thousands of dollars to buy an identical replacement, then spends decades scrimping and saving to repay the loan, only to learn at the climax of the story that the locket she lost was a worthless fake. Stephens was impressed with "The Locket", although he found the dialogue stilted and the Hornsby setting poorly drawn. He cut two hundred words, retitled it "True Blue" and published it in the *Bulletin* in December 1898. This success encouraged Stratford to submit thirteen more short stories to the journal over the next decade, under his full name. His family and his colleagues were somewhat awed by his appearances in the *Bulletin*, and Stratford began to be spoken of by the Sydney literati in the same breath as Addison Tiller and Henry Lawson. It was only with the submission of "Ball of Grease" in 1907 that Stephens became suspicious. He rejected the story as being overlong and over familiar, telling Stratford he was sure he had read it somewhere before. Stephens was not mistaken; "Ball of Grease", like "The Locket" and every other piece he had accepted from Stratford, was copied almost word for word from the collected stories of Guy de Maupassant, which Stratford had confiscated, and which Stephens himself had bought and paid for.

The rejection of "Ball of Grease" marked the end of the first stage of Stratford's career in plagiarism. While he still socialised with other writers, he "wrote" nothing for over a decade, instead working diligently in his position as a customs inspector.

During the Great War he was excused from military duty due to his employment, and was quickly promoted through the ranks until 1918, when he replaced his father as director of the customs and excise office after Laurence Stratford's retirement. In May 1922 Stratford began the second, and most audacious, period of his literary larceny, using his authority as director to order the seizure of all copies of James Joyce's recently published *Ulysses* that came into the country. Stratford burned every copy of the novel bar one, which he took home and retyped over the next six months, replacing references to Dublin with Sydney and removing vulgar language. In November he submitted the retitled *Odysseus* to Allenby & Godwin. Lloyd Allenby found large parts of the novel incomprehensible, but was still able to recognise its tremendous skill and originality. After some hesitation he accepted the novel, which was received with equal parts bafflement and acclaim when it was published in March 1923. *Odysseus* entered a second printing in April, the sales at least partly driven by the fact that it contained lewd passages that Stratford hadn't excised because he was ignorant of the sexual practices Joyce described.

With the publication of *Odysseus*, Stratford became the darling of the Sydney literary scene, a position cemented by the critical and commercial success of *A Journey to India*, published little more than a year later. He came to the attention of the powerful, and there was talk of him standing for parliament. He attended parties and soirées held in the capital's grandest houses. Reporters hounded him; they demanded to know why he didn't retire from the customs service to write full-time. Stratford would reply that he wanted to serve his country as well as his art. In reality, retiring from the service was out of the question; his literary career depended on his being able to seize novels as they entered the country and destroying all but one copy, which he would then plagiarise. The books he published over the next few years exhausted the superlatives of Australian critics: *The Enchanted Mountain* (1924), *The Prodigious Gatsby* and *Mrs Galloway* (both 1925), *The Sun Comes Up Too* (1926) and *Hooroo to All That* (1929). One perceptive reviewer for the *Western Star*, noting Stratford's perfect control of an almost inconceivably varied range of styles and voices, commented, "It is as if Frederick Stratford were not one writer, but many."

In February 1926 Stratford married Norah Seaman, a society beauty he had met at one of Vivian Darkbloom's literary salons, and within three years they had a son, Giorgio, and a daughter, Lucia. The recently published *The Sun Comes Up Too* had been proclaimed as another triumph, and Stratford's chances of being the first Australian to win the Nobel Prize in Literature were widely discussed. That same year, however, his deceptions showed signs of unravelling. Critics drew attention to examples of carelessness in Stratford's oeuvre; the sanatorium in *The Enchanted Mountain* was in Katoomba on one page and Davos in Switzerland the next, and the Brisbane of *Mrs Galloway* had not only a British Museum but also a Piccadilly Circus. Stratford's defenders pointed out that Shakespeare had clocks striking the hour in Ancient Rome, which didn't make him any less of a genius. The most serious charge against Stratford came in an article published in August 1926 in the *Journal of Australian Literature*. "The Cries of Polyphemus: Australian Criticism and Frederick Stratford's *Odysseus*" by Peter Darkbloom set out the argument that Stratford had plagiarised James Joyce's *Ulysses*. Stratford angrily denied the charge, as did a number of prominent critics, rallying together as "Stratfordians" who hailed *Odysseus* as a uniquely Australian masterpiece. Darkbloom was threatened with a libel action. Although he suspected Stratford of being a serial plagiarist, he did not want to further humiliate Lloyd Allenby, Stratford's publisher and Darkbloom's own father-in-law. He had warned Allenby about Stratford's literary thieving, but the old man would not believe him.

Stratford, made cautious by Darkbloom's article, published nothing for three years. After the appearance of *Hooroo to All That* in 1929, he agreed to an interview with Quincy Gunn, editor of the *Southern Cross*. Stratford considered Gunn a friend; he knew and liked Gunn's wife, Claudia, and had been their honoured guest at their beautifully appointed house, "Mysteriosa". Stratford was therefore shocked and revolted when Gunn demanded five thousand pounds from him to keep quiet; Gunn had irrefutable proof that not only *Odysseus* but all Stratford's novels had been plagiarised from work published in the United States and Great Britain. Stratford refused to pay, instead publishing a brazen statement in the *Bulletin* in May 1929, announcing his recent discovery that his work was being poached by overseas writers. Retaining lawyers in the United States, France, Germany and Great Britain, Stratford launched lawsuits against E.M. Forster, Virginia Woolf, Robert Graves, Ernest Hemingway, Thomas Mann, F. Scott Fitzgerald and James Joyce for breach of copyright.

The remainder of Stratford's life was taken up by protracted legal battles, as the authors he had attacked launched countersuits against him. Hemingway sent Stratford a telegram in November 1930, threatening to come to Australia for the pleasure of punching him on the nose. Fitzgerald's response to the blizzard of suits and countersuits was to get blind drunk; after one long weekend of dissipation in July 1929, he started to believe that Stratford had indeed written *The Great Gatsby*, and he, Fitzgerald, was the plagiarist. Nathanael West had to restrain Fitzgerald from throwing himself from a moving automobile. In London, Virginia Woolf recorded in her diary that "Stratford is a dirty little liar, and in all likelihood a Jew." James Joyce's response to the lawsuit is not recorded, but it is perhaps no coincidence that in the second part of *Finnegans Wake* (1939), written in 1929, the following can be found: "he was dud. Dumb! Mastabatoom, mastabadtomm, when a mon stratford shat his self all long. For whole the world to see."

At first Stratford's publishers and a host of Stratfordian critics united in their support for the beleaguered Australian prodigy whose work had been cannibalised by foreigners. Yet it was not long before mountains of evidence proved beyond all doubt that Stratford was a liar and a cheat. His friends turned their backs on him. Allenby & Godwin, crippled by legal fees, recalled all of Stratford's books that they could and pulped them. The firm went bankrupt in February 1932; Lloyd Allenby killed himself a few weeks later. Stratford, unashamed and unrepentant, revelled in the notoriety the case brought him, making ever more outlandish claims about the writers he had accused of copying him: Joyce's *Dubliners* (1914), Stratford maintained, had been stolen from his Sydney home in a burglary in 1910. In interviews, Stratford continued to press his claims against Hemingway and the others, stating jocosely, "If I am not the author of those books, why have I suffered from such terrible writer's cramp these last ten years?" Stratford did indeed suffer increasing pain in his right hand for the last decade of his life. In late 1932 it was realised that this pain was due to a chondrosarcoma, a cancer originating in the fingers. The diagnosis came too late for treatment, and Frederick Stratford died on 19 January 1933, disgraced and shunned by his erstwhile supporters but protesting his authorship of the disputed novels to the last.

After his death, Stratford was all but forgotten until 1961, when the pamphlet *Shames Joyce: The Great Plagiarist* by Arthur ruhtrA was published in France. ruhtrA argued passionately, if not entirely convincingly, that Frederick Stratford had indeed written *Odysseus* before Joyce had published *Ulysses*, citing numerous examples from the novel that coincided exactly with Stratford's life. ruhtrA's argument remained unknown in Australia until 1974, when the pamphlet was reprinted by New Dimensions, to derision from academics. Despite this, ruhtrA's idea gained currency throughout that decade and the next, kept alive by the Frederick Stratford Society, which had emerged from the ashes of ruhtrA's failed experimental writing collective, Kangaroulipo. The rise of the internet in the 1990s, which saw the proliferation of outlandish conspiracy theories, gave new impetus to the question of who really wrote *Ulysses/Odysseus*. By the turn of the century the Frederick Stratford Society had almost two thousand members in Australia and a further ten thousand worldwide. On 16 June every year, Stratfordians across the globe celebrate "Humesday", named after Archibald Hume, the protagonist of *Odysseus*, and toast Stratford with the last words of his great novel, as spoken by Vivvy Hume: "And dinkum I said fair dinkum I will Dinkum."

Edward Gayle in Alice Springs, May 2001

Edward Gayle [signature]

(1928–2008)

*It is tempting to suggest that since so-called "indigenous"
Australians are now so quick to take offence, they should be
renamed "indignant" Australians.*
From *Terror Nullius: How the Left's Intimidation and Lies
Distort Australian History* (1999)

ONE OF AUSTRALIA'S MOST CONTENTIOUS HISTORIANS, EDWARD
Gayle was born on 9 May 1928 on a cattle station twenty miles
from the town of Stuart, in the heart of the Northern Territory.
His mother, Rowena, died when he was an infant, and Edward
was raised by his father, Theodore. The station employed a
dozen men and women, mostly Central Arrernte Aboriginal
people, who lived in cabins a ten-minute walk from the Gayle
house. Theodore Gayle was an unhappy, irascible man, and his
son learned to stay out of his way. Edward, a dreamy, sensitive
boy, spent most of his time in the station kitchen, where he was
looked after by Katie Gurnabil, a young Aboriginal woman who
served as housekeeper and cook for Gayle. Katie's daughter,
Alice, was Edward's playmate, born just a day after he was.

The boy enjoyed a large measure of freedom in his early
years, and he and Alice would spend hours roaming the
property, building cubbies and playing house. The two were

inseparable, though Theodore Gayle would tell the girl to "piss off" if he found her playing with his son. Edward loved Katie like a mother, but most of all he loved Alice. In 1933, when the town of Stuart was officially renamed Alice Springs, Edward believed that it had been named for her. Alice did not go to school. Edward, after he turned five, had lessons with his father. Gayle taught his son to read from the only books in the house: the *King James Bible* (1611) and Edward Gibbon's *The History of the Decline and Fall of the Roman Empire* (1776). Though the lessons always ended with Gayle berating his son for his block-headedness, it was clear the boy was highly intelligent.

By the time he was eight Edward had read Gibbon twice and the Bible five times; he could recite the book of Genesis from memory. Occasionally he would come across an old pulp maga-zine left by a passing jackaroo – *Bonzer Science Stories* or *Saucy Mystery* – and he would hide them away from his father and read them in secret again and again until the cheap paper disinte-grated in his hands. When Alice asked him if he could teach her to read, Edward was enchanted. She was a quick study, and after only a few months had amazed him with her progress. In return for his tutoring he asked Alice to teach him stories about the Dreamtime, which he had overheard Katie talking about. Edward was captivated by the traditional stories, and after Alice's lessons he would carefully note them down so he could learn them by heart. Unfortunately, his father saw these notes and, after whipping Edward for blasphemy, decided it was time his son should go to school.

In February 1937 Edward was sent to St Ambrose's College, a boarding school on the outskirts of Alice Springs. Although pleased to be away from his father, Edward missed Alice and

Katie dreadfully, and sent them letters whenever one of his father's workers came to town. Edward was terrible at mathematics, chemistry, biology and all the other subjects his father had never touched upon in their lessons, but he excelled at history and English. Even at nine his prose was fluid and elegantly constructed, yet it would never quite shake off the mustiness of the eighteenth century. During the school holidays Edward would return home to Katie and Alice and his father, who became ever more petulant as he aged. The outbreak of the Second World War saw Alice Springs develop rapidly to accommodate the hundreds of thousands of American troops passing through the town. Edward barely noticed; on his most recent visit home, at the age of fifteen, he had realised he was hopelessly in love with Alice.

He intended to tell her when he returned home that Christmas, and had rehearsed what he would say a thousand times, but Alice was not there. Katie told him she had found a well-paying job in the military kitchens in town. Taking one of his father's horses without permission, Edward rode into Alice Springs and loitered outside the gates of the military base until he saw Alice leaving. She was strolling and laughing with an American GI. Without saying a word, Edward attacked the soldier, hitting him on the forehead with a rock he had picked up from the roadside. The stroke was only glancing. Alice screamed and tried to pull her companion away but the GI retaliated viciously, breaking Edward's nose, then kicking and stamping on his chest as the boy lay helpless on the ground. Finally, some other soldiers pulled the GI away, and Edward was taken to hospital. When his father found out what had happened, he gave Alice some money and ordered her away to her grandmother, who lived in Darwin. When Edward was released from hospital, his father refused to tell him where Alice was. Neither would Katie, no matter how much Edward ranted and wept. In spite of his emotional turmoil, Edward did exceptionally well in his final exams that year. His father told him he could either stay and help run the station (although he vowed that Alice would never return), or continue his studies in Sydney.

In 1945 Edward Gayle was admitted to the University of Sydney to study history. He was a brilliant student, although his unorthodox opinions were mocked by his peers and lecturers. In particular, his contention that the doctrine of *terra nullius* could not be applied to Australia because of the Indigenous population's previous claims to the land became a standing joke. During his semester breaks Gayle would travel to Darwin and search for Alice. In early 1947 he finally found Alice's grandmother living in a shack on the edge of the city, but the old woman told him that Alice had left for Melbourne the month before. Gayle spent his next vacation in Melbourne, but he found no trace of her there. He never gave up looking for Alice, but as time passed he began to lose hope. Once in a while Katie wrote to him to tell him she had received a postcard from Alice. Sometimes Katie forgot herself and mentioned where Alice was living: Perth, Coober Pedy, Newcastle. As quickly as he could, Gayle would go there and hunt for her. Over time, these occasional trips had assumed the character of holidays. He wondered if he would even recognise Alice if he passed her on the street.

Gayle completed his undergraduate degree in 1949 and began a PhD in Australian history, surveying the agricultural techniques of the First Fleet settlers. The years passed slowly. After

completing his doctorate Gayle became a lecturer at the university, neither liked nor disliked by his students, content to publish
a handful of articles a year on unexciting and uncontroversial
topics of Australian history. Once or twice his work criticised
the invisibility of Indigenous people in the country's historiog-
raphy, but these papers were always rejected, and contributed to
a reputation for eccentricity that meant he was passed over for
promotion more than once. He continued searching for Alice,
visiting and revisiting each of Australia's largest cities.

Gayle did not return to Alice Springs until January 1954,
when his father died of internal injuries after being crushed
against a truck by a bull. Gayle had not seen his father for
more than a decade, and felt nothing as he watched his coffin
being covered with dirt, but he comforted Katie, who sobbed
throughout the service. Without being asked, Katie told him
she had not heard from Alice in months. After the funeral
Gayle stayed on for a few days to put his father's affairs in order.
On the desk in his father's study he came across the *King James
Bible* from which he had been taught to read. When he opened
it, Gayle found an old, yellowed letter serving as a marker for
Proverbs 6:32, "Whoso committeth adultery with a woman
lacketh understanding: he that doeth it destroyeth his own
soul." The letter, dated April 1928, was from Gayle's mother,
Rowena, to his father, reprimanding him for his shameless relations with "that sluttish gin" Katie Gurnabil. It described the
humiliation and shame Rowena felt at seeing "her condition"
shared by the cook, and begged Theodore to send Katie away
somewhere so that she would not have to endure the sight of her
husband's half-caste bastard running around the farm with her
own child. After reading the letter, Gayle went for a long walk

around the property. At twilight, he came upon a broken-down wooden structure, the remains of one of the dozens of cubbies he and Alice had cobbled together during their childhood. He kicked it down. The next morning he left the property early, without speaking to anyone. Before the funeral, Gayle had told the Aboriginal men and women who had worked for his father that they could stay on with full pay for six months before he would sell the farm. But on the way to the airport, he stopped at the property agent's office in Alice Springs and instructed him to clear off the lot of them and put the place on the market. At the airport, Gayle read a note that the solicitor had given him when his father's will was read out. In it, Theodore Gayle asked his son to ensure Katie was looked after in her old age. Theodore had evidently been too embarrassed to leave Katie any formal bequest. Edward Gayle tore up the letter, and Katie was left with nothing.

Gayle's return to Sydney after his father's death marked a new phase in his academic life. Previously, his research had been sound but half-hearted; now he threw all his energy and time into it. There were no more trips to search for Alice. His published work on the early settlers became less critical and more celebratory in tone, as reflected in articles such as "The Taming of Tasmania" (1955) and "A Desert for Every Purpose: The Settlement of the Hunter Valley" (1956). Where once he had attempted, haltingly and clumsily, to include Aboriginal people in his work, now he either did not mention them at all, or emphasised the benefits European civilisation had brought them. From publishing only a couple of articles a year before 1954, he now published fifteen or twenty. His students noticed a change in Gayle, and some complained about his attitude; he had become impatient, dismissive and hostile to new ideas. In 1956 he published his first book, *Australian Colonial Agriculture*, which won praise for the clarity and beauty of its prose, but drew criticism for its outdated methodologies and conservative bias. The book was favourably reviewed in *Quarter*, the right-wing literary journal recently founded by Rand Washington, who invited Gayle to submit work. Over the next two years, a number of Gayle's essays appeared in *Quarter*, on a range of literary and historical themes, including "Addison Tiller: Holding a Mirror to the Past", "The Literary and Political Crimes of Francis X. McVeigh" and "Myth and Mistake: The Absurdity of the Aboriginal Dreamtime", in which Gayle made satirical use of the sacred knowledge Alice had taught him years before. Washington and Gayle became friends, with Gayle a regular guest at Washington's home. Washington dedicated *The Dark Hordes of Cor* (1958) to Gayle and in 1960 offered him the editorship of *Quarter*. With Gayle at the helm, the magazine enjoyed a renaissance, publishing writing of a noticeably higher quality than under Washington's tenure, and also becoming pronouncedly more conservative. Gayle introduced a new motto for the journal: *Damus Parci*, or "We give no quarter."

Promotion followed hard at the heels of Gayle's move towards the right. In 1964 he was made an associate professor and deputy head of the history department at the University of Sydney. Despite this new responsibility and his continuing work for *Quarter*, he produced a substantial body of research in the next few years, though of an increasingly divisive nature. Gayle's detractors argued that he was allowing his political views to distort his historical judgments, but this did not prevent his rise. In 1968 he was appointed professor and head of history at Sydney, in the same month that eminent anthropologist Professor W.E.H. Stanner gave the Boyer Lecture in which he coined the term "the Great Australian Silence". Stanner argued that Australian historians had chosen to ignore the violence inflicted on the Aboriginal population by European settlers in the nineteenth century, and continued to disregard the presence of the country's Indigenous peoples in their histories, essentially practising a "cult of forgetfulness".

Gayle was present at Stanner's lecture, and within three weeks had responded with a lecture of his own. "The Great Australian Licence: W.E.H. Stanner's Disdain for the Facts" forcefully argued against each of the points Stanner had raised, concluding that the advent of European rule had ended "a prehistory of barbarity and ignorance" in Australia. The lecture was widely reported in the press and reprinted in the November 1968 issue of *Quarter*. This was to be the last of Gayle's work to appear in the journal for some time; he continued as editor until October 1969, when he resigned in protest against his publisher's insistence that *Quarter* provide space to advertise the newly revealed religion of Transvoidism.

Throughout the 1970s Gayle wrote a number of increasingly partisan articles for newspapers and academic journals, and a trio of books on the question of the British settlement of Australia, often in response to the work of Manning Clark. In 1976 two articles he submitted to journals on this topic were rejected after peer review on the basis of their selective and cavalier attitude to primary sources. In response Gayle wrote *Abhorigines: The Manufacturing of Racism in Australia* (1977), which was published by Berkeley & Hunt after being rejected by every university press in the country. In this book Gayle argued that there was no racism or discrimination against Indigenous Australians and there never had been; in complicity with the left, the idea had been invented in order to extract more handouts from the government. In the following furore other historians wrote dozens of articles exposing the fallacies and inaccuracies in Gayle's book, and in all his published work after 1954. Gayle's professional reputation suffered severe damage, which was compounded by the events of 1980.

When confronted by his critics with the undeniable evidence of many massacres of Indigenous Australians throughout the nineteenth century, including the infamous slaughter at Myall Creek in June 1838, Gayle responded with *Murder or Self-Murder: A Theory on the Nineteenth-Century European "Atrocities"* (1980). No publisher in Australia would consider this work; it was finally serialised in *History and Thought*, a far-right magazine published in Chile. In *Murder or Self-Murder*, Gayle asserted the "more than likely possibility, indeed, the high probability" that massacres of Indigenous Australians in the colonial era were in fact mass suicides provoked by the "existential despair of the primitive Aboriginal culture on encountering a civilisation superior to it in every way". Gayle argued that pity should be reserved for the Europeans who were present at these "orgies of self-destruction, when crazed Aboriginal men, women and children, with malice aforethought, skewered themselves on the swords of horrified settlers". In conclusion, Gayle urged the government to pardon the seven colonists who had been wrongly convicted and hanged for their part in the "so-called" Myall Creek massacre, and to raise a memorial in their honour.

A year passed before *Murder or Self-Murder* was taken note of in Australia, when it was broadly denounced for its outrageous, racist claims, claims that were quickly analysed by other historians and found to be entirely without foundation. Indeed, Gayle was accused of fabricating the pitifully few shreds of evidence he had used to bolster his "theory". There were calls for his dismissal and Gayle's office at the university was picketed by hundreds of students. Amid rumours that his sacking was imminent, Gayle released a statement that he was taking early retirement, after writing a bitter article for *Quarter* about the "leftist witch-hunt" he had had to endure. Then he fell silent, remaining out of the public eye until March 1986, when he again appeared on the front page of newspapers, this time after his arrest for soliciting a prostitute. Gayle told the press he had only approached the woman to ask what people she came from; he was conducting research for a scholarly article on urban Aboriginality. Gayle's defence was accepted by the court, the charges were dismissed, and the historian disappeared back into anonymity.

Gayle's exile ended with the election of the conservative Howard government in 1996, and the firing of the first shots in the so-called "History Wars". Gayle was an enthusiastic advocate of the prime minister's view that too many historians had adopted a "black armband" view of Australian history, painting the country's past in an overwhelmingly negative light. Gayle was inspired by Howard to write his first essay in years, "On the Many Uses of a Black Armband", which elaborated on the prime minister's analogy. In the essay, Gayle claimed that left-wing historians also wore the armband as a blindfold, to hide their eyes from the truth, and to fight unfairly, by using it to tie the hands of their opponents behind their backs. At Gayle's re-emergence into historical debate, opponents resurrected his entirely discredited claims about the Myall Creek massacre, but nevertheless Gayle was embraced by the right as a fearless iconoclast. Emboldened by this support, in 1998 he weighed into the Stolen Generations debate with "The Stolen Inspiration", an incendiary article in *Quarter*, in which he claimed that there was no empirical evidence whatsoever for the Stolen Generations, and that "it was all nothing more than a concoction by the Aboriginal Industry". This was followed by *Terror Nullius: How the Left's Intimidation and Lies Distort Australian History* (1999), in which Gayle reprinted and rebutted the attacks made on him in the previous year by journalists and academics.

In 2000 Gayle's long association with *Quarter* came to an end. His last published article, "The Washington Consensus", a tribute to the recently deceased Rand Washington, appeared in the journal's April issue. The next essay Gayle submitted, "A New Timeline of Australian History", suggested that Indigenous Australians, rather than being present in this country for forty thousand years before the landing of Europeans, had arrived "at most, a month before the First Fleet". Gayle offered no sources to validate this peculiar claim and the editor of *Quarter* regretfully informed him that, much as they respected his work, they could not publish his latest submission. The rejection caused Gayle to break with *Quarter* for good, though the journal devoted a special issue to his life and work when Gayle was awarded the Medal of the Order of Australia for his service to Australian history on Australia Day 2001.

Gayle's final work, *Truth Goes Walkabout: The Great Aboriginal Lie*, an expanded version of his rejected *Quarter* article, was published by a vanity press in a run of three hundred copies and released on 1 April 2001. The book was badly written, almost nonsensically so for large sections, as Gayle repeatedly lost and painstakingly retrieved the thread of his thesis from a morass of conjecture, bias and invention – his argument being that Aboriginal people had no claim whatsoever to Australia. The leftist journal *Overground* published a gleeful twelve-page analysis of the book, made up of equal parts derision and disbelief, and announced that the right had fired the last shot of the History Wars, into its own foot. Amid the uproar, Gayle was nowhere to be seen. *Quarter* launched an energetic counter-attack, declaring in an editorial that *Truth Goes Walkabout* was a laughably obvious forgery, part of a Marxist conspiracy designed to destroy Professor Gayle's reputation. Even Gayle's most vehement opponents, they said, had always conceded the suppleness and gracefulness of his prose, while *Truth Goes Walkabout* appeared to have been written by someone who had only recently started taking English language lessons. *Quarter* also pointed to the publication date, April the first, as a sure sign of a tasteless practical joke.

The controversy raged on until June, when Edward Gayle reappeared in public. He called a press conference to explain that he had spent the last two months in Alice Springs working on his memoirs, and had been unaware of the war of words his book had provoked. In a lengthy, rambling statement he told reporters that the book was indeed his, and he stood by every word. In July, only a few months after the special issue celebrating Gayle's achievements, *Quarter* featured essays denouncing the historian "more in sorrow than in anger" and lamenting the decline of a once powerful intellect. Gayle was unabashed by the publicity, and the petitions demanding that he be stripped of his Medal of the Order of Australia. The initial small print run of *Truth Goes Walkabout* sold out, and the book was reprinted three times throughout the year, eventually selling over two thousand copies. This was more than the circulation of *Quarter*, Gayle noted, and a sign that ordinary Australians were more open-minded than the city's elites.

Gayle's foremost critic since his return to public life in 1996 had been Professor Adam Kingston, Chair in Australian History at the University of Newcastle and himself an Indigenous Australian. In a long series of articles published in academic journals and in *Overground*, he had spent hundreds of pages demolishing the false premises, lies, misrepresentations and inaccuracies that riddled Gayle's work. At the height of the *Truth Goes Walkabout* debacle, Kingston challenged Gayle to a public debate on not only the claims Gayle made in his latest book, but also *Murder or Self-Murder*, a work which Gayle had never repudiated, despite all of its central contentions being proven, unequivocally, to be false. Gayle accepted Kingston's challenge and the debate was scheduled to take place in the Great Hall of the University of Newcastle on the evening of 19 August 2001.

At seven o'clock, the scheduled time for the debate, Kingston stood on the stage alone. Gayle finally arrived twenty minutes late. He appeared flustered; his shoelaces were undone, as were the top two buttons of his shirt, and his tie was askew. Gayle slowly climbed the stairs to the stage, passing Kingston as he went to his podium. He ignored Kingston's proffered hand and looked around confusedly when the crowd booed him. With difficulty, the moderator restored order, and after a short introduction Professor Gayle was invited to outline his views on Australian history, specifically those concerning the country's

Indigenous inhabitants. Gayle began, in an unsteady voice, by saying he had significantly revised his conclusions since the publication of *Truth Goes Walkabout*. This prompted scattered applause from the audience, who believed Gayle was about to apologise for and retract his offensive thesis. After waiting for quiet, Gayle continued; having weighed all the evidence, he had come to the conclusion that he had been gravely mistaken in his beliefs that Aboriginals had arrived in Australia a short time before Europeans, and that the massacres of the nineteenth century were mass suicides. He was mistaken, he went on, because Aboriginals did not exist. They had not been massacred because they had never been in Australia at all.

There was silence in the auditorium as Gayle explained his recent realisation that Aboriginal people were nothing more than a figment of the imagination, like Father Christmas or the Easter Bunny. Here, Professor Kingston tried to interrupt him, but Gayle spoke over him, citing as evidence for his claim the fact that there was supposed to be an Aboriginal beside him here tonight, but as everyone could see, Gayle was on the stage alone. Kingston walked over to Gayle and stood directly in front of him. The old man looked through him, his voice trailing as he presented his proofs that the Indigenous population of Australia was nothing more than a collective hallucination. The crowd began to jeer, and Kingston turned to them to ask for their forbearance; Professor Gayle was obviously very unwell. Gayle went on speaking for another moment before lapsing into unintelligibility. Kingston called for an ambulance just before Gayle collapsed on the stage. He was taken to the John Hunter Hospital, where he was diagnosed as having suffered a stroke, as well as being in the late stages of dementia.

In October 2001, Gayle was released from hospital and moved to a nursing home in Sydney, where he would spend the rest of his life. He required constant care, having been paralysed down his left side by the stroke, and made bewildered and often angry as his dementia progressed. In his last years Gayle was to have only one visitor. In June 2004 an elderly Aboriginal woman came to see him. According to one of the nurses, she remained in his room for two hours, sitting by his bed and holding his hand. Gayle was asleep for most of this time, but when he opened his eyes once, the woman leaned over and whispered something in his ear. Gayle showed no sign that he heard her. Finally, she kissed him on the cheek and left.

Edward Gayle died on 26 May 2008.

Vivian Darkbloom, with husband Peter, circa 1936

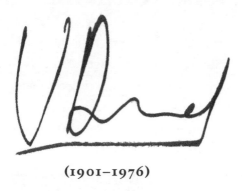

(1901–1976)

... the bare shoulders of a hawk-like black-haired strikingly tall woman ...

From *Lolita* (1955) by Vladimir Nabokov

VIVIAN DARKBLOOM, NOVELIST AND SELF-PROCLAIMED MUSE, was born in Parramatta, New South Wales, on 13 March 1901. Her father was the editor and publisher Lloyd Allenby, founder of Allenby & Godwin, Australia's foremost publishing house from the end of the nineteenth century to the 1930s. Her mother, Thalia, died giving birth to Vivian and the girl was brought up by her father, who never remarried. Vivian's childhood was an extraordinarily happy one. Her father doted on her, as did the writers drawn to his sumptuous Point Piper home, including Banjo Paterson, Barbara Baynton and Sydney Steele, Vivian's godfather, who composed many poems in Vivian's honour, now sadly lost.

Allenby, though renowned for his acuity in business matters, could not see how he was spoiling his daughter. He was convinced she was a prodigy; when she was six months old he started to involve her in editorial decisions, reading aloud novels he was considering publishing and rejecting them if Vivian fell asleep within ten minutes. Writers eager to curry Allenby's favour learned that he never tired of hearing his daughter praised. He once rejected a book about a plucky little girl as "sentimental bilge of the lowest order" but accepted the story six months later when the writer resubmitted it, having made only one alteration: she changed the name of the protagonist to "Little Viv". Allenby purchased the rights to the "Little Viv" character, and numerous other *Little Viv* children's stories followed in elaborately illustrated clothbound editions, with Vivian Allenby modelling for the pictures. Vivian only came to realise that not every little girl had books written about her when she went to school and asked one of her classmates which books in the library she appeared in.

Allenby's indulgence of his daughter was to have disastrous consequences for Australian literature when, in December 1910, Sydney Steele visited the publisher with the only manuscript of his short-story collection, *Charlie Cobb's Cobbers*, which Allenby had promised to publish. Allenby and Steele shared a bottle of whisky to celebrate the new book, before lapsing into unconsciousness in front of the fireplace in the library. Awoken by their laughter, Vivian had slipped downstairs and watched the two men from the doorway until they were asleep. Then she crept into the room and delicately removed the manuscript from Steele's lap. Though she found his handwriting difficult to decipher, Vivian quickly realised that "Uncle Sydney's" book was not about her; indeed it featured no character called Vivian at all. Disappointed, she threw the manuscript onto the fire and returned to bed.

Her father's cries woke her early next morning. The cook and the housemaid had already given notice before Vivian came downstairs and confessed that it was she who had destroyed Steele's manuscript. When she refused to apologise, her father struck her for the first time in her life and sent her to her room. However, Steele was mollified by the large cheque Allenby gave him, and confident that he could rewrite *Charlie Cobb's Cobbers* in just a few weeks. (Tragically, the book was lost for good.) Vivian's disgrace lasted for only an hour. Lloyd Allenby sat in the draughty hallway beside her locked bedroom door, begging the nine-year-old to forgive him. Only the promise that he would commission *Little Viv's Book of Days*, *Little Viv's Favourite Things* and *Little Viv's Garden of Verses* brought about a rapprochement.

After the twelfth *Little Viv* book appeared, Vivian demanded more involvement in their composition, and so Allenby would send a writer to talk to Vivian at home, who would then transform her chatter into a book. If Vivian was not pleased with what was written about her, she would tell her father, and the unfortunate writer would be dismissed. However, the series, which had once turned a small profit, soon tried the patience of the reading public, and the commercial failure of *Little Viv Tells the Time*, *Little Viv Goes for a Walk* and *Little Viv Grows and Grows* cost Allenby a considerable amount of money. In 1911 he had the idea of only publishing one copy of each subsequent *Little Viv* book, which would then be presented to his daughter. To spare her feelings, this new arrangement was kept from Vivian, who continued to believe that thousands of copies of the *Little Viv* books were being sold every year.

The *Little Viv* stories published in 1916 provide clues to Vivian's experiences during her late adolescence: *Little Viv Puts On Perfume*, *Little Viv's Hand Is Kissed*, *Little Viv Grows Hair in*

Peculiar Places and *Little Viv Meets an Author*. By this time Vivian had grown taller than her father and matured physically so that she appeared years older than she actually was. The writer in *Little Viv Meets an Author* is assumed to be Addison Tiller, the creator of the popular *Homestead* stories, whom Vivian met at a party given by Quincy and Claudia Gunn in 1916 to celebrate sales of *On Our Homestead* reaching 200,000. *Little Viv Meets an Author* describes Viv's coquettish attempts to catch the eye of a surly middle-aged writer. There seems little doubt that this meeting led to a sexual relationship between the 42-year-old Tiller and the sixteen-year-old Vivian as early as June 1917, although Tiller's definitive biography, *Addison Tiller: Australia's Chekhov* (1963), makes no mention of it. The textual evidence for their affair is compelling, if circumstantial. July 1917 saw the publication of *Little Viv Becomes a Woman*. Four months later Tiller's *Off Our Homestead* appeared, featuring a short story called "Kissing Kousins" in which Pete Tiller falls in love with his cosmopolitan younger cousin Vi, a "tall, dark-haired girl with fearless black eyes". The lovelorn Pete eventually declares his feelings for Vi in a passage that the critic Peter Crawley called "the nadir of Australian comedy writing".

> "I love you, Vi!" stammered Pete. "You get under me skin like the quills of a-a-a—"
>> "Echidna?" Vi smiled, batting her dark eyes at him.
>> "Nah, I'm not kiddin' ya!" Pete protested.

Tiller's biographer, Stephen Pennington, acknowledges that "Kissing Kousins" was a late addition to the collection, the poor sales of which were in large part due to Allenby & Godwin's failure to promote it. After the publication of *Off Our Homestead* Tiller was released from his contract with his publisher, and there is no record of him ever speaking with Allenby again.

Allenby let it be known that *Little Viv Becomes a Woman* would be the last of the *Little Viv* stories, perhaps a sign of his displeasure at his daughter's behaviour. When a month of pouting and sulking did not change her father's mind, Vivian decided on a different approach. If her father would not publish a book featuring her, she would write one herself. Vivian began work on *Ivy Van Allbine* on her seventeenth birthday, and by the time she had completed her first draft six months later it had acquired the grandiloquent subtitle *An Australian Vanity Fair*. The novel, a *Bildungsroman*, follows the romantic adventures of the beautiful and mesmerising young ingénue Ivy, whose charms cause an endless procession of novelists, poets and playwrights to fall at her feet. The plot borrowed heavily from Max Beerbohm's *Zuleika Dobson* (1911), though without the English novel's humour or wit. Vivian was convinced that her novel was a masterpiece, but decided that engaging the services of an editor could not hurt. Her father refused her request that he assign one from Allenby & Godwin, so Vivian turned instead to Peter Darkbloom, a young writer from Melbourne whose collection of short stories, *The Flyscreen* (1915), had been published by Allenby's firm to respectable reviews. Darkbloom, known to his friends as Pin, had first met Vivian at the same party that had marked the beginning of her relationship with Addison Tiller; although she had barely spoken to him, Pin had become infatuated with her. Grateful for any chance to spend time with her, he agreed to edit her novel for nothing, his first task being to replace the dozens of instances of "Vivian" with

"Ivy". Darkbloom sweated over the manuscript for weeks, but when he returned it with over a thousand suggested alterations and cuts, Vivian burst into tears and ordered him from the house, vowing she would never speak to him again. A dejected Darkbloom returned to Melbourne and tried to lose himself in his writing, the result of which would be the classic novel *Dancing in the Shadows* (1920).

Ivy Van Allbine: An Australian Vanity Fair was published by Allenby & Godwin, without editorial interference, in June 1919. The novel sold only one hundred and nine copies from a print run of three thousand, and it was rumoured that these were all purchased by Vivian herself. Reviewers were unanimous in their hostility. The *Mercury*'s critic lamented that George Meredith's novel had already used the title of *The Egoist*, as it would have been perfect for Vivian Allenby's book. The *Western Star* argued, "If Narcissus had written a novel, it would read much like this one," while the *Antipodean* railed, "This is not *An Australian Vanity Fair*, but rather *An Australian Vanity Foul.*"

Stung by the criticism, Vivian swore never to write another word of fiction. For months she was not at home to visitors and refused all invitations to balls and parties. She suffered from insomnia and lost her appetite, becoming so thin that her anxious father summoned Sydney's most expensive physicians to examine her. Vivian was a model patient, happy to discuss her symptoms for hours with anyone who cared to listen. Her slow decline appeared as irreversible as it was mysterious, until one morning in March 1920. Vivian's night nurse had left behind a novel she was reading, and Vivian took it up listlessly, without even glancing at the cover. At the third chapter she was about to throw it aside, when the character of Vivian Allden was

introduced. Flirtatious, maddening, quixotic and darkly allur-
ing, the fictional Vivian captured her namesake's heart within
only a few pages. The novel was *Dancing in the Shadows* by Peter
Darkbloom. Though only a minor character, Vivian Allden
was rendered immortal by Darkbloom's desperate passion for
Vivian Allenby, the woman who had told him in 1918 that she
would never care a pin for him. Vivian read the book throughout that day and stayed up all night to finish it. When she closed
the novel she had what she later described as an epiphany: "To
write takes talent. To be written about takes genius." That
morning she met her father for breakfast and declared that she
was cured.

Darkbloom's debut novel had sold well, going through four
printings in its first year of publication. The reviews were as
congratulatory as any writer could wish, though some critics
felt that Cecilia Bourne, the ostensible heroine of the novel,
was utterly eclipsed by Vivian Allden, marring an otherwise
perfectly structured work. Lloyd Allenby, pestered by his
daughter, invited Darkbloom to dinner, and the young writer
was a frequent visitor thereafter. Within two months, he had
proposed to Vivian, who accepted at once, and the couple
were married in September 1920. Pin had already finished the
handwritten first draft of his next novel, *Crossroads at Dawn*, a
formally ambitious modernist work following the fragmented
lives of a group of Australian soldiers on their return from the
Great War. When his new wife offered to type out the manuscript for him, he could not have been more pleased. At first,
Vivian's influence on the book was negligible. The unimportant
character of Edna Huntingtower, wife of one of the protagonists, was cured of her alcoholism and renamed "Vivian" in the

second draft. By the fourth draft, "Vivian" appeared in half of the book's twenty-six chapters; by the fifth she was no longer a soldier's wife, but a writer's, and by the eighth she had become the main character. Pin, though aware Vivian was ruining his novel, felt powerless to stop her. He could refuse his wife nothing, not even her request that he destroy the earliest drafts of the book now retitled *For the Love of a Beautiful Woman*. Only a few scraps of *Crossroads at Dawn* survive, and its loss is considered a calamity for Australian literature, only on a par with that of the destruction of the works of Sydney Steele.

The publication of *For the Love of a Beautiful Woman* in 1922 ended Peter Darkbloom's career as a novelist and irrevocably damaged his marriage. Vivian never forgave her husband for the novel's failure; she accused him of deliberately writing badly, wrecking her chance of literary immortality. She briefly considered divorce, but she knew that her father, a Roman Catholic and member of the Knights of St Columba, would disown her if she carried out her threat. Instead she moved into the spare bedroom of their house, utterly ignoring her husband unless visitors were present. Pin found himself unable to begin another novel, and was grateful when he was offered employment at the University of Sydney as a lecturer in English literature. Vivian no longer referred to him, when speaking to her friends, as a writer, but as a teacher, and Pin did not contradict her. He acquired a small measure of attention in academic circles for his critical work, including the seminal comparison of Agatha Christie and Claudia Gunn, "The Mysterious Affair of Literary Styles" (1925), and "The Cries of Polyphemus: Australian Criticism and Frederick Stratford's *Odysseus*" (1926), which sought to prove that the Australian novelist had plagiarised

James Joyce's *Ulysses*. The caustic tone of the latter article was no doubt due at least in part to Vivian's intimate relationship with Stratford. Stratford's mammoth novel *Odysseus* had been submitted to Allenby & Godwin in November 1922, and Lloyd Allenby had sought Peter Darkbloom's opinion on the manuscript. Pin recognised it as a work of genius, but told Allenby he was certain he had read some of the novel before, serialised in a literary journal during the war. After Pin was introduced to Stratford, his suspicions were confirmed; he could not imagine such a man writing such a book. Allenby ignored Pin's concerns and *Odysseus* was scheduled for publication in March 1923. In the meantime, Vivian had come to hear of the manuscript from her father, and she threw a New Year's Eve party with the express intention of meeting Stratford. The two began an affair shortly afterwards. By the end of January, as *Odysseus* was going to press, Stratford insisted that the character of Molly Hume be renamed "Vivvy". Pin, whom Allenby had begged to help copyedit the vast manuscript, realised what the change must have meant but said nothing. His later contention that *Odysseus* had been almost entirely poached from *Ulysses* was not a popular one, and was rejected by many eminent Australian critics and academics who had only just crowned Stratford the greatest novelist of the Southern Hemisphere.

Following the publication of "The Cries of Polyphemus", pressure from Stratfordians led to Pin losing his job at the university. In 1926 the Darkblooms moved to Brisbane, much to Vivian's dismay, where Allenby's influence had secured for Pin a position as a tutor in the University of Queensland's English department. Their home became the centre of artistic life in the city, as Vivian hosted an endless round of dinner parties, poetry readings and debates. During this time she saw her husband rarely; Pin preferred to stay in his small, gloomy office, working on scholarly articles, rather than endure the company of the writers, artists and composers who gathered around his wife. On the rare occasions Pin returned home, Vivian was either asleep or too busy with her friends to take any notice of her husband as he stole past to find refuge in his bedroom. Once Pin overheard Vivian reading aloud, in a ridiculously solemn tone, a love scene from *Dancing in the Shadows* to the hilarity of her guests.

Vivian's extravagances inevitably depleted their small stock of savings, and she often resorted to applying to her father for loans, which she never disclosed to her husband. Lloyd Allenby, now in his eighties and in poor health, rarely refused her, though the tone of his letters to his daughter grew ever more querulous, demanding she provide him with a grandchild before he died. In February 1928, Vivian wrote to her father that she and Pin were expecting. Their daughter, Polyhymnia (Polly), was born in September of that year. Pin did not ask Vivian who the father was; he simply read all the books she had purchased in the last two years, at last coming across a suggestive love scene in the title story of the communist writer Francis X. McVeigh's short-story collection *The Red Flag* (1928). Although Polly was not his, Pin loved the child. Vivian was distant, employing a nanny to look after Polly while she met with her literary friends for long lunches and dinner parties.

Pin lost his teaching post at the University of Queensland in July 1929 after his ecstatic review of Matilda Young's collection *Poems* (1928) alienated the conservative vice-chancellor, who had ordered the book's removal from the university library after reading its first three pages. From 1929 to 1937 the Darkblooms lived a peripatetic life, as Pin found, and lost, teaching work in universities and colleges across Western Australia, New South Wales and Queensland. Matters were made worse by the bankruptcy of Allenby & Godwin in February 1932, and the suicide of Lloyd Allenby less than a month later. Allenby's death meant the end of the "loans" that Vivian had relied on to fund her patronage. Although her father left her all his property and possessions, there was little remaining once his creditors had been paid off. Now wholly reliant on Pin's modest salary, Vivian complained to her husband about his habit of losing perfectly good jobs because of the silly articles he insisted on writing, and demanded to edit them before they were submitted. Although Pin would grant his wife almost anything, he refused to acquiesce to this. In retaliation, Vivian became less discreet about her love affairs. In July 1935, when the Darkblooms were living in Perth, Vivian invited the novelist Alexander Fernsby to stay with her for a month at a hotel only a few minutes' walk from Pin's office. When Pin bumped into Fernsby in the street one day, Pin invited the novelist out for dinner, and brought along his first editions of the author's *Broken Sunlight* (1925) and *The King Died and Then the Queen Died of Grief* (1928) to sign. Mortified, Fernsby left the next morning. The publication of Fernsby's *The Bloodshot Chameleon* (1949), which fictionalised aspects of Fernsby's liaison with Vivian, confirmed Pin's suspicions that their youngest daughter Urania (Rainy), born in November 1935, was not his but Fernsby's. As with Polly, Pin kept this knowledge from Rainy for as long as he lived.

In 1937 an anti-Stratfordian was appointed vice-chancellor of the University of Sydney. Pin, on the strength of his critical publications, was offered a senior lectureship in the English department. To his wife's elation, the Darkblooms returned to Sydney towards the end of the year, and Vivian lost no time in setting up her salon once again, keeping open house for the city's intelligentsia. Her affairs were marked by the publication of poems, plays and novels written in her honour, always featuring a sensuous, tall, dark-haired woman. One of Vivian's innumerable conquests was Rand Washington, then at the beginning of his long career as a science-fiction writer. Their relationship lasted for a tempestuous month in 1939, resulting in the novel *Vivyan of Cor*, in which the hero, Buck Whiteman, is lured away from his Princess BelleFemme Blanch by a "marble-skinned brunette temptress". The novel is notable for its tender (if mawkish) treatment of romantic love, almost unique in Washington's oeuvre. After Vivian ended the affair, Washington responded by writing the sadistic fever dream *Torturers of Cor* (1940), in which Vivyan is captured and slowly dissected alive by the villainous Argobolin. Washington also claimed credit for a joke about Vivian Darkbloom that made the rounds of the Sydney literati in 1939 and 1940:

FIRST BLOKE: Have you seen Bob lately?
SECOND BLOKE: No, I heard he has a bad case of VD.

At the outbreak of the Second World War, many writers in Vivian's circle joined the army, and correspondingly she made far fewer appearances in print during the first half of the 1940s. Pin, on the other hand, published over fifty critical articles and three books during this decade, including *Swastikas and Ray-Guns: Australian Scientifiction and Fascism* (1942), a magisterial denunciation of the *Cor* novels, and "The Clock Will Strike" (1947), an examination of the legend of Sydney Steele's contract with the devil, of which, sadly, only the abstract survives. By the end of the war Pin was appointed a professor and head of the University of Sydney's English department. With the conflict over, Vivian expected her life to return to what it had been, but she was disappointed. Now in her late forties, although still handsome, she did not find it as easy as she once had to attract men. To her disgust, some younger poets insisted on seeing her as a mother figure. This perhaps explains her brief fling with the mystery writer Claudia Gunn in 1946, Vivian's only known same-sex relationship. Though not particularly attracted to women, and even less so to one sixteen years her senior, Vivian nevertheless engineered a brief affair with Gunn, a liaison that produced the novel *Death in Full Bloom* (1948), in which Gunn obligingly killed off the femme fatale "Vivian Bloom" by eviscerating her with a stalactite.

In 1948 Pin was offered the post of professor of Australian literature at Cornell University in New York State. The role had been created specifically for him by the dean of the Faculty of Arts, who had been impressed by Pin's research published throughout the 1940s. The Darkblooms arrived at the university on 9 November 1948, two days before Vladimir Nabokov, who had recently been appointed to teach Russian and English literature at Cornell. The Darkblooms and the Nabokovs met for the first time at a party to welcome new teaching staff. Nabokov took an instant liking to the diffident Pin, who had read and admired Nabokov's *Bend Sinister*, published the year before. After a few cocktails, Vivian interrupted the conversation between the two men to whisper that there seemed to be a lot of Jews at the party. She then proceeded to air some of the racial theories she had picked up from Rand Washington. Nabokov did not inform Vivian that his wife, Vera, was Jewish, but from that moment on he treated her with polite disdain whenever they met. After learning that Nabokov was a celebrated writer, Vivian flagrantly pursued him throughout 1949 and 1950, exploiting her husband's friendship with the Russian to throw herself in his way as much as possible, even using the pretext of her daughter Polly's crush on Nabokov's son, Dmitri, to visit the Nabokovs' home as often as she could. Nabokov, in turns amused, angered and aghast, rebuffed Vivian's advances, which only ceased when Pin, for the first and last time in their marriage, threatened to leave her.

Pin and Volodya (as Nabokov was known to his close friends) would meet twice a week to take long walks together. Nabokov, to Pin's embarrassment, praised *Dancing in the Shadows*, a copy of which he had found in the university library, and would good-naturedly needle Pin about when he would write another novel. Pin demurred but enjoyed listening to Nabokov's plans for his next book, *The Kingdom by the Sea*. Pin's encouragement and enthusiasm for this work, which eventually became the notorious *Lolita* (1955), helped to sustain Nabokov during the early stages of the novel's composition when he was, uncharacteristically, afflicted with self-doubt. Nabokov's fondness for Pin is clear in his letters to his friend Edmund Wilson, the editor and writer. In a letter dated 17 April 1952, Nabokov describes a conversation with Pin in which the Australian had mechanically enumerated his wife's many lovers, concluding, "And yet, I still think of her as an angel." Nabokov had responded, "Yes, an angel dancing on the head of a pin."

During their years at Cornell, Vivian's only appearances in print were three articles in the university newspaper, the *Cornell Daily Sun*, whose nineteen-year-old editor she had seduced in March 1950 after a three-month campaign. The first article was an interview with Vivian, which described her as a "famous Australian novelist" and "good friend of the Nabokovs", while her other appearances were limited to brief mentions in the newspaper's "Spied around Campus" column. Though Nabokov did his utmost to disguise his loathing for Vivian in deference to his friend's feelings, he was perversely fascinated by the couple's relationship, and delighted when Pin pointed out to him that Vivian's full name was a perfect anagram of "Vladimir Nabokov". The Russian writer was incapable of resisting such a delicious play on words, which explains the brief appearance of the character "Vivian Darkbloom" in *Lolita*, where she is the lover and biographer of Humbert Humbert's nemesis, Clare Quilty. Later, the character would resurface as the annotator of Nabokov's longest novel *Ada or Ardor: A Family Chronicle* (1969). Vivian remained unaware of her appearances in Nabokov's books until the 1970s.

One morning in early June 1954, Pin was on his way to meet Vivian for lunch at a diner in Ithaca when he suffered a massive brain haemorrhage and collapsed in the street, directly outside the funeral parlour where his body would lie, and where his memorial service would take place, four days later. Pin, Nabokov noted in a letter to Edmund Wilson, had died as he had lived, not wishing to put anyone to any trouble. Before the funeral, Nabokov and Vera visited Vivian to pay their respects. The children, Polly and Rainy, were sitting silent and numb in the kitchen. Vera made the girls some soup and tried to comfort them. Nabokov found Vivian weeping in Pin's study, a room she had never set foot in before. Littered around her, Nabokov noted, were stacks and stacks of her book, *Ivy Van Allbine: An Australian Vanity Fair*. As Vera helped Vivian to bed, Nabokov replaced the books on the shelves, pondering what had possessed his friend to keep precisely one hundred and nine copies of his wife's horrendous novel.

Vivian and Rainy returned to Australia in September 1954, but Polly elected to remain in America, having fallen in love with one of her father's protégés in the English department. She stayed with the Nabokovs for five months before marrying her sweetheart in February 1955; Vivian chose not to attend the wedding. She used the money from Pin's life-insurance policy to buy a comfortable home in Sydney's Double Bay. Rainy stayed with her until the beginning of the academic year, then left to study drama at the University of Western Australia. Three years later she met Will Deverall, a mystery critic, and the two married. Free at last of her daughters, Vivian set about re-establishing her literary gatherings, but she found it much more difficult now to attract any but the most obscure writers and artists. Her one coup was a brief visit in December 1955 from Nobel laureate Matilda Young, who bored Vivian by talking about how much she owed to Peter Darkbloom's early championing of her work, and resisted Vivian's suggestion that the best way to honour Pin would be by writing a poem about his widow.

By 1956 Vivian had grown tired of the inability of the writers she patronised to publish anything. Using most of her savings, she established the Darkbloom Press. Six collections of verse by various undistinguished poets appeared throughout 1956 and 1957, all containing gushing dedications to Vivian and a mandatory poem or two immortalising her beauty. The books did not sell, and the press went bankrupt in the summer of 1957, forcing Vivian to auction her house and move to an apartment in Blacktown. Later that year Nabokov sent her a courteous note, along with a copy of his latest novel, *Pnin* (1957). This book, arguably Nabokov's most humorous and poignant, describes the misadventures of the clumsy, balding lecturer Timofey Pnin, a man who retains his essential decency and kindness despite being shabbily treated by the world at large, and by his manipulative ex-wife in particular. Though Nabokov had made Pnin Russian instead of Australian, the resemblance to Vivian's Pin was clear. The commercial and critical success of Nabokov's novel enraged Vivian, who could not understand why the Russian had chosen to write about her husband rather than her.

Without any money to bestow on authors, or hospitality to attract them to her poky apartment, Vivian found herself alone for the first time in decades. Her old lovers, among them Rand Washington and Claudia Gunn, wanted nothing to do with her. Her spirits were briefly lifted when *Dancing in the Shadows*, which had been out of print for twenty years, was brought out in a new edition by Berkeley & Hunt in 1961, complete with a rare, admiring quote by Nabokov on the cover. Vivian granted interviews to journalists and academics, who called to talk about Peter Darkbloom but left with shorthand notes and audio tapes full of Vivian's recollections of herself. The University of Sydney contacted Vivian to purchase her husband's papers, but she had left them in the basement of their house in Cornell, where they had been burned by a janitor. Undaunted, Vivian offered the university her collection of the novels, poems, stories, paintings and sculptures she had inspired, but they declined. Vivian then turned to the noted biographer Stephen Pennington, asking him if he would be interested in writing her life. Pennington refused Vivian's persistent requests for a meeting until she told him that she was in possession of Alexander Fernsby's love letters to her. Pennington had just begun work on Fernsby's biography and could not resist the bait. He visited Vivian in June 1964, but she refused to show him the letters unless he signed a contract to write her biography. After a futile hour of flattery, which included tactfully deflecting Vivian's attempts to seduce him, Pennington made his excuses and left, convinced the letters did not exist. Pennington's brief and uncharacteristically vicious description of Vivian in his *Biographical Sketches 1953–2003* read: "Vivian Darkbloom. A lanky oversexed crone, with the faltering, high-pitched voice of an unconvincing female impersonator."

A month after Pennington's visit Vivian was reading the morning newspapers, checking for any mention of herself, as was her lifelong habit, when she came across a review of a recently published science-fiction novel, *An Imperfect Vacuum* by P.V. Darkbloom. A letter to the publisher confirmed the author as Vivian's daughter Polly. Vivian borrowed the book from the library, but to her disappointment could find no trace of herself among its spaceships and aliens. She had made no effort to contact her children in years, and so was unaware that Polly had become a cult science-fiction novelist, and Rainy a playwright whose farces had been successfully staged in Sydney and London. Neither was Vivian aware that she had three young grandchildren.

Vivian sent letters to her daughters asking them to visit her in Sydney. Polly was living in San Francisco, but agreed to meet her mother since it coincided with her returning to Australia to promote her latest novel. Rainy, it transpired, was living only a short bus ride from Vivian's flat. The reunion took place in a café near Vivian's home in late November 1965. Polly and Rainy had barely sat down before their mother began berating them for their selfishness in not mentioning her in their work; between them they had dedicated two plays and a short-story collection to their father, but nothing to her. Polly and Rainy listened in silence as Vivian outlined her plans: they should each write a memoir of their childhood, in which she would play a major role. This was too much for her daughters, and as they went to leave Vivian pleaded with them, telling them it would be easy as there was so much to write about; for instance, Pin wasn't their father. The news appalled the sisters, and an incensed Polly led Rainy, crying, from the café. Polly returned to America six weeks later and never spoke to her mother again. The second volume of Stephen Pennington's exhaustive biography *The Life of Alexander Fernsby* made public Rainy's parentage in 1972. Although Fernsby, her biological father, would attempt to contact Rainy in the 1970s and 1980s, she refused to meet with him.

In the last years of her life Vivian made repeated efforts to republish her novel *Ivy Van Allbine*. She would spend each weekday at the offices of a different publisher, clutching her manuscript and demanding to be seen. Sometimes a kindly receptionist would accept the manuscript and promise to give it to an editor, but Vivian would return a week or two later, having forgotten the incident, and the charade was repeated. In January 1975 Vivian fell and broke her hip outside a supermarket in Blacktown. She was hospitalised for nine weeks, and during her stay was diagnosed with Alzheimer's disease. Her eldest daughter, Polly, continued to refuse to have anything to do with her, but Rainy visited her in hospital, though her mother no longer recognised her. After Vivian's hip replacement, Rainy installed her in a comfortable care home in Liverpool in western Sydney. Vivian appeared happy in her new surroundings, especially after her books and papers were brought from her flat once it had been sold. Rainy and her daughter Rachel would visit one afternoon each month, and Vivian would ask her granddaughter to read her a story. Rachel read to her from *Little Viv's Birthday Party*, or *Dancing in the Shadows*, or one of the many hundreds of poems which featured Vivian Darkbloom, while Vivian listened with her eyes closed. When Rachel finished, Vivian would open her eyes and thank her. "I like stories about Vivian," she would say. "Vivian is my favourite."

Vivian Darkbloom died of heart failure on the evening of 13 June 1976.

Helen Harkaway, in Robert Bush's flat, October 1963

(1940–1993)

The Bell Jar in the Rye . . .

> Robert Bush, describing Harkaway's novel
> *Parade of the Harlequins* (1965) in his autobiography
> *Bastard Title* (2004)

THE RECLUSIVE NOVELIST HELEN HARKAWAY WAS BORN IN Canberra on 29 June 1940. Her father, Iain, was a federal member of parliament for the seat of Lyne, New South Wales, representing the United Australia Party. Her mother, Diana, was a former model, still occasionally recognised as the "Gunn Girl" who had appeared in advertisements for the mystery novels of Claudia Gunn in the 1930s. The Harkaways were wealthy, owning two houses in Canberra, three in Sydney, and a thousand acres of land in the Barrington Tops. Helen enjoyed a privileged upbringing, but in contrast to her sociable parents she was an introvert. As she grew into an exceptionally beautiful young woman, however, she found attention more and more difficult to escape. Helen preferred to stay in the family's farmhouse in the Barrington Tops rather than in Canberra, but her parents only went there for a few weeks every year.

At the private school she attended in the capital she made few friends; girls seemed to take an instinctive dislike to her, and boys were simply an annoyance. Like many lonely children before and since, she found refuge in reading. Among her favourite books were *The Magic Pudding* (1918) by Norman Lindsay, *A Child's Jane Eyre* (1950) by Naomi Plume and *Tales of Snugglepot and Cuddlepie* by May Gibbs (1918). Helen also enjoyed such pulp magazines as *Nurse Sheila Romances* and *Famous Sheilas of Filmland*, published by Fountainhead Press. They inspired her to write her own stories in exercise books, but she would allow no one to read them. Helen was a perfectionist; even the simplest homework took hours, and she would often destroy her work if it was returned with any corrections from the teacher. By the time she was fourteen she was taller than her father and was already developing her mother's figure. Helen hated her height and deliberately cultivated a slight stoop; she refused to wear the fashionable dresses her mother bought for her, preferring dowdy clothes. This did nothing to deter the increasing number of male visitors who came to court her. She was thrilled when her poor eyesight required her to wear thick glasses, and she tried unsuccessfully to develop a squint. Her parents blamed Helen's continuing eye problems on her constant reading and writing, and forced her to attend parties and balls; Helen would spend these evenings hiding in a bathroom. She received her first marriage proposal before she turned seventeen. She rejected her puzzled suitor with lines borrowed from *A Child's Jane Eyre*:

I am no bird; and no net ensnares me: I am a free human being with an independent will. I have an inward treasure born with me, which can keep me alive if all extraneous delights should be withheld, or offered only at a price I cannot afford to give.

Helen's "inward treasure" was her growing sense of vocation as a writer.

When she was eighteen she began attending the Australian National University in Canberra to study English literature. Two male undergraduates were expelled for fighting over her, and a sixty-year-old lecturer was forced to resign when Helen reported the love letters and compromising photographs he had sent her. After a few unhappy months she stumbled upon a forgotten corner of the library where she was never disturbed by either students or staff: the Australian literature section. When she realised that her lecturers would never give her a failing mark, no matter how poorly she performed in exams, Helen spent all her time in her secret place in the library, reading. In her years at university she filled in hundreds of call slips requesting books from the stacks, including one that much influenced her, *The Catcher in the Rye* (1951) by J.D. Salinger, which had been banned in Australia until 1958.

Harkaway's idyll was destroyed in December 1961 when she returned from the stacks to her usual desk to find an admirer had placed a note there for her. She only read the first line – "Was this the face that launched a thousand slips?" – and was so upset that she left and never went back. Instead of reading, she took up writing again, this time in earnest. Much as she disliked the experience, she attended lectures and tutorials once more, recording scraps of overheard conversation in her notebooks, as well as ideas for poems and short stories. She even overcame her distaste for parties so that she could meet people and gather more material. During her last semester she began work on at least three novels, only to discard them after a few chapters. In October 1962, shortly before her final exams, Harkaway's parents perished in a light-plane crash over the Barrington Tops. After the funeral, she left university without completing her degree and put the houses in Canberra and Sydney on the market, where they sold quickly. With this money, and the sum she inherited from her mother and father, Helen Harkaway had become a very rich young woman. She retreated to the family property in the Barrington Tops to concentrate on her writing.

Harkaway wrote for four hours a day, five days a week, spending the rest of her time maintaining the property and taking long walks in the rainforest that bordered it. Once a month she drove into Gloucester to stock up on food and supplies. Apart from that, she had no contact with the outside world; she did not own a radio, telephone or television, and her nearest neighbours lived miles away. In June 1962 she completed her novel, a *roman à clef* called *Parade of the Harlequins*. The story's protagonist is Blythe Walker, a striking young debutante who strives to escape the suffocating influence of her family, and to avoid being snared by the attractive tricksters, or "harlequins", of the world. By the end of the novel Blythe has been betrayed by everyone she loves, and the final scene shows her walking fully clothed into the surf at Bondi. Harkaway submitted the novel to Sydney publishers Berkeley & Hunt in February 1963, where it came to the attention of Robert Bush, then a junior editor. Bush felt the book showed some talent, if little originality, and believed that it might sell due to the prevailing vogue for stories featuring alienated young people. He wrote to Harkaway that he was interested in her book, but emphasised that it required substantial rewriting. The satirical depictions of lightly fictionalised Canberra and Sydney society figures were well done, but the protagonist, Blythe Walker, was problematic, being more of a cipher than a character. Harkaway

responded by asking if she could see Bush to discuss his sugges-
tions, and in June 1963 she caught the train to Sydney, where she
met the editor at a restaurant near the Berkeley & Hunt offices.

Bush arrived at the restaurant with Harkaway's manuscript,
each page marked with suggested changes and deletions in his
preferred purple ink. In his autobiography, *Bastard Title*, written decades later, Bush recalled his initial encounter with Helen
Harkaway:

> I realised then the truth behind the clichés I had spent the
> last week ferreting out of *Parade of the Harlequins*. When I
> first saw Helen Harkaway, peering at the small print of the
> menu and frowning with concentration, I stopped in my
> tracks. My heart skipped a beat. The blood rushed to my
> face. I was thunderstruck. It was love at first sight.

Bush, who was fast developing a reputation for the thorough-
ness and stringency of his editing, was helpless against
Harkaway, unable to contradict her when she calmly stated
that she had decided the manuscript would be published as it
stood. By the end of their lunch, Bush had promised Harkaway
absolute control over every aspect of the book, from the cover
design to the layout, typography, blurb and advertising campaign. Even Berkeley & Hunt's top-selling writer, Claudia
Gunn, was never granted such authority. Harkaway remained
in Sydney while Bush prepared her novel for publication. He
told no one at Berkeley & Hunt that he had ceded so much
power to an unknown writer, and it has been suggested that
he diverted resources and money away from some of his other
authors to help publicise *Parade of the Harlequins*. By August,

Bush was fretting that his lies would be found out, and that it could cost him his job. He went to Harkaway's hotel to tell her he was going to confess everything to Claude Berkeley. As he was about to leave, Harkaway pushed him against the wall and kissed him. Although he was later to describe their sexual relations as "like making love to a hardback book", Bush continued to sleep with Harkaway at every opportunity over the next six months, while she used him as a proxy to oversee her book's publication. Bush never told Claude Berkeley what he had done.

Harkaway was convinced that her novel would cause a scandal and perhaps even trigger court cases for libel, featuring as it did unflattering and barely disguised pen portraits of the many famous politicians, sportsmen and society figures she had been introduced to by her parents. *Parade of the Harlequins* was published in February 1964, a month after Harkaway had retreated once again to her farm in the Barrington Tops, where she intended to remain until the storm had passed. On publication day, Harkaway wrote to Bush to tell him that their personal relationship was over, although she had no objections to his continuing as her editor, if he promised not to bother her with "all that grunting and sweating" again. In his autobiography Bush once again resorted to clichés to describe his feelings at receiving Harkaway's letter: "My heart was broken. I was absolutely devastated. But then, I burned for revenge."

Parade of the Harlequins sold poorly, despite Berkeley & Hunt's costly advertising campaign, and received almost no attention in the press. The one review of the book, in the *North Sydney Advocate*, consisted of only six words, "A flawed but promising first novel." Before Bush could compose himself to reply to Harkaway's letter ending their relationship, he received three more missives from her demanding to know about the latest sales numbers, the reviews, and if any public figure had yet condemned the novel. Bush waited a week, then sent Harkaway a letter telling her the wonderful news: *Parade of the Harlequins* was a smash hit. The reviews could not have been any more favourable if he had written them himself. Furthermore, questions about the novel had been asked in parliament, with more than one MP demanding that it be banned. A crowd of reporters were besieging the offices of Berkeley & Hunt even as he wrote, baying for an interview with the author of the *cause célèbre* of 1964.

Harkaway had no reason to doubt Bush, especially after receiving a package from him containing press clippings from dozens of journals and newspapers. Bush had written these effusive reviews, then had the art department mock up the clippings in the precise style of the *Antipodean*, *Overground* and others. He even sent her numerous fan letters, written in different hands, from Harkaway's readers, telling her how the book had changed their lives forever. While Harkaway was well pleased with the stir her book had caused, she still abhorred personal publicity, and instructed Bush to refuse on her behalf all requests for interviews. She also asked that no more fan mail be sent to her, gratifying as it was. She did not have time to respond to the trickle of letters, which had no doubt by now become a flood.

Three weeks after *Parade of the Harlequins* was published, the National Parks and Wildlife Service opened a new walking track that skirted the edge of Harkaway's property. The track was poorly signposted, and lost bushwalkers would often wander onto Harkaway's land, sometimes approaching the house to ask their way. Harkaway was not fooled; she knew that they must be reporters in disguise. She refused to open her door to such people. If they approached her while she was checking the letterbox at her gate she would rush past them, covering her face with her hands and muttering, "No comment!" To deter these pests Harkaway put up large "No Trespassing" signs around her property, as well as hiring a handyman from Gloucester to fix razor wire along her fence line. Her excursions to town became more infrequent; in 1964 she made the two-hour round trip only five times. Once, outside a shop on the main street, a man handed her a leaflet advertising the next Gloucester Show. Before he could say anything, Harkaway had signed his leaflet, thrust it back at him, and walked brusquely away. The attention was unbearable, she wrote to Bush, and was distracting her from her new work, a collection of short stories.

Having always been retiring, Harkaway now became a recluse. The only contact she had with the outside world was with Bush. The tone of her letters to him suggests she had no idea how severely she had hurt him. Bush, never of a forgiving nature, took a sadistic pleasure in maintaining the illusion of Harkaway's success. He continued to send her reviews he had written himself as well as inflated royalty statements; knowing how careless she was with money, he correctly foresaw that she would never bank the cheques he sent. Events also conspired to convince Harkaway of her literary fame when she became embroiled in the disappearance of the prime minister, Harold Holt.

On 17 December 1967 Holt had gone to Cheviot beach near Portsea, Victoria. Despite the dangerously heavy surf and the protests of his friends, he insisted on going for a swim. Soon he was lost to view; his body was never recovered. In the days after his disappearance, the public was obsessed with any information relating to the prime minister's last hours, no matter how trivial. On 21 December the *Daily Trumpet* revealed that at the time of his death, Holt had been halfway through a little-known novel called *Parade of the Harlequins* by Helen Harkaway, "a sexy story about a lusty lovely". A reporter from the newspaper contacted Berkeley & Hunt, and Bush supplied him with Harkaway's address. Since she had no telephone, the reporter drove to the Barrington Tops to get a comment from the writer about her minor connection with Holt's disappearance. The gates of the Harkaway property were locked and topped with razor wire, but the reporter decided to wait, having travelled all the way from Sydney. He was fortunate in having chosen one of the rare days when Harkaway was going into Gloucester, and within a short time the writer appeared in her filthy ute. As she opened the gates, the reporter introduced himself and asked her for her thoughts on her novel being the last book the prime minister had read before his disappearance and possible suicide. Harkaway was horrified. She had not known of Holt's vanishing, and thought the reporter was blaming *Parade of the Harlequins* for Holt's taking his own life. She shut the gates, got into her ute and raced back up the road to her house, but not before the reporter had snapped a photograph.

The resulting article, "Holt Hottie Harkaway Hurries Homeward", appeared in the *Daily Trumpet* with accompanying picture on 28 December 1967. By coincidence Harkaway was in town that day, and the woman who worked at the post office showed her the paper. Harkaway fled, and was not seen in Gloucester again for five months. In mid-1968 she wrote to Bush to tell him that she had completed her short-story collection and another novel; she had been about to send them to him, but the furore over *Parade of the Harlequins* had so revolted her that she had decided not to publish anything for the time being. Harkaway had persuaded herself that the novel had played a part in the death of Harold Holt, and demanded that Berkeley & Hunt suppress it. The novel had been out of print for years, but Bush wrote to assure her that they had removed it from bookshops, despite the protests of her devoted readership. Harkaway wrote back thanking Bush for his swift action. This was the last he was to hear from her for over a decade.

In 1969 the 300-acre property adjacent to Harkaway's was purchased by Rand Washington, who intended to establish a religious commune there. A month later, Washington's wife, Joyce, introduced herself to Harkaway when the two ran into each other on the fence line of their properties. Joyce Washington was one of the few people to gain Harkaway's friendship, perhaps because, as Harkaway learned in passing, Joyce had written for many of the pulp magazines Harkaway had so enjoyed reading as a little girl. Through Joyce, Harkaway was introduced to Rand (whom she found captivating) and to the tenets of Transvoidism. Harkaway donated a significant amount of money to the cause, becoming the only one of Washington's followers to attain the third level of Transvoidism. The sudden death of Joyce Washington in a car crash in May 1970 marked the end of Harkaway's involvement with the cult. After the collapse of Transvoidism in 1974, Harkaway purchased Washington's property to ensure she would never have near neighbours again.

In 1976 Harkaway was dragged into the spotlight once more, when it came to her attention that the experimental writer

Arthur ruhtrA had appropriated her *Parade of the Harlequins*, retaining two-thirds of the original text and interlacing it with long chapters of "erotica". The resulting "composite novel", *The Coming of the Harlequins*, had been released by New Dimensions earlier that year. Harkaway retained the Sydney law firm Bolton & Todd and took ruhtrA to court, claiming breach of copyright. ruhtrA, representing himself, argued that no one had even heard of the original novel, and moreover his additions had immeasurably improved the book. Harkaway was present throughout the proceedings, but to her great relief was not called to give testimony. ruhtrA was ordered to pay Harkaway two thousand dollars and costs.

Three years after the ruhtrA affair, Harkaway received an invitation from Berkeley & Hunt to a dinner in honour of Alexander Fernsby, generally considered to be Australia's greatest living novelist, who had recently returned to his homeland after a lengthy self-imposed exile. Harkaway had long enjoyed Fernsby's work and decided to attend, leaving the Gloucester area for the first time in seventeen years. The dinner took place in late May 1980 at a restaurant on Circular Quay. Harkaway, fearing she would be recognised, showed up wearing a headscarf and dark glasses. Bush introduced Harkaway to his wife, Lydia McGinnis, and although Harkaway spoke civilly, Bush noted her utter self-absorption was intact; she did not notice that he now walked with a limp and used a cane. Bush had invited Harkaway because he had grown tired of the trick he had played on her. He thought that if she went unrecognised at the dinner, she would gradually come to realise that *Parade of the Harlequins* had not been the success he had convinced her it was. Bush observed her as she met other writers and publishers who expressed nothing more than ordinary politeness when they heard her name. He could see Harkaway becoming unsettled as the evening wore on.

After dinner, Alexander Fernsby gave a brilliant speech to the hundred and fifty guests before moving from table to table with Bush. When they reached Harkaway's table, before Bush could introduce them, Fernsby astounded everyone by kissing Harkaway's hand and saying, "Why, it's the stunning Helen Harkaway, of course." When Bush's wife made to take a photo of the encounter, Harkaway, ever protective of her privacy, slapped Fernsby on the cheek and stormed out of the restaurant. Later, when Bush questioned Fernsby, it emerged that Fernsby did not know Harkaway was a writer; he had recognised her because he had often seen her in the library of the Australian National University in 1961, when he was carrying out research for what would become his novel *Donkey Hotel* (1965). Fernsby had never forgotten the beautiful young woman, although she had spurned the note he had left on her desk.

Harkaway did not contact Bush again until 1982, and then only to complain about a request for an autograph she had received from "some forward girl called Deverall". Bush did not reply to this letter, nor to others that Harkaway sent him querying foreign publication contracts or reminding him that film rights to her novel must never be sold. In 1989, enmeshed in scandal over his late wife's suicide, Bush resigned from Berkeley & Hunt; he died the following February. Harkaway learned of his death two months later, when her letters to him were returned. She continued to write to Berkeley & Hunt, but Bush had destroyed all files relating to *Parade of the Harlequins*, and her former publisher told Harkaway they could provide no further information about her book. Despite this annoyance, Harkaway's solitary life continued as before. She walked at least eight miles each day, carefully avoiding the journalists who continued to pose as bushwalkers. Once back home, she would write for four hours. Every six or seven weeks she would stock up on supplies at the same half-dozen shops in Gloucester she had patronised since 1962, exchanging small talk with the shop owners. Although she was now in her early fifties, she could pass for a forty-year-old; she still turned mens' heads, in spite of her large, thick, ugly glasses. Occasionally she would write to Berkeley & Hunt to tell them she had finished another novel but was not quite ready to publish it. She received no replies.

On 25 May 1993 Stephen Pennington, the biographer of Alexander Fernsby, arrived in Gloucester. The dogged Pennington was then working on the sixth volume of Fernsby's biography and was seeking information about Fernsby's celebration dinner in 1980, when Harkaway had cuffed the famous author. Pennington's research had revealed that Harkaway was also a writer, although he had never heard of her. Out of curiosity, after weeks of searching, he had managed to procure a copy of her book. It was not much easier to locate her property. The Gloucester locals had become fond of the eccentric woman and, knowing how much she hated attention, refused to tell Pennington where she lived. When he finally arrived at the entrance to the Harkaway property, Pennington ignored the signs warning him against trespassing. The old padlock on the rusty gates gave way at a push and Pennington, without a four-wheel drive, walked up the long, steep, potholed road to the ramshackle farmhouse, dragging his briefcase with him.

When he knocked on the front door there was no answer, but he thought he heard a faint voice from inside. Pennington

opened the door and went down a dim hallway to a small bedroom, where he found a delirious woman, burning with a fever,
lying in filthy clothes across the bed. Pennington dropped his
case and rushed to her side. From her ramblings, Pennington
understood that a morning ago, or perhaps two, Harkaway had
been out walking in the rainforest when she had dropped her
glasses. While searching for them she had fallen down a ravine,
breaking both her legs. It had taken her a full day to drag herself back to the house through heavy rain. She had been too
exhausted, and her legs too badly injured, to drive her car anywhere. Pennington gave her some water and aspirin and tried
to make her comfortable, but she was terribly weak and sick.
After a frantic search, he realised there was no telephone in the
house. Pennington explained to the woman that he was going
for help and would return at once. She smiled but said nothing.
Pennington, unfit and infirm as he was, limped back to his car
and drove for twenty minutes to the nearest neighbour, where
he was able to call for an ambulance. When he returned to the
Harkaway house, Helen Harkaway was dead. Beside her, on the
floor, was the copy of *Parade of the Harlequins* that had fallen
from Pennington's briefcase. It was only that night, as he lay in
bed in a Gloucester hotel room, that Pennington realised she
had signed it.

Helen Harkaway left six novels and a short-story collection
in the care of her Sydney lawyers and literary executors, Bolton
& Todd, with instructions that they be published at intervals
one hundred and one years after her death. The first of these
books, a sequel to *Parade of the Harlequins*, is expected to appear
in May 2094.

Donald Chapman?

Donald Chapman

(1903?–1937?)

The feckless waves coolly adore
The shark's barbaric gloaming.

From "The Red Stumps of Memory" (1936?)

DONALD CHAPMAN, POET, WAS BORN IN TAREE, NEW SOUTH Wales on 19 August 1903, a few minutes after his twin sister, Deirdre. Chapman's father was a plumber and his mother a seamstress. Donald showed little interest in literature in his youth, although in secondary school he reportedly enjoyed the short stories of Addison Tiller. After finishing his education he became a telegram boy, then a shoe salesman, a stevedore and – finally, in 1925 – an insurance clerk. Chapman lived a quiet life. On his parents' death he moved in with his sister and her family, sleeping in a small spare room that he always kept neat and tidy. He seemingly had no interest in the opposite sex, or in dancing, music or the cinema. Sometimes he would return home furtively carrying a small package wrapped in brown paper; when Deirdre confronted him, he showed her with some embarrassment the poetry collections he had bought.

On 22 September 1937 Chapman was struck by a bus and killed as he was walking home from his office. Several months after his funeral a tearful Deirdre was going through her brother's few possessions when she happened on three note-books filled with the poetry Chapman had written in his last years. Wanting to preserve something of her brother's memory, Deirdre decided to send a few of his poems to a publisher to ask their opinion. In December 1938 Paul Berryman, editor of the *Modrenist* magazine, opened a large envelope containing a let-ter from Deirdre Chapman, which gave the outline of her late brother's life described above, a photograph of Donald, and six poems she had torn from his notebooks. Berryman glanced at the letter and briefly considered returning the poems without reading them, but finally decided to skim the first lines of "The Red Stumps of Memory".

As well as being the founding editor of the *Modrenist*, Australia's leading journal of avant-garde poetry and prose, Berryman was himself a poet. Born in Newcastle in 1900, he had been brought up on the bush verse of Paterson and Lawson. His first published poems, in the *Newcastle Herald* when he was sixteen, were traditional bush ballads with titles such as "Drenching the Cows" and "The Joy of Fencing". Berryman's approach to his craft was transformed when he moved to Sydney in 1918 to study literature at university, where he made friends with fledgling poets Jack Sargent and Matilda Young. In post-war Sydney the arts blossomed as never before, and doz-ens of poetry movements burst into life. Among them were the Onomatopoets, who held the sound of a poem to be supreme, as well as the cross-dressing, surrealist Mamaists, and the Metallurgists, who claimed Sydney Steele's lost masterpiece, *Bush, Beer and Ballads*, as their canonical text. Jack Sargent was involved with many of these groups, and Berryman became something of a disciple to the handsome Sargent, earning the nickname "Private" from Sargent's wife, Matilda. Berryman's experimental verse enjoyed a brief vogue in the early 1920s, and he was hailed as one of the most promising of the new generation of Australian poets.

When Matilda Young left Sargent in 1924, Berryman was suspected of helping his friend write and distribute an obscene poem about his estranged wife. After Sargent's death, Berryman used his influence in the Sydney poetry world to isolate Young, attacking her in print at every opportunity and spreading rumours that she had driven Sargent to drink and an early grave. In 1929 Berryman was made deputy editor of the literary journal *Northerly*, whose editor, Albert Mackintosh, shared his dislike of Young. Though the regular wages were welcome, Berryman despised the traditional verse *Northerly* favoured. He attempted to persuade Mackintosh that readers hungered for a new kind of poetry, as exemplified by the work of Ezra Pound. Mackintosh would not listen to him, and in a June 1930 editorial dismissed Pound and the poetry of "Modrenism" (a printer's error) as "an imposture perpetrated on a credulous public".

Berryman's tenure at *Northerly* came to an abrupt end in July 1931 when Mackintosh learned that his deputy editor had destroyed a number of poems submitted to the magazine by Sydney Steele, then living in London. Mackintosh also suspected Berryman of having disposed of the work of other conservative poets rather than publish them, and Berryman was dismissed. A month before, Berryman had made a copy of *Northerly*'s subscriber list. He now used this information to send out a manifesto advertising a new poetry journal, the *Modrenist*, which Berryman would publish and edit. He promised an innovative brand of

Australian poetry that would no longer rely on the old poetic conventions and threadbare themes of bush poetry.

The first issue of the *Modrenist* was a success, selling out its initial run of five hundred copies, and a number of avant-garde poets began to cluster around Berryman. In response, Mackintosh, who lived in the Sydney suburb of Arcadia, formed a poetry club called "The Arcadians", who valued poetry with regular rhyme and metre that dealt with traditional Australian themes – the kind of poetry that Mackintosh continued to champion in *Northerly*. The feud between the two men continued for years in editorials and articles, with each attempting to recruit poets to their side. By 1938 the erratic publishing schedule of the *Modrenist* had diminished to once a year, and Berryman was frantically seeking writers who would arouse the interest of his dwindling number of subscribers. It was at this time that he received the letter from Deirdre Chapman and encountered Donald Chapman's verse.

"The Red Stumps of Memory" impressed Berryman, and on reading "The Jabberwock Saunters Along Taree Main Street" his excitement grew, but it was the third poem, a sonnet in fifteen lines, that convinced him of Chapman's immense talents:

The Thaumaturgist's Complaint
As I am made a killing instrument
Lust and decay vie in my heart's dark race.
Ill thought is born amid the bride's intent
And eldritch gales devour the sailor's face.
So you gulp grotesque dreams beneath the ground
Therefore goodbye, go bother weaker hearts.
If there are rabid swans along the sound

Let them before your tomb unveil their arts.
Desiring nothing more than splintered tears,
Although my undecided self's a verb
Your secret hope results in unheard cheers.
Oh basil is the most untruthful herb,
Unless you would create a kinder lie.
Now courting owls by you my darkness cry
God knows that only gods know when they die.

Chapman's nihilistic, ambiguous poems were unlike anything Berryman had come across as editor of the *Modrenist*, and
they could not have fallen into his hands at a better time. He
wrote at once to Deirdre Chapman, asking that she send the
rest of her brother's notebooks as soon as practicable. Without
waiting for a reply, he dedicated the January 1939 issue of the
Modrenist to Donald Chapman, including a short biography of
the poet, which he adapted from Deirdre's letter, his photograph, and all six of Chapman's pieces, which he rearranged
and corrected under the title *The Red Stumps of Memory*. "The
Thaumaturgist's Complaint", which was to become the best
known of Chapman's poems, appeared first. In his editorial,
Berryman did not hesitate to call Chapman's opaque, allusive
verse the work of a genius, and he challenged Albert Mackintosh
to produce an Arcadian poet with even half as much talent.

Mackintosh's reply was swift. In his editorial to the
February issue of *Northerly* he smugly explained how he had
found two poets with half of Chapman's talent. Indeed, the
two poets together had made up Chapman. Mackintosh then
printed in full a letter he had received from Les Mitchell and
Tom Stirling, two bush poets from Bacchus Marsh, "proud

Arcadians" and favourites of Mackintosh, whose work, including "The Fossickers", "Only a Timber Cutter's Daughter", and "'E Woz Me Best Mate, 'E Woz" had appeared regularly in *Northerly* since 1929. In their letter, Mitchell and Stirling explained how they had grown tired of Berryman's insulting attacks and had resolved to show him up. Over the course of "an idle afternoon" they had composed the half-dozen poems attributed to Donald Chapman, and the letter from his equally fictitious sister. The photograph was of a local milkman. The two bush poets had not, they said, expected Berryman to be so naive as to publish their "experimental" poetry, and they had been most entertained when their creation had taken up an entire issue of the *Modrenist*. Mackintosh added that since the moral and poetical bankruptcy of the modernist movement had been revealed to the public, he presumed those involved would now have the good taste to remove themselves from the literary world. Predictably, while crowing over Berryman's gullibility, Mackintosh made no mention of how he himself had been tricked by Matilda Young into heralding the Sans Souci school of poetry a decade earlier.

The Chapman affair, as it came to be known, attracted the attention of the Australian press. Berryman gave sullen interviews to newspapers defending the poems despite their origins, while having to endure Mackintosh's taunting in *Northerly*. The humbled Berryman's allies deserted him and subscriptions for the *Modrenist* collapsed. Berryman brooded in silence for months and it was assumed that his literary career, along with the Chapman affair, would now fade into oblivion. However, a new issue of the *Modrenist*, which Berryman had financed by selling his Sydney flat, appeared in May 1939, heralding yet another twist in the saga. Berryman's triumphant editorial explained that he had recently received a letter containing "incontrovertible proof" that its author, Bruno Claypool, was the mastermind behind the Chapman affair. Claypool, a self-proclaimed "avant-garde arriviste", whose work had appeared in the *Modrenist* throughout the 1930s, asserted that he had written not only the Donald Chapman poems, but also the letter published in *Northerly* from Les Mitchell and Tom Stirling. Claypool had formed a plan to humble Albert Mackintosh years before, when Mackintosh had sneeringly rejected one of his poems. Claypool revealed that he had created the personas of the Bacchus Marsh poets Mitchell and Stirling and had submitted a number of "infantile" poems under their names, which Mackintosh had happily published in *Northerly*. Then he had spent two years crafting his "masterpieces", the six Donald Chapman poems, and had submitted them to the *Modrenist*, before writing to Mackintosh, in the guise of Mitchell and Stirling, to tell him that Chapman was a sham. Claypool had wished to demonstrate that Mackintosh had no eye for poetry, condemning as he did the brilliance of Claypool's Chapman poems while celebrating the mediocrity of Mitchell's and Stirling's verse, work which, Claypool claimed, had been written with the help of his four-year-old son. As if that were not enough, Claypool revealed that Mitchell and Stirling were not his only creations; he was behind almost every poem that had appeared in *Northerly* since 1933.

The June 1939 issue of *Northerly* contained no poetry, and the Chapman affair was addressed only in Mackintosh's uncharacteristically brief editorial, which deplored the vile deception that had been practised on him and his readers, while

stubbornly insisting on the merits of the work he had published
by Claypool's aliases. Privately, Mackintosh began an investigation into the Chapman affair. At great expense he hired a
team of private detectives to look into the matter, providing
them with a shortlist of suspects including Rex Ingamells, A.D.
Hope and Hal Porter, all of whom had reason to dislike the
editor of *Northerly*. (Mackintosh was evidently certain of one
thing: only a man would have the intellect, talent and patience
to carry out such an involved ruse.) Meanwhile, Berryman
enjoyed his moment in the sun: the *Modrenist* issue revealing
Claypool's deception had sold out, and the mainstream press
now lampooned Mackintosh in their cartoons. But Berryman's
victory would prove to be shortlived.

In the third week of August 1939 new issues of *Northerly* and
the *Modrenist* appeared, by coincidence, on the same day, each
reproducing yet another letter, this time from the poet who
claimed to be behind Chapman, Mitchell, Stirling and Claypool.
The letters, signed "X", were identical in every respect, except
the one published in *Northerly* claimed that Berryman had
orchestrated the hoax all along, and the one published in the
Modrenist claimed that Mackintosh was the originator of the
deception. Berryman blamed Mackintosh, Mackintosh blamed
Berryman, and each vehemently proclaimed his own innocence.
By this time the press were bored with the affair, and news of
impending war in Europe meant the most recent revelations
received little mention in the newspapers. Enraged by this latest
humiliation, and convinced of Mackintosh's guilt, Berryman
spent days trying to find the *Northerly* editor, finally running
him to ground as Mackintosh made a call from a telephone
booth in George Street. Brandishing a butterknife, Berryman

attacked Mackintosh. The men struggled in the booth for a moment or two before a passing policeman arrested them both. Mackintosh was later released, but Berryman was charged with aggravated assault and sentenced to two years in gaol.

Berryman's imprisonment, and the outbreak of the war, marked the end of the Chapman affair. In 1940, Berryman was released and straightaway enlisted in the Australian Army. He saw action in North Africa and was badly wounded in a skirmish in December 1941, losing his right eye. On his return to Australia after an honourable discharge, he attempted to re-establish the *Modrenist* but was unable to compete with the new magazine of experimental writing, *Angry Penguins*. Instead, Berryman submitted a number of his avant-garde poems to Max Harris, the editor of *Angry Penguins*, but they were rejected as too old-fashioned. Berryman then turned to prose; in 1942 he began his account of the Chapman affair, *On First Looking into Chapman's*, in which he outlined his theories as to the true identity of Chapman/Mitchell/Stirling/Claypool/X. He now no longer believed Mackintosh to be the culprit; he did not think him a good enough poet to have written *The Red Stumps of Memory*. Instead, Berryman's prime suspects were William Baylebridge and Kenneth Slessor, two writers he had frequently attacked in reviews throughout the 1930s. Berryman finished his book in January 1944 but was unable to find a publisher. In June of that year he bought the latest issue of *Angry Penguins* and read, with an increasing sense of déjà vu, the Ern Malley poems. Although he was convinced the Malley poems were a prank, he decided not to warn Harris. When the trick was revealed, Berryman wrote to newspapers, highlighting the similarities between the Malley and Chapman affairs, but his correspondence attracted little interest. Berryman continued to live in Sydney until his death in 1953 from throat cancer.

Albert Mackintosh remained editor of *Northerly* but refused to publish any more poetry on principle. After the assault by Berryman, Mackintosh never again referred to the Chapman affair. Despite falling sales and accusations of irrelevance, *Northerly* limped along through the 1950s, when it lost many of its readers to Rand Washington's journal *Quarter*. By January 1961, *Northerly* was selling fewer than five hundred copies a month. The final blow, however, did not come from poor sales. In late 1961 Mackintosh was involved in another scandal when an anonymous source provided the *Daily Trumpet* with evidence of his enormous private collection of pornography. Every day for the first week of December 1961 there was another salacious story about "Dirty Mackintosh". He resigned a few days before Christmas and the last issue of *Northerly* appeared in January 1962. Mackintosh died from a heart attack nine months later.

The 1960s saw a renewed interest in the Chapman affair, sparked by the controversial inclusion of "The Thaumaturgist's Complaint" in the canonical anthologies *Classic Australian Poems* (1961), *The Classic Poems of Australia* (1965) and *Australia's Classic Poems* (1969). Since that time at least a dozen books have appeared elaborating different theories as to the identity of X; Banjo Paterson, Douglas Stewart and Roland Robinson have all been put forward as candidates, and even prose writers such as Francis X. McVeigh and Rand Washington have come under suspicion. The figure in the Chapman photograph has never been identified. Perhaps the most bizarre theory was originated by Arthur ruhtrA, who maintained that *The Red Stumps of Memory* had been written from beyond the grave by Frederick Stratford.

The Chapman affair continues to fascinate Australian writers; perhaps most famously, it appeared in fictionalised form in Peter Carey's *My Life as a Fake* (2003), as well as inspiring recent novels and short stories by Tim Winton, Gail Jones, Gerald Murnane and Charlotte Wood. In 2009 researchers at the University of Sydney carried out a series of linguistic analyses of the Chapman corpus in an attempt to determine their authorship, but the results were inconclusive. The identity of "Donald Chapman" remains, and quite possibly will forever remain, a riddle.

Stephen Pennington at home, 11 April 2003

Stephen Pennington

(1935–2009)

I now envisage completing the Fernsby biography by the end of 1967 at the very latest...
From a letter to Robert Bush, 5 January 1965

STEPHEN PENNINGTON, BIOGRAPHER OF SYDNEY STEELE, Addison Tiller and, most famously, Alexander Fernsby, was born in Eden, New South Wales, on 12 September 1935. His childhood was far from idyllic; his mother, Eve, was undemonstrative and his father, Robert, resentful and quick to anger. The Pennington family lived in a two-bedroom cottage with a small kitchen and an outhouse. Eve Pennington was the daughter of a wealthy local landowner, and Robert was captain of a fishing vessel; with so little in common, it is understandable that their marriage was made up of brief, violent arguments and extended periods of silence.

Stephen's parents became the subject of his first, unauthorised biographies. From the few civil conversations they had, the boy reconstructed and consolidated everything he knew of their lives in one of his school notebooks in order to avoid mentioning any subject that might cause discord between them. He established that his mother was happy only when she recalled her life before marrying his father, and that to ask about their wedding, or how they met, was to earn a thrashing with a wooden spoon. His father was a more difficult study; Stephen never ascertained much about him, only that he should never appear before his father carrying a book, as the sight of one enraged him. Robert Pennington despised learning and was determined to make a fisherman of his son, but Stephen's frequent ear infections meant that he was rarely well enough to go out on the boat.

Stephen felt little grief when, in August 1948, Robert Pennington drowned after being washed overboard in a storm off Cape Conran. Within the month Stephen and his mother left Eden and moved to the Sydney suburb of Point Piper. Stephen was dispatched to Calvin Grammar, an exclusive boys' boarding school; it was only then that he grasped the fact that his family was rich, despite his father's miserly ways. At school, Stephen showed great promise in English and his lifelong love of history was kindled by reading Naomi Plume's popular abridgements *A Child's Parallel Lives by Plutarch* and *A Child's Secret History by Procopius* (both 1947). In his second year at the school, and every year thereafter, Stephen won the Addison Tiller Prize, a writing award named after his school's most famous alumnus, for his essays on Australian history and literature.

Stephen's grandfather, whom he had never met, died in 1949, leaving a substantial bequest to his only child, Eve Pennington. Not long after, Eve reverted to her maiden name of Forester and soon became a noted figure in Sydney's social scene, taking up where Vivian Darkbloom had left off on her departure for America the previous year. Eve seldom replied to Stephen's letters and never visited him during term time, though the school was only a short walk from their home. Unhappy and lonely, Stephen begged his mother to allow him to become a day pupil, but she refused. Stephen spent his sixteenth birthday, which his mother had forgotten, in the school library. It was there that he came across Alexander Fernsby's *The Bloodshot Chameleon* (1949). This novel, Fernsby's fifth, tells the story of Terry Finnegan, a self-educated drifter working on a trawler in the waters off Broome in Western Australia. At the beginning of the novel, Finnegan considers himself to be a chameleon, able to adapt perfectly to his surroundings, whether a working-class pub or a society cocktail party. Ultimately, his experiences in Broome, from falling in love with a married woman to almost killing a man in a bar brawl, change him, and when he returns to Sydney he feels that he can no longer fit in there, or anywhere. He has become an outcast.

Stephen read the short novel in one morning; the character of the fascinating, feckless Finnegan so impressed him that he went to a nearby bookshop to seek out Fernsby's other novels: *Broken Sunlight* (1925), *The King Died and Then the Queen Died of Grief* (1928), *Today, Tonight, Tomorrow* (1933) and *The Square Circle* (1934). After reading all four books in one sleepless weekend, Stephen wrote a long letter to Fernsby, care of the novelist's publisher, pouring out his feelings of isolation and resentment. When months passed and no reply came, Stephen assumed the letter had gone astray, or the writer did not care to answer it. Stephen spent the next term rereading Fernsby's novels, and much of his free time scouring bookshops for back issues of literary magazines containing Fernsby's short fiction, which was at that time uncollected. Then, in September 1952 Stephen received a letter with a London postmark. He presumed it was from an English book dealer he had contacted to enquire about the price of a signed first edition of *The Bloodshot Chameleon*, but found instead that it was from Alexander Fernsby himself. The author apologised for the delay in replying; he had been travelling in Africa and Europe and Stephen's letter had finally caught up with him in England. He offered sympathy and counsel, encouraging the young man to write, and to get away from his family and school as fast as he could. Echoing one of his novels, Fernsby concluded by telling Stephen, "Like me, you're a circle. Don't let them turn you into a square." Stephen carefully preserved the letter in one of his history books, and years later had it framed and hung over his desk when he commenced his biography of Fernsby.

A month after the delivery of the Fernsby letter, Stephen's mother was killed in a car accident; Eve Forester had crashed her Auburn 851 Speedster into a lamppost as she raced home drunk from a party. Somewhat to his surprise, Stephen found himself stricken by her loss. Her funeral was attended by the cream of Sydney society. Stephen did not know any of the mourners, and during the service overheard a couple arguing about who the young man in the front row was; Eve had told everyone she was childless. For his last year of school, Stephen became a day pupil and lived in the large house he had inherited, keeping on his mother's cook and maid to look after the place. Inspired by Fernsby, he had determined to become a writer, and that summer he began scores of short stories and poems but was unable to finish any of them.

In 1953 Pennington began studying history and English literature at the University of Sydney, consistently achieving the top marks in his year. He continued to write poetry and even began a novel, but it became painfully obvious to him that he did not have the imaginative gift for fiction, and he decided instead to become a biographer. He asked his fellow students innumerable questions, amassing information to write brief, biographical outlines. Pennington's relationship with his first girlfriend was blighted when she happened upon her file, which recorded everything from her father's nearsightedness, to her mother's birthplace, to her own bra size. Despite this, Pennington was to continue his practice of writing capsule biographies of the many people he encountered throughout his life; his posthumously published three-volume *Biographical Sketches 1953–2003* (2010) contains over a thousand pen portraits of the famous and the unknown, from an encyclopaedia salesman Pennington once sat next to on a brief bus trip in London in 1966, to prominent literary figures including Robert Drewe, Lydia McGinnis, David Malouf and Claudia Gunn.

In his third year at university, during a lecture on the Napoleonic Wars, Pennington suddenly came to the realisation that he knew infinitely more about the life of Napoleon than he did about his own mother and father. He made the decision to resume the unauthorised biographies of his parents he had begun as a child, and to spend the winter break finding out more about their lives. Consequently, in July 1955 he returned to Eden for the first time since he was thirteen; he stayed in the old cottage his mother had never bothered to sell, which was now in a state of disrepair. There Pennington chanced on relics of his father – a spare pair of gloves, an oilskin jacket and sou'wester, his bank book – but of his mother there was little sign. Finally, in an old chest under his parents' bed, Pennington found a mouldering pile of documents, including an ancient photograph of a smiling debutante whom Pennington eventually recognised as his mother, and a copy of Stephen's birth certificate, mottled with damp, which listed "Eve Forester" as his mother and his father as "Unknown".

As Pennington later wrote in his unpublished *Autobiography of a Biographer*:

> Everything became clear to me at that moment; now I understood why my father hated me and the reason for the complete absence of love between my parents. The birth certificate, taken together with my father's old bankbook, which showed a deposit of a thousand pounds in the month after I was born, could only mean that Robert Pennington had been bought off, paid to marry my mother and to raise another man's son as his own.

Pennington was more relieved than shocked by his discovery, and also electrified by the thought that his real father might still be alive. After months of investigation, which involved questioning his few surviving relatives, Pennington believed he had identified his father: all evidence pointed to a man called Harry Valentine, who had once worked as a deckhand on Robert Pennington's ship. But Valentine had vanished without a trace in January 1935.

Upon completing his degree in 1956, Pennington undertook a doctorate in Australian literature, although his initial proposal to study the development of the Oedipus myth in the novels of Alexander Fernsby was rejected. At this time, seven years before the publication of *The Sydney Trilogy*, Fernsby was still regarded as a minor writer. Instead Pennington chose Sydney Steele as his thesis topic, and it was as a direct result of his painstaking archival research that the only surviving works in Steele's hand were uncovered: a shopping list from May 1899 and Steele's signature on the original contract for *Charlie Cobb's Cobbers*. Pennington eventually revised and extended his thesis as *Sydney Steele: Australia's Homer* (1961), published by Kookaburra Books. His chapter on the so-called "Curse of Sydney Steele" reportedly challenged the notion that Steele, and those who chose to write about him, were doomed to mishaps and adversity. (Unfortunately, the entire print run of the book perished in a mysterious explosion at the printing works before it could be distributed.) After the completion of his doctorate in 1960, Pennington was offered a lecturing post at the university but turned it down, preferring to devote his time to another biography, this time of the perennially popular short-story writer Addison Tiller.

Pennington spent a month in Coolabah and almost a year in Bath, England, researching Tiller's life, and the resulting exhaustive 1200-page biography, completed in the remarkably short period of two years, proved hugely controversial, bringing to light Tiller's real name and nationality, and his often unflattering opinions of his adopted country. Copies of *Addison Tiller: Australia's Chekhov* (1963) were burned outside Tiller's supposed childhood home on the edge of Coolabah during the annual Tiller festival, as the town's mayor refuted Pennington's claim that not only had Tiller not been born there, he had never even been to Coolabah until his burial in 1929. Pennington's biography was credited with sparking a renewed interest in Tiller's stories, including a television adaptation of *On Our Homestead* commissioned by the ABC, on which Pennington served as creative consultant.

Although not yet thirty, Stephen Pennington had established himself as the pre-eminent literary biographer in the country. By September 1963 he was considering his next project, tentatively titled *Frederick Stratford: Australia's Laurence Sterne*, when he was approached by Berkeley & Hunt to write a biography of Fernsby, whose recently published *The Sydney Trilogy*, comprising *Yellow Blue Vase*, *A Day Trip* and *The Kissing of the Cross* (1963), had finally brought the writer to national and international attention. Remarkably, Pennington vacillated for almost a month over the commission. Although he still treasured Fernsby's letter to him, and continued to regard Fernsby's early novels as masterpieces, Pennington had been disappointed by the stark modernism of *The Country of Mirrors* (1959) and frankly befuddled by the stylistic and narrative experiments of *The Sydney Trilogy*. He was also concerned that his idealised image of Fernsby would necessarily be sacrificed in the process of writing a biography. Undoubtedly, too, his hesitation also owed something to the sheer scope of the task. Fernsby had lived an almost absurdly full life across four continents, and Pennington surmised, correctly as it turned out, that a biography of Fernsby would require more research and more time to complete than his biographies of Sydney Steele and Addison Tiller combined. When Pennington expressed his reluctance to commit to the project, he received a letter from Alexander Fernsby himself, who told him how much he had enjoyed his biography of Tiller and begged Pennington to reconsider:

I can tell you how the book will end, if that makes things any easier. According to the medicos, I have a grapefruit-sized tumour growing in my noggin, and it's only a matter of weeks before it goes off, or whatever it is that tumours do. *Alexander Fernsby: 1903 to 1963 (Or 1964 with Any Luck)*. There's your title. What do you say?

Pennington could not refuse the dying man's wish, and at the end of October 1963 he signed a contract with Berkeley & Hunt for "a two-volume biography of Alexander Fernsby, volume one to be delivered on or before 1 July 1965 and volume two on or before 1 July 1967". The biographer and his subject met for the first time on 29 November at St Luke's Hospital in Sydney, where Fernsby was spending his last days. Pennington was struck by how youthful Fernsby appeared, and how closely he resembled the author photograph on the first edition of *The Bloodshot Chameleon*, taken almost fifteen previously, which Pennington had brought for him to sign. Fernsby greeted his biographer genially, but obviously did not recognise Pennington as the boy who had written to him years before, and Pennington did not remind him. He liked the old man immensely, and for several weeks Pennington spent his days by Fernsby's bedside, recording on an expensive, unwieldy tape recorder Fernsby's memories of his childhood in Beijing and his travels across India, Africa, Europe and Australia.

When Fernsby was alone he spent his every waking moment on what he presumed would be his final book, *The Blind Sunrise*, a collection of short fiction which he was revising for publication. The doctors had told him he would not live to see the new year but he was still alive by the end of January 1964, having completed revisions of *The Blind Sunrise* and begun an ambitious new novel, *The Papercut* (1965). Pennington continued to visit Fernsby throughout February, but after a weekend spent organising and transcribing their interviews, he returned to the hospital to be informed the writer had disappeared. Robert Bush, Fernsby's editor, told the biographer that further tests had revealed Fernsby was perfectly healthy; his X-rays had been mixed up with those of another patient, who had since died. On hearing the news, Fernsby had discharged himself from hospital. News of his whereabouts did not come until September 1964 when Berkeley & Hunt received a postcard and the completed manuscript of *The Papercut*, sent from Bolivia.

Pennington began his research in earnest after Fernsby's reprieve, spending all of 1964 and most of 1965 gathering information on the writer's years in Australia. Fernsby was born in Randwick, Sydney, on 11 April 1903. The Fernsbys were an old and well-respected Sydney family; Alexander's great-grandfather had been a midshipman on the HMS *Sirius*, one of the ships in the First Fleet; his grandfather had been a magistrate, and his father was a successful businessman. When Fernsby was two, his family moved to Beijing, where his father opened several factories. Fernsby did not return to Australia until 1921; when he did, he spent twenty-eight years living a rootless life as a farmhand, fencer, fruit picker, fisherman, jackaroo, labourer, bin man, cook and shepherd, among dozens of other jobs, while at the same time writing and publishing five novels. In 1949 Fernsby left Australia once more, living first in Africa and then Europe, returning to his homeland in 1961. Upon his diagnosis of a brain tumour he elected to remain in Australia, expecting to die at any time.

With their hospital conversations as his guide, Pennington attempted to retrace the writer's travels across Australia in the 1920s, 1930s and 1940s, interviewing as many of his friends and acquaintances from that period as he could find. Fernsby had crisscrossed the continent dozens if not hundreds of times, and despite his meticulous research Pennington was unable to account for months of Fernsby's life in 1923, 1927 and 1929. He wrote to Fernsby care of his last known address in Bolivia and received a reply six months later, postmarked from El Salvador. In it, Fernsby attempted to puzzle out from memory his movements during these lost years. In an almost illegible postscript, he told Pennington of his sudden recollection that he had hidden the only copy of his first, unpublished novel, *The Huntigowk*, in the library of the University of Sydney while working there as a janitor in 1923. Pennington was in Perth when Fernsby's letter was forwarded to him and he returned to Sydney without delay. He spent the next nine weeks inspecting every inch of the library stacks, hoping the lost manuscript might be recovered. When Robert Bush mentioned Pennington's assiduous search in his correspondence with the writer, Fernsby telegrammed Pennington. He had written the letter, he explained sheepishly, on April Fool's Day, and the postscript when he was drunk. "Huntigowk" was the old Scots word for an April Fool. Fernsby had learned it while crofting on the Isle of Skye in 1920. He sent his sincere apologies to Pennington for wasting so much of his time.

Pennington's abortive search for *The Huntigowk* meant that he had fallen behind his strict writing schedule. With the submission date for the first volume looming, he spent the second half of 1964 toiling fourteen-hour days, seven days a week, organising his notes, transcribing interviews, sifting archives and working on the first draft. In January 1965, Pennington was finally granted a visa to visit China, where Fernsby had lived between the ages of two and sixteen. Pennington flew to Beijing on 24 January 1965 and, with the help of a translator and government chaperone, was able to track down two of the domestic staff who had worked for the Fernsbys. Although now very old, they could still recall the frolics of the young Alexander. In a letter to Fernsby dated 14 February 1965 Pennington described, with some satisfaction, the trove of anecdotes about the writer he had amassed during his stay.

Pennington's repeated requests to visit Fernsby's childhood home in the Xicheng district were politely but firmly refused by his Chinese guardians. On the day before he was due to depart for Sydney, Pennington slipped away from his hotel room for the afternoon and, with the aid of a map, found Fernsby's old house for himself. He took a photograph of it, but before he had replaced his camera in its case was accosted by soldiers of the People's Liberation Army, who prevented him from leaving. Within the hour police arrived, and Pennington was arrested. The Australian government was not informed of his detention until a week had passed; despite their formal protests, at the end of February Stephen Pennington was charged with espionage and his trial set for July. (Later it was revealed that Fernsby's childhood home now housed the favourite mistress of Mao Zedong, Chairman of the Communist Party.)

The Australian government downplayed the situation, believing that publicity would only make matters worse. In secret negotiations throughout March 1965, the Chinese were finally convinced of Pennington's innocence and scheduled his release for 6 April. Unluckily, Alexander Fernsby, by then living in Mexico, was already circulating an immoderately worded letter protesting Pennington's arrest, signed by American, Australian and European writers and intellectuals, including Norman Mailer, Edward Gayle and Susan Sontag. The letter was published in the *New York Times* on 5 April, prompting a swift response from the Chinese government: a statement was released declaring that Pennington's trial would be brought forward to the end of the month, and prosecutors would be seeking the death penalty. The matter was raised at the United Nations, with Great Britain, France and Canada taking Australia's side. Soon after, the espionage charges were dropped, but Pennington was sent to the Shayang Re-Education Through Labour camp in Hubei province, where he spent the next eight months. During one of his daily interrogation sessions, three of Pennington's fingers and his thumb on his right hand were broken; without adequate medical treatment, they healed badly. The deadline for the first volume of the biography passed while Pennington was in the camp, as did his thirtieth birthday.

After months of sensitive negotiations between the Chinese and Australian governments, Pennington was released and deported to Australia at the beginning of December 1965. He spent a month in hospital, where he was treated for malnutrition and scurvy, and began the frustrating process of learning to write with his left hand. When he was discharged he wasted no time getting back to work, determined to complete the first volume of the biography before the year was out. Pennington spent only three months recuperating in Australia before setting off for Bombay, where Fernsby had lived for a year after being thrown out by his father at the age of sixteen. Despite contracting amoebic dysentery, Pennington was elated to find that the model for the unforgettable Father O'Malley in Fernsby's first novel, *Broken Sunlight*, was still alive and running an orphanage in Calcutta. The old priest proved eager to share his memories of the young, idealistic Fernsby.

In June 1966 Pennington left India for Great Britain, where Fernsby had lived briefly in 1920–1921 and then again from 1951 through to 1960. Pennington was based in London for the rest of

1966, interviewing Fernsby's surviving friends and associates and gradually nearing the end of his second draft of the first volume. To Fernsby's amusement, Pennington even succeeded in recovering the US Army revolver Ernest Hemingway had given Fernsby in November 1921, when the pair of ambitious writers had met at a bar in Cheapside as Hemingway was en route to Paris. Fernsby had wrapped the gun in oilskin and buried it in a private park in Hampstead, intending to go back for it later. But when he did return to England three decades later, he had been unable to find the weapon. Pennington, after Fernsby's reassurances that the gun was not another "Huntigowk", had crept into the park every night for a week, digging and then filling dozens of holes before finally unearthing the firearm.

Despite Fernsby's gratitude for the find, by the beginning of 1967 Pennington was trying his subject's patience. In his haste to complete the first volume, Pennington had sent over a hundred letters to the writer in November 1966 alone, requesting further information and clarification about his youthful exploits in China, India and London. Fernsby's replies from Ecuador were at first swift and jocose, gradually becoming more abrupt and fewer and farther between, until finally, in January 1967, the writer, who was editing an early draft of his most linguistically dense and psychologically complex novel, *Donkey Hotel* (1969), sent Pennington a page torn from Boswell's *The Life of Samuel Johnson* (1791) with two sentences underlined in red ink: "Sir, you have but two topics, yourself and me. I am sick of both." Fernsby later apologised, even going so far as to dedicate *Donkey Hotel* to Pennington, but after the biographer's many ordeals the exchange proved a serious strain on their relationship, which was arguably never the same afterwards.

Pennington arrived back in Australia in March 1967 and delivered the finished first volume to Berkeley & Hunt in June. Thanks to the heroic efforts of its editor, Robert Bush, *The Life of Alexander Fernsby: Volume One: 1903–1925* was published just four months later. Adulatory reviews and brisk sales went some way towards assuaging Pennington's fury that his preferred title for the book, *Alexander Fernsby: Australia's Graham Greene: Volume One 1903–1925*, had been changed by Bush without his consent. Fernsby, in a letter from Argentina congratulating Pennington on his winning the Laurence Steed Prize for Biography in December, commiserated, recalling that his publisher had made him discard the original title of *The Bloodshot Chameleon*, which he could now not even recall.

As Pennington embarked on the second volume of the biography, it became clear that one book would not be enough to cover the remaining thirty-two years of Fernsby's life, including as they did his travels across Australia, Africa and South America and the writing of his most important novels. Pennington was therefore contracted to write an additional third volume, which was expected to be finished in time for Fernsby's seventieth birthday in April 1973. On hearing the news, Fernsby, who had narrowly escaped being executed with Che Guevara in Bolivia in October 1967, wrote to Pennington expressing his hope that he would live long enough to see the third volume published. Fernsby had long held a suspicion he would die before the age of sixty-nine.

Having earlier been sidetracked from Fernsby's wanderings across Australia by the abortive search for *The Huntigowk*, Pennington spent the next three years retracing Fernsby's travels, from Alice Springs to Perth, Brisbane to Launceston,

Darwin to Melbourne, Canberra to Cairns, Townsville to Coober Pedy, Broome to Mackay. During his lengthy nomadic period, between 1926 and 1949, Fernsby had written some of his best work, including *The King Died and Then the Queen Died of Grief* (1928) and *The Bloodshot Chameleon* (1949). While his writing had brought him admiring reviews, and a few hundred pounds in royalties and advances, Fernsby supported himself by doing a range of jobs across the country; in one month he could go from being a political speechwriter in Canberra to being a pimp in Adelaide. Fernsby's diverse experiences in these years informed his novels, allowing him to create dozens of memorable characters, from the doomed self-loathing bisexual policeman Sergeant Hobby in *The Square Circle* to the saintly elderly Methodist Mrs Farrell in *Today, Tonight, Tomorrow*.

Pennington, despite never again enjoying good health after his experiences in India and China, continued to work long hours for months at a time without a break. He crisscrossed the continent by car, train, bus, helicopter, boat and aeroplane, travelling an estimated 55,000 miles between 1967 and 1971. His perseverance was amply rewarded: he found a lost poem Fernsby had inscribed with a diamond on the window of a Newcastle boarding house in 1932, six forgotten short stories that had appeared in a Catholic church newsletter in Kalgoorlie in 1929, and even the medical records detailing Fernsby's treatment for gonorrhoea in February 1935 at a medical clinic in Boydtown, New South Wales, a small town not far from Pennington's birthplace. Pennington's chief discovery was that Fernsby's brief dalliance with Vivian Darkbloom that same year had produced a daughter, Rainy, whom Darkbloom's husband had raised as his own. Fernsby had no idea he had fathered a child, but his intermittent attempts to contact Rainy on learning of her existence were rebuffed.

The Life of Alexander Fernsby: Volume Two: 1926–1935 appeared on 11 April 1972, Fernsby's sixty-ninth birthday. The writer cabled his congratulations to Pennington from Tijuana, Mexico, expressing his great pleasure that he was still alive to read it. Neither Fernsby nor his publisher, Berkeley & Hunt, spoke any longer of the delays that plagued the biography, or its excessive length; the first two volumes alone amounted to nearly nineteen hundred pages of closely printed text. To their credit, Berkeley & Hunt never considered abandoning the project, even when the company's fortunes were at their lowest in the mid-1970s after the death of Claudia Gunn. It helped that Pennington's work continued to win various literary prizes, and that both volumes had sold in respectable numbers, enough even to generate a small profit.

From 1973 to 1977 Pennington remained in Sydney, working steadily on the third and projected last volume of the biography, which would follow Fernsby through the writing and publication of *The Bloodshot Chameleon* to the present day. Although he was now reluctant to bother Fernsby with questions, Pennington found the writer eager to discuss the composition of his most famous novel. The film rights to *The Bloodshot Chameleon* had been purchased by Paramount in 1972, and Fernsby hired to write the screenplay. Fernsby arrived in Hollywood in July 1973 and was put up in a palatial house in Bel Air. Yet after months of effort he had made little progress. When he mentioned a structural issue he was struggling with in a letter to Pennington, the biographer's reply gave him the direction he needed to solve the problem. Over the next four months Fernsby continued to seek Pennington's assistance on matters of dialogue, pacing and characterisation, telling his biographer, "You know the damn thing better than I do."

Although initially flattered to be of use, Pennington came to resent Fernsby's constant queries by letter, telephone and telegram, as he was anxious to finish off volume three of the biography before he turned forty in 1975. Rather than answering any more of Fernsby's queries, Pennington wrote a complete screenplay for *The Bloodshot Chameleon* in five days in May 1974 and sent it to Fernsby with a curt note requesting that he now be allowed to concentrate on the biography. Fernsby submitted Pennington's script under his own name, and the studio expressed its satisfaction by giving the writer a $10,000 bonus. By December 1975 the film was in production, with Robert Redford as Terry Finnegan and Diane Keaton as Alicia McDowell. *The Bloodshot Chameleon* was released in America to critical acclaim and respectable box office returns in April 1977, the same month *The Life of Alexander Fernsby: Volume Three: 1936–1949* was published in Sydney. After tense discussions with Pennington, his publishers had bowed to the inevitable and authorised a further two volumes. Pennington was too busy either to attend the launch of the third volume or to see *The Bloodshot Chameleon* when it was released in Australian cinemas in July 1977. By the time Fernsby won an Academy Award for best adapted screenplay in April 1978, Pennington was in Malawi, visiting the small primary school in Blantyre where Fernsby had taught English from 1949 to 1951, and which had provided the setting for *The Country of Mirrors* (1959). Pennington learned of Fernsby's Oscar triumph in June, from an old copy of the *Washington Post* that he came across while having dinner with the Australian consul in Lilongwe. In Fernsby's self-deprecating acceptance speech, the writer had thanked his agent, his editor and even his cleaning lady, but there was no mention of Pennington.

After six months in Africa, Pennington travelled by boat to South America, arriving in Rio de Janeiro in August 1978. The next year and a half was spent in the various backwaters that Fernsby had frequented during his travels on the continent from 1964 to 1972. Though Fernsby had lived a charmed life in South America, Pennington was not so fortunate. He was kidnapped and held to ransom twice, once in Paraguay and once in Chile, with his publisher paying the ransom on both occasions. As well as contracting, at different times, malaria, yellow fever, dengue fever, cholera and typhoid, Pennington lost three toes on his left foot to piranhas while fording the Bermejo River in Argentina, and was hospitalised with suspected rabies after being savaged by a dog in Bogotá. Pennington continued to work during his stays in hospitals and clinics, and despite his hardships made great progress with the fourth volume of the biography, completing it shortly before returning to Australia in May 1980. Having spent long periods travelling far from civilisation, Pennington had not received any of Fernsby's increasingly querulous letters from Hollywood during this time. After the success of *The Bloodshot Chameleon*, in 1979 Fernsby had been commissioned to adapt William Gaddis's *The Recognitions* (1955) for Twentieth Century Fox, but he was lost without Pennington's advice and unable to submit a finished screenplay. Fernsby's acrimonious disputes with Fox and the studio's threat of legal action to recover the $200,000 advance it had paid him were behind the novelist's returning to

Australia in May 1980. It was the first time he had been in the country since his cancer scare sixteen years earlier.

Fernsby and Pennington met in Robert Bush's office in the Berkeley & Hunt building on 31 July 1980. Much had changed since their last meeting in 1964. Fernsby was now seventy-seven and Pennington forty-four. In Bush's autobiography, *Bastard Title* (2004), he gives a short description of the encounter. Pennington was late and limped into the room, scowling. Fernsby clasped his biographer's hand, causing Pennington to yelp in pain from the arthritis that had resulted from his injuries in China. Pennington said little, save to finish Fernsby's sentences, a habit that annoyed and discomfited the writer. Pennington's ability to predict what Fernsby was going to say was uncanny. Bush was puzzled by Pennington's moroseness; Pennington had earlier told the editor how much he was looking forward to seeing Fernsby again after so long. Pennington's attitude can be explained by his chancing on a note in Berkeley & Hunt's archives only an hour earlier, which he copied into his diary. The note, which Fernsby had written to publisher Claude Berkeley in 1963, revealed Pennington had not been the first choice to write Fernsby's biography:

> It's a crying shame that Richard Ellmann isn't available.
> Still, can't be helped. Anyway, have you read the new
> biography of Addison Tiller? My God, it's tedious. The
> writer makes the fundamental mistake of assuming
> that Tiller was a good writer, rather than a hack. Still,
> Pannington [sic] can just about put a readable sentence
> together, when it comes down to it, and we may as well
> get him as anyone else. The doctor says I won't be around

to read it anyway. For the love of Christ, though, make sure you put in the contract that he can't call it *Alexander Fernsby: Australia's Graham Greene*.

All three men were visibly relieved when a journalist from the *Daily Trumpet* arrived to interview Fernsby, ending their meeting.

Remarkably, volume four (1950–1964) of Fernsby's biography, which dealt with his years in Africa, return to Europe, and the famous brain tumour misdiagnosis, and volume five (1965–1973), which focused on his travels in South America and the writing of *Donkey Hotel*, were published within six months of each other, in January and July 1982. Pennington had no doubt that the sixth volume, covering Fernsby's years in California and his return to Australia, would be the last. The biographer set off for Hollywood in November 1982, the same month that Fernsby was invited to take part in an expedition retracing the route of the explorers Burke and Wills from Melbourne to the Gulf of Carpentaria. Fernsby jumped at the chance, and despite his age easily passed a rigorous medical examination for insurance purposes. The journey, by camel, foot and four-wheel drive, took over ten months; Fernsby wrote about his experiences in his first work of nonfiction, *Footsteps in the Sand* (1984). He completed this book while staying at Australia's Mawson Antarctic Research Station in Mac. Robertson Land, where he had been offered the post of writer in residence for six months from January to June 1984.

Pennington spent most of 1983 in the Paramount Studio archives. If he had not known before, he must have realised then that the screenplay that had won Fernsby his Oscar in 1978 was the one Pennington had written for him. Whatever his feelings, Pennington never commented on the matter. Through Fernsby's Hollywood agent, Pennington was granted interviews with the stars of *The Bloodshot Chameleon*. Redford and Keaton spoke to Pennington at length about their experiences of working with Alexander Fernsby, and it must have been somewhat gratifying to Pennington when Redford told him, "To be perfectly frank, I couldn't get through the novel. But the script ... The man who wrote the script for *The Bloodshot Chameleon* ... He's a genius. No other word."

Pennington had to cut short his stay in Hollywood in October 1983 so that he could join a second expedition that intended to follow in the footsteps of Burke and Wills. Poorly planned and funded, this caravan ran into trouble after travelling only fifteen hundred kilometres, and Pennington almost died from dehydration before they were rescued. After recovering for four months in Sydney, Pennington resumed his usual working habits. The biography was now only a few months behind the actual life of Alexander Fernsby, a fact of which Fernsby himself was becoming uncomfortably aware. Writing in his journal in the third month of his stay in Antarctica, Fernsby confessed a recurring nightmare of looking through the thick glass of his hut and seeing Stephen Pennington, with his sinister limp and twisted right hand, approaching inexorably through the blizzard. Always superstitious, Fernsby came to believe that the day his biography caught up with him would mark the day of his death.

Fernsby returned to Sydney in late June 1984, having completed the final draft of *Footsteps in the Sand* and the initial draft of its companion volume *Footsteps in the Snow* (1986, edited by Pennington), a nonfiction account of his stay in Antarctica. That same month Pennington applied for and was denied permission to visit the Antarctic research station that had hosted Fernsby, delaying the progress of the biography. Only by chance, much later, was Pennington to learn that Fernsby, whom he had listed as a referee in his application, had written that Pennington was a violent alcoholic and on no account should be allowed into the station. Pennington pressed forward with the application, and after his publisher interceded was eventually allowed to stay at the research station for a month, under strict supervision, in December 1984.

Pennington had been in Antarctica for three weeks when he was informed of Fernsby's accident. The writer had been crossing Pitt Street in Sydney when he was clipped by a van. The impact threw Fernsby three metres across the road; he suffered numerous compound fractures and serious head injuries. At the hospital Fernsby slipped into a coma from which he was not expected to awaken. Pennington returned to Australia in January 1985 and went straight to the hospital. He stayed by the old man's side throughout the night, mentally revising the opening of volume six of the biography. The doctors assured him that due to the nature of Fernsby's injuries and his advanced age, he would almost certainly pass away in the next few weeks. Pennington visited Fernsby every day for the following three months, but the old man refused to die.

Pennington took a month off from the biography: his first holiday in over two decades. He returned to Eden, where he found that his old family home had collapsed from termite damage, so he had to stay in a local hotel. From habit, he awoke at half past five each morning, but instead of commencing work on the biography, as he had done almost every morning for twenty-two years, he went for long walks on the beach. On his third morning he nodded hello to a woman strolling in the opposite direction. On the fifth morning, they had a short conversation about the weather. Later that day, Pennington realised this marked the first time in years he had talked to someone for more than two minutes without mentioning Alexander Fernsby. By the seventh morning Pennington and the woman on the beach had exchanged names. Hers was Susannah Pope; she was forty-two, and a nurse. On the tenth morning, Susannah asked Pennington what he did, and he told her he was writing a biography of Alexander Fernsby. "I've never heard of him," she replied, and not long afterwards Pennington asked her to marry him.

The couple returned to Sydney in July 1985 and were married three months later. Instead of slaving for most of the day on the biography, Pennington now worked only three hours in the morning, spending the rest of his time doing repairs around their dilapidated house or tending to the long-neglected garden. Susannah found employment in the same hospital where Fernsby still languished in a coma. On the days she worked, Pennington would have lunch with her at the hospital canteen, then spend half an hour reading to the comatose writer from one of Addison Tiller's short-story collections. Pennington was later to recall this as the most carefree time of his life.

Work on the sixth and final volume of the biography progressed slowly throughout the late 1980s, and was interrupted when Pennington and his wife took a five-month luxury cruise. In 1990 Berkeley & Hunt, who had shown commendable patience throughout the long life of the project, began to pressure Pennington to complete it. Finally, in 1991 Pennington informed his publishers that he had only one more chapter to write, which would describe Fernsby's road accident and tragic fate. Three days later, Pennington sat by Alexander Fernsby's bedside on what he intended to be his final visit and, as he had done in the past, started to read an Addison Tiller story aloud. On this occasion, Fernsby slowly opened one eye and croaked, "Will you please stop reading that fucking tripe?"

Fernsby's astonishing recovery, at the age of eighty-eight, from a seven-year coma would become the subject of heated discussion in the *Lancet*, as well as the subject of Fernsby's next book, *The Comma*, in which he described his period of unconsciousness as nothing more than a pause between two clauses in his life. After months of physical therapy, Fernsby, though confined to a wheelchair, was able to leave hospital and return to his home in Randwick, where he continued to live independently. This marked the beginning of Fernsby's remarkable late period, which saw the publication of *The Comma* (1992) as well as the novels *The Rooms* (1993), *The Newcastle Fragment* (1995), *Falling into Space* (1996) and *The Amputee* (1998), his second short-story collection *Tapestries of Light* (2000), and his first poetry collection, *A Crown of Lantana* (2001). Fernsby also stood unsuccessfully as the Greens' candidate for Randwick in the 1993 and 1998 federal elections, an experience which informed his memoir, *The Red, Red Dust of Home* (2003), published on his hundredth birthday.

Not long after Fernsby's recovery, Stephen Pennington suffered a nervous breakdown and spent seven months recuperating in a sanatorium. Against the advice of his psychiatrists, he insisted on resuming work on volume six of the biography during his stay. When told he needed to rest, Pennington responded agitatedly, "I can't. Every time I sit down for five minutes, the

bastard writes another book." Eventually Pennington experienced a psychotic break, coming to believe that Fernsby was
immortal. During this period he attacked and injured a doctor whom he mistook for the writer. Pennington's recovery was
slow. In his last two months at the sanatorium, he refused to
see his wife, and on his release moved into a motel and began
divorce proceedings. Although Susannah attempted to contact
Pennington, he ignored her appeals. Finally he sent her a note
that simply said, "Stop distracting me." Susannah agreed to
their divorce and returned to Eden, leaving Pennington alone.
He went back to his house, and *The Life of Alexander Fernsby:
Volume Six: 1974–1991* was published in 1994.

To the wonder of many, Pennington did not participate in the
elaborate festivities which Berkeley & Hunt and the University
of Sydney had organised for Fernsby's hundredth birthday in
2003. The university presented Fernsby with an honorary doctorate and hosted a three-day conference on his work, which
attracted scholars from all over the world. There was also a gala
banquet to mark the reprinting of all of Fernsby's books as part
of Berkeley & Hunt's new *Antipodean Classics* line. Pennington
sent a paper to be presented at the conference but offered his
apologies, claiming he was too busy with volume seven of the
biography (1992 onwards). Now sixty-eight, frail and suffer-
ing from a persistent racking cough, Pennington nevertheless
continued to work at an accelerated pace in the hope of finally
concluding his great work. Throughout 2004 Fernsby had been
uncharacteristically quiet, and Pennington made great progress
in catching up to him, but in February 2005 the writer made two
announcements: he had almost completed *Unfinished Stories*, the
sequel to *The Bloodshot Chameleon*; and he had booked a seat on

Virgin Galactic's first commercial space flight, with the launch predicted for 2009.

After reading Fernsby's statements in the newspaper, Pennington suffered a heart attack and spent a week in the intensive care unit of St Mark's Hospital in Sydney. While in recovery, routine tests revealed that he had stage-three lung cancer. His prognosis, with chemotherapy, was six months. Pennington had never smoked and suspected the cancer had been caused by the three weeks he had spent in Maralinga, South Australia, in 1974; Fernsby had worked in Maralinga as a labourer in the late 1930s. It was later revealed that the area had been the site of secret British nuclear tests in the 1950s. Upon his release from hospital on 17 March 2005, Pennington took a taxi to a storage unit in Ryde, where he kept his mammoth Fernsby archives in two hundred filing cabinets, spread over eight large units. He asked the driver to wait and returned fifteen minutes later carrying a bulky envelope. He then gave the driver Fernsby's home address in Randwick.

When he arrived, Pennington found the front door unlocked and let himself in. Fernsby was in his study upstairs, working on the final chapter of *Unfinished Stories*. The old man was almost deaf and did not hear Pennington as the latter stood a few feet behind him and tore open the envelope he had taken from the archives. Pennington brought out the revolver Hemingway had given Fernsby in London in 1921, then walked up behind Fernsby, placed the barrel against the back of the writer's head and pulled the trigger. Despite its great age, the gun went off, killing Fernsby instantly. The barrel of the gun also exploded, taking with it the four fingers of Pennington's good hand, his left. The biographer called the police and waited for ten minutes

beside Fernsby's body until they arrived. Pennington was discovered with his jacket wrapped around his bleeding hand,
reading Fernsby's gore-covered manuscript and jotting down
notes on a piece of paper with a pen held between his teeth.

Pennington was arrested and charged with murder, to which
he pleaded guilty. Despite submissions to the court testifying
to his good character, and his terminal cancer, the judge had no
choice but to sentence him to twenty years in prison. He was sent
to the minimum-security wing of Long Bay Correctional Centre
in Malabar, where he was made a trusty in the prison library and
held classes to help inmates improve their reading and writing
skills. Although Pennington's injuries meant he could no longer
write longhand or type, a number of inmates volunteered to be
his assistants, and once again progress on the biography resumed,
albeit slowly. Pennington refused all treatment for his cancer but,
rather than expiring within the predicted six months, he survived
for four years. He completed the seventh and final volume of his
monumental project in December 2008. *The Life of Alexander
Fernsby: Volume Seven: 1992–2005* was published on 1 February
2009, and Pennington died three weeks later.

Fernsby's murder, by his own biographer, created an intense
interest in the life and work of the novelist. *The Bloodshot
Chameleon, The Country of Mirrors* and *The Comma* all became
bestsellers in 2005. Pennington's biography would never
achieve such sales, in part because the complete seven-volume
set cost $349 and Pennington's contract with Berkeley & Hunt
stipulated that his work could not be abridged. Its status as a
classic was nonetheless assured, as critics frequently compared
Pennington's biography to Boswell's *Life of Johnson*. The success
of the sumptuous twelve-part ABC adaptation of *The Country*

of Mirrors (2007) and its companion documentary on Fernsby demonstrated the spell the writer continued to exercise over many Australians.

In November 2009 New Dimensions commissioned the author of this book to write a one-volume biography of Fernsby. *Alexander Fernsby: The Definitive Biography* (2010) necessarily drew a great deal from Pennington's classic work, while revealing one fact about Fernsby's life that Pennington had inexplicably overlooked. Among the papers left by Vivian Darkbloom after her death in 1976 were two dozen letters she had received from Fernsby. Pennington had, of course, already disclosed that Darkbloom and Fernsby's brief affair in 1935 had resulted in the birth of a daughter, Rainy, yet Pennington was unaware that Fernsby had kept in touch sporadically with Vivian Darkbloom in the years afterwards. In a letter sent from Paris in May 1954, Fernsby told Darkbloom that while he had based the physical characteristics of *The Bloodshot Chameleon*'s Alicia McDowell on her:

> . . . as for [Alicia's] passionate, repressed nature, that came from a woman I had a dalliance with over Christmas 1934 in a little town called Eden when I was living under the romantic alias of Harry Valentine. Her surname was Forster? Foster? Forester? I loved her with all my heart (for that single, wonderful week), but now I can't remember her last name. Isn't memory a terrible thing? Her father found out about us and I had to make a dash for it. But I will never forget her first name. Eve.

ACKNOWLEDGMENTS

The genesis of this book can be traced back to the night of 5 October 2001, when I attended the Pennington Prize for Nonfiction awards ceremony in Melbourne. My provocative history of Australian short fiction, *Ordinary People Doing Everyday Things in Commonplace Settings*, was shortlisted, and having garnered enthusiastic reviews and generated robust critical debate was the obvious favourite. As it transpired, the prize was won by Rachel Deverall for her study of Lydia McGinnis's short stories. I was, I admit, disappointed, but since the judging panel included two writers whose work I had disparaged in my book, I was not entirely surprised. (This experience was to be repeated in 2012, when *The Weight of a Human Heart* was shortlisted for the Addison Tiller Short Story Collection Award and lost under similarly dubious circumstances, this time to a book belonging to that neither-here-nor-there genre, a "linked short-story collection".)

At the end of the ceremony, after an unpleasant altercation with Tim Winton, I went to congratulate Deverall. Rachel was then in her early thirties and already had a reputation for her outspokenness as much as for her brilliant research. She said she had enjoyed my book, but did not hesitate to tell me it was skewed too much towards men: eighteen pages on Price Warung and only one on Barbara Baynton was a travesty. I disagreed with Rachel then, as I was to do throughout our relationship, and we spent the next three hours at the bar arguing over the merits of Lydia McGinnis and Henry Lawson. During our lengthy conversation we touched on those Australian writers who had inspired us (Young, Swan) and repulsed us (Washington, Gayle), some of them famous (Tiller), some notorious (Pennington, Gunn), and others almost entirely blotted out by time (McVeigh). Walking to my hotel that night with Rachel, the idea for this book began to crystallise: a series of short biographies that would place these fascinating figures in their historical and literary contexts. Rachel and I saw each other more and more over the next few months, as I exploited her vast knowledge of Australian literature to assist me in selecting the writers to be included in my book; it was Rachel who suggested Vivian Darkbloom, her grandmother, as a possible subject for study. Aware of how much I owed Rachel, I tried, in vain, to persuade her to be my co-author, but she was too caught up in her own research.

Rachel and I were married in 2003 and we were happy, until Rachel's fascination with Wilhelmina Campbell, an unknown nineteenth-century writer, became a mania. Our belated honeymoon in Paris was simply an excuse for my new wife to continue her research, a circumstance that became clear when Rachel refused to return to Australia with me. During many phone conversations over the next year, I begged her to come home. Finally, in June 2005 I issued her an ultimatum, demanding she choose between her husband and a long-dead writer. She chose the long-dead writer. Although forced to admit that this did not bode well for our marriage, I could not face the prospect of divorcing her.

I did not see Rachel again until after her breakdown in 2009, when she had lost everything. (Sometimes I blame myself for dissuading her from publishing her findings on Campbell earlier, but they were so incredible, I felt she had to leave no shadow of a doubt as to their authenticity.) After Rachel's release from psychiatric care, I tried to help her, though in her paranoia she was now pitifully suspicious of everyone. In December 2011, hoping to divert her from her melancholy fixation on Campbell, I employed Rachel as an assistant on my seminal volume of literary criticism, *Sacred Kangaroos: Fifty Overrated Australian Novels* (2013), a book whose sales were equalled only by the number of enemies it made me in the literary world. (Geordie Williamson's description of me as "a jackass of all trades" in his review is sadly typical of the vitriol it attracted.) Serious research was beyond Rachel by then; she was incapable of writing a paragraph without mentioning Wilhelmina Campbell. When Rachel was diagnosed with cancer, I vowed to save what small part of her I could by including her in this book, and I was deeply moved when, despite her illness, she offered to compile its index. During the long talks we had in her final months I was able to complete her life, even as her life was ending. Rachel, my darling, I owe my brilliant career to you.

I could not have written the life of Robert Bush without the aid of Patrick Cullen, whose reminiscences of Bush proved invaluable to me as I fleshed out a portrait of this singular man. Similarly, my research on Arthur ruhtrA was enriched immeasurably by Lazaros Zigomanis's generosity. As one of the founding members of Kangaroulipo, and current vice-president of the Frederick Stratford Society in Australia, Zigomanis granted me full access to ruhtrA's surviving letters and notebooks. Laura Elvery, Annabel Smith and Amanda Betts were the only friends of my late wife who consented to speak to me, and I suppose for this they should be thanked, even if it was only to shower insults upon myself and Anne Zoellner. I owe a great debt to A.S. Patric for his generosity in sharing the rare papers in his Matilda Young archive. Patric's 2010 poetry collection *Music for Broken Instruments* is an inventive and insightful reworking of Young's verse that, I am certain, would have delighted the Nobel laureate. My thanks must also go to Roberto Bolaño, whose *Nazi Literature in the Americas* (1996), a series of biographical sketches of right-wing and fascist writers, provided essential background information for the life of Rand Washington. The Australian was known to have corresponded with many of the writers Bolaño featured in his book, including Harry Sibelius and Thomas R. Murchison. I am especially indebted to Bolaño for his biographical sketch of the pathological plagiarist Max Mirebalais, which served as a model for my own life of Frederick Stratford. Thomas Mallon's classic study *Stolen Words: Forays into the Origins and Ravages of Plagiarism* (1989) also provided indispensable, if sometimes inaccurate, information about Stratford. (Speaking of plagiarism, critics will no doubt use the life of Stephen Pennington to resurrect accusations that my *Alexander Fernsby: The Definitive Biography* appropriated large sections of Pennington's classic work. I have always acknowledged that I owe a great debt to Pennington; if

---

I have seen further it is by standing on the shoulders of giants such as he. I am not, however, a plagiarist.) Thanks also to my editors, Chris Feik and Denise O'Dea, especially for their forbearance in the matter of the Sydney Steele chapter. A run of bad luck, which included computer viruses, software malfunctions and my research assistant Robert Skinner being struck by lightning, plagued this piece right up to the deadline. It seemed at one point we might lose the life of Steele altogether, something that would, no doubt, have gratified those who subscribe to the legend that the great writer was some sort of Antipodean Faust. I trust that the publication of Steele's biography here will finally lay to rest the foolish idea of Steele, and by extension those who write about him, being cursed.

I must also extend my heartfelt gratitude to the Australian Federal Police. Six weeks after my wife's death, just before this book went to press, the police contacted me to say that, acting on a tip from an anonymous source, they had found thirty boxes marked "Property of Rachel Deverall" at a storage unit in a warehouse in Ryde. Rental for the unit had been paid for, in cash, for five years in advance, by someone giving the name John Smith. As Rachel's next of kin, I was invited to claim her property. When I visited the unit I was flabbergasted to find the boxes comprised Rachel's research into the life and work of Wilhelmina Campbell, including the Degraël trove, and Rachel's priceless copies of *The Summer Journey* and *The Autumn Journey*, which had been believed lost in the mysterious fire that consumed her house in the first week of November 2009.

Finally, Anne Zoellner. I simply don't have the words to thank you for your generosity and friendship. You were there in the good times when Rachel and I first met. You were there in the dark times after Rachel left me, when I thought my life had ended. You were there when my groundbreaking work was snubbed again and again by the critics and their "literary" awards. In countless letters and articles you defended me from unsubstantiated charges of plagiarism. You remembered, crucially, that we had dinner together on the evening of 7 November 2009, and so prevented a terrible travesty of justice. When Rachel broke apart, you were beside me, and together we tried to pick up the pieces. And you are here, now, as we embark on a new book together, one that will bring about the rewriting of every literary history of France, Great Britain and Australia.

Thank you, Anne, for everything, but especially those things of which I cannot write.

INDEX

INDEX

Eden, New South Wales 231, 232,
235, 253, 256, 259
egomaniac, *see* O'Neill, Ryan
Eliot, T.S. 26, 65
Engin, Erol 42
errors 12, 25, 67–8, 79, 103, 115, 135,
137, 142, 192, 238, 240

falsifications 121–37
Fancy Jack, *see* Sargent, Jack
Fernsby, Alexander 73, 74, 75, 76, 78,
83, 84, 102, 191, 198, 199, 213, 214,
215, 231, 233, 234, 236, 238–59
First World War, *see* Great War
Fitzgerald, F. Scott 160, 161
Forester, Eve, *see* Pennington, Eve
Forster, E.M. 65, 160
Fountainhead Press 5, 6, 7, 145, 204

Garner, Helen 24, 32, 125
Gayle, Edward
death 179
early life 165–8
Murder or Self-Murder 173, 177
Terror Nullius 175
Truth Goes Walkabout 125, 175–8
Gayle, Rowena 165, 169
Gayle, Theodore 165, 168, 169, 170
Gladkgov, Fyodor 112
Gorky, Maxim 112, 113, 119
Great War 26, 63, 108, 130, 132, 158,
187
Greene, Graham 67, 245, 251
Greer, Germaine 32, 89
Groovy! 46
Gunn, Dame Claudia
death 103
The Death of Vincent Prowse 93,
96–100
early life 93–5

An Icicle for an Icicle 80, 103
marriage 96
A Red Herring 93, 94, 97, 101
Gunn, Quincy 75, 95, 96, 99, 101,
102, 104, 160, 184
Gurnabil, Alice 165–9, 170, 171, 179
Gurnabil, Katie 165–167, 168, 169, 170

hackwork 28, 37–9, 66, 95–9
Hardacre, J.R., *see* Washington,
Joyce
Harkaway, Helen
Parade of the Harlequins 74, 203,
206, 207, 208, 209, 211–14, 216
Harkaway, Iain 114, 203
Harris, Max 227
Hitler, Adolf 4, 5, 114
Holt, Harold 210–12
howlers 24, 87, 88, 214, 244
Hugo Award 12, 13
Hunter, Richard, *see* Young, Matilda

incorrect chronology 24–6, 214, 221,
223–6, 244
Indigenous writers, lack of 1–176,
179–259

Jolley, Elizabeth 125
Joyce, James 38, 110, 158, 159, 160,
161, 189
Judas, *see* Zoellner, Anne

Kangaroulipo 35, 42–6, 121, 126, 162
Katoomba, New South Wales 27, 159
Keats, John 16
Kings Cross 3, 55, 97, 114, 144
Kingston, Adam 177, 178
Kookaburra Books 7, 59, 60, 63, 64,
66, 76, 146, 147, 148, 151, 237
Kristel, Sylvia 43

Laurence Steed Prize for Biography
245
Lawson, Henry 52, 54, 56, 58, 111,
123, 127, 128, 157, 220
Le Voyage d'hiver, see Degraël,
Vincent
Lone Hand 29, 52, 96, 129
Lovecraft, H.P. 2–3

Mackellar, Dorothea 22
Mackintosh, Albert 19, 20, 23, 24,
29, 102, 221–8
Malley, Ern 227
Manly, Robert, *see* Young, Matilda
Mann, Thomas 160
McAllister, Tex, *see* Swan, Catherine
McGinnis, Lydia
  A Kingly Kind of Trade 84, 85, 87
  Basilica 81–2, 84, 85, 87, 89, 123, 125
  death 88
  first marriage 78
  marriage to Robert Bush 81
  Ryan O'Neill's misinterpre-
  tation of 78–82, 84–8
  Ultimo Thule 88, 89, 123, 125
McVeigh, Francis X.
  death 117–19
  early life 107–9
  The Red Flag 111, 112, 122, 190
  Return to Animal Farm 116–17
Melbourne, Victoria 27, 28, 60, 121,
168, 185, 186, 246, 251
misreadings 20, 25, 41, 61, 82, 176
mistakes 1–259
mistress, *see* Zoellner, Anne
Modrenist 27, 220, 221, 222, 223, 224,
225, 226
Montague, Aubrey 16, 17, 21
Moorhouse, Frank 40, 44, 47, 77
Moscow 111, 112, 113, 114, 117, 119

Murray, Max 24, 25–8
Musgrave, Oscar 102, 144, 145, 147,
151

Nabokov, Vladimir
  Ada or Ardor: A Family Chronicle 195
  friendship with Peter
  Darkbloom 193–5
  Lolita 194
  Pnin 197
Nebula Award 12, 13
New Dimensions 13, 43, 45, 85, 104,
105, 151, 162, 213, 259
Northerly 18–20, 23–5, 102, 221–6,
228

O'Neill, Ryan 126, 129, 130, 137, 259
Onomatopoets 18, 23, 220
Overground 8, 176, 177, 209
oversimplifications 169–79
*Oulipo (Ouvroir de littérature
  potentielle)* 40–2
Oxley, Queensland 15, 21

padding 182–7
Paris 38, 39, 42, 47, 130, 131, 132, 133,
136, 244, 259
Parramatta, New South Wales 55,
93, 129, 181
Pascoe, W.D. 36
Paterson, Banjo 52, 54, 127, 181, 228
Paterson, Henry, *see* Young, Matilda
Pennington, Eve 231–4
Pennington Prize for Nonfiction
105, 125
Pennington, Robert 231–2
Pennington, Stephen
  *Addison Tiller: Australia's
  Chekhov* 75, 184, 237
  death 258

iINDEX

early life 231–4
    marriage 254
Perec, Georges 35, 39–42, 47
Pieburn, Alan 13
Pin see Darkbloom, Peter
plagiarisms
    of Rachel Deverall 15–32, 93–105,
    127–35, 141–51, 181–201, 203–16
    of Roberto Bolaño 154–6, 158,
    161
    of Stephen Pennington 238–58
Plume, Naomi, see Swan, Catherine
Poe Edgar Allan 94
Pound, Ezra 221
pyromaniac, see O'Neill, Ryan

Quarter 7–10, 12, 30, 31, 171, 172,
    174–7, 228
Queneau, Raymond 39, 40, 44

Reith, Joyce see Washington, Joyce
Richardson, Henry Handel 128
Robinson, Arthur, see ruhtrA,
    Arthur
ruhtrA, Arthur
    death 47
    early life 35–8
    Long Time No See 41, 43, 46
    Shames Joyce: The Great Plagiarist
    39, 162
    The Coming of the Harlequins 45, 213
Runyon, Percy 57

Salinger, J.D. 205
"Sans Souci School" 24–5, 22
Sargent, Jack 18–24, 220
Second World War 27, 65, 101,
    114, 115, 167,
shameless self-promotion 126, 137,
    259

shoddy research 4–7, 37–41, 94–101,
    154–9, 183–94, 209–18
Sholokov, Mikhail 112
Siegfried Press, see Fountainhead
    Press
Solzhenitsyn, Alexander 118
Sontag, Susan 242
Southern Cross 51, 96, 160
Stanner, W.E.H. 172
Steele, Sydney
Steelman Press 28, 29, 114–16
Stephens, A.G. 58, 156, 157
Sterne, Laurence 35
Stratford, Frederick
    The Enchanted Mountain 159
    Mrs Galloway 153, 159
    Odysseus 38, 41, 46, 122, 158–60,
    162, 188–9
    The Prodigious Gatsby 44, 159
    The Sun Comes Up Too 38, 159
Strong, Guy, see Swan, Catherine
Sutcliffe, Kiralee 42, 43, 47
Stuart, Northern Territory 165,
    166
Swan, Catherine   146
    A Child's Finnegans W of Things
    A Child's Rememb
    Past 146
    Cor Blimey
    death 15 141–3
    early   145
    ...n, Claire 141, 144
Swan, Septimus 141, 143
Sydney Review 44, 90, 124, 127
Sydney Steele Centre 76, 77

Taree, New South Wales 219, 222
Taylor, Jim 23, 53, 155–6
"The Truants" 23

273